STUDY GUIDE
Henry Borne

MARRIAGES
&
FAMILIES

Diversity and Change

Second Edition

Mary Ann Schwartz

BarBara Marliene Scott

PRENTICE HALL, *Upper Saddle River, NJ 07458*

© 1997 by PRENTICE-HALL, INC.
Simon & Schuster / A Viacom Company
Upper Saddle River, New Jersey 07458

10 9 8 7 6 5 4 3 2 1

ISBN 0-13-259268-1
Printed in the United States of America

Table of Contents

Preface

This Study Guide has been written to enhance the foundation of sociological ideas and issues which are presented in the text, *Marriages and Families* by Mary Ann Schwartz and Barbara Marliene Scott. To help you review and think about the material found in the text, the Study Guide has been organized into several different sections to accompany each chapter in the text.

A *Chapter Outline* provides a basis for organizing segments of information from each chapter in the text. A section on *Learning Objectives* identifies the basic knowledge, explanations, comparisons, and understandings students should have after reading and studying each chapter in the text. A section entitled *Chapter Review--Key Points* consists of a brief review of the chapter in paragraph form, following the outline of each chapter. This is followed by a section entitles *Key Terms* in which the important concepts from each chapter are listed, with space provided for the student to write out the definition for each of the terms. This section is followed by the *Important Researchers* section. Researchers cited in the text are listed, with space provided for students to write out important ideas, findings, etc. for each researcher. The next section provides *Study Questions*, including true-false, multiple-choice, fill-in, definition, and short-answer type questions. The following section provides the *Answers to Study Questions*, including a listing of the page numbers where the answers to these questions can be found. The final section, *Analysis and Comment*, provides space for students to raise questions and make comments on the boxes in the text.

This Study Guide is intended to be a concise review and learning tool to accompany the text *Marriages and Families*. It is complementary to this text and is not intended to stand alone as a brief text. It will provide the student with opportunities to more deeply benefit from the knowledge of sociology which the authors offer concerning marriage and family life.

On a personal not I want to congratulate Dr. Schwartz and Dr. Scott for writing such an excellent text on marriages and families. They offer students a very meaningful perspective on many important issues involved in marriage and family life. I believe students will be excited by this text, and rewarded by what it has to offer them both personally and academically. It has been a pleasure for me to write this Study Guide. I would like to also thank Sharon Chambliss, Editor--Sociology and Anthropology of Prentice Hall for her insight, guidance and support. It is a joy working for people such as her. Finally, my love to my family--Cincy, Ben, and Abby--for their support and love.

HB

Marriages and Families Over Time

PART II: LEARNING OBJECTIVES

1. To recognize the diversity of marriage and family forms that exist in the United States and around the world.
2. To develop broader and more socially relevant definitions to the institutions of marriage and family.
3. To recognize the important social functions served by the institution of the family.
4. To discuss contrasting views of families and how these relate to important cultural values in society.
5. To critically assess one's assumptions about the social institutions of marriage and the family, and in so doing debunk myths about them.
6. To develop a historical understanding of families in the United States, including the experiences of African Americans, Native Americans, Mexican Americans, and European immigrants.
7. To consider issues relating to gender, age, and social class as they have affected family experiences during the 19th and 20th centuries.
8. To review important historical events during the 20th century that have helped shape family life in the United States.
9. To develop a sense of the sociological imagination and begin to recognize the benefits such a perspective can have in our personal lives.
10. To begin to systematically evaluate your feelings and desires regarding the life choices you have made or will be making over the course of your lifetime.

PART III. CHAPTER REVIEW--KEY POINTS

The opening vignette illustrates how definitions for what constitutes a family vary greatly, and can affect people and their lives.

CONTEMPORARY DEFINITIONS OF MARRIAGES AND FAMILIES

What is your definition for marriage? For family? Accurate definitions must take into account many different forms of these institutions that have exited historically and still exist today here in the United States and globally.

What Is Marriage?

Marriage has been defined in the United States as *a legal contract between a woman and a man who are at or above a specified age and who are not already legally married to someone else.* Our authors suggest that this definition is too narrow and will utilize a more encompassing and *reality-based* definition for the text. **Marriage** is being defined here as *a union between people (whether widely or legally recognized or not) that unites partners sexually, socially, and economically; that is relatively consistent over time; and that accords each member certain agreed upon rights.*

Several **types of marriages** are found cross culturally. Generally, marriages are either monogamous or polygynous. Legally, **monogamy** refers to *heterosexual relationships between one woman and one man.* However, any couple can be monogamous if they are committed exclusively to each other sexually and otherwise during the course of their relationship. **Polygamy** is a broad category that refers to *one person of one sex married to several people of the other sex.* It can take to forms: **Polygyny**, in which *one man has two or more wives*, or **polyandry**, in which *one woman has two or more husbands*.

A third form of marriage is **cenogamy**, or *group marriage, in which all of the women and men in a group are simultaneously married to one another.*

What Is a Family?

A family can be defined in many ways. An important issue to investigate concerns who defines or who has the right to define *family*. The U.S. Bureau of the Census defines a family as *two or more persons living together and related by blood, marriage, or adoption.* Our authors suggest this definition is too limiting, failing to recognize the diversity of family forms that exist today. The family is being defined in the text as *any relatively stable group of people who are related to one another through blood, marriage or adoption, or who simply live together, and who provide one another with economic and emotional support.* Polls indicate that most Americans seem to agree with this broader definition.

There are several different **types of families** identified in the text. The **family of orientation** refers to *the family into which a person is born and raised.* In contrast, the **family of procreation** refers to *when we marry or have an intimate relationship with someone, or have children.* A **nuclear family** as traditionally been understood as *consisting of a mother, father, and siblings.* Further, there are **extended** or *multigenerational families consisting of one or both partners, our siblings, if any, and other relatives, including grandparents.* Other family types identified include *modified extended, voluntarily child-free, single-parent, reconstituted, blended, or stepfamilies, foster families, and surrogate or chosen families,* and *patriarchal families.*

Race, Class, and Gender

Race, class, and gender are three of the most important social categories of experience for individuals and families in the United States, and are related to both oppression and privilege. Opportunities and choices for families are shaped by representation in these categories. These are interrelated or interactive categories of social experience that affect all aspects of human life.

FAMILY FUNCTIONS AND THE DEBATE OVER FAMILY VALUES

Social Functions on Families

Several social functions of the family are identified and illustrated, including: *regulation of sexual behavior, reproduction, social placement, socialization, economic cooperation,* and *care, protection, and intimacy.*

Every society is concerned about sexual behavior of its members. For example, of *all societies prohibit sexual relations between blood or close relatives,* this is known as the **incest taboo**. Societies also are concerned about procreation. Practices in different societies are designed to promote fertility, such as tax credits for children, or inhibit procreation, as found in the one-child policy in China. Families provide status for their members, such as religious affiliation, race, ethnicity, and social class. Families are also the primary transmitters of culture to each new generation. Families also are productive economic units, though much of the labor provided by women in the home is overlooked. Finally, and most critically, the family provide children with warmth and affection.

The **Global Perspectives** box (p. 6) discusses issues relating to traditional wedding in rural India. The father of the bride must spend a considerable amount of money on a dowry and the wedding ceremony to secure a suitable husband for his daughter.

Contrasting Views of Families

Two views of the changing nature of families are considered in this section, one pessimistic and another more optimistic. The former perspective focuses our attention on issues concerning the loss of family functions and encroachment of outside institutions, especially the state, on the family are addressed. Further, evidence of the moral decay of families, such as family violence and unwed motherhood. The latter perspective focuses our attention on the context of changing social, economic, and political circumstances and trends that surround families. While proponents of this view are concerned about problems involving families, they also suggest that families are still extremely important and resilient.

DEBUNKING MYTHS ABOUT MARRIAGES AND FAMILIES

Several myths about the traditional family are identified and confronted in this section of the text, including *the self-reliant traditional family, the naturalness of different spheres for wives and husbands, the private and autonomous family, the unstable African American family,* and *the idealized nuclear family of the 1950s.* Evidence that contradicts these views (myths) about families is discussed.

4

FAMILIES IN EARLY AMERICA

Colonial Families

Information on this historical period in America comes from three sources:

        (1)   surviving material artifacts
        (2)   diaries, wills, letters, etc.
        (3)   census data and other public records.

The text focuses on three general areas of family life during this historical period, including:

        (1)   household composition
        (2)   marital roles
        (3)   childhood

Three generalizations made concerning household composition are that the nuclear family structure dominated family life, the family formed the basic economic unit of society, and family functions were interwoven within the larger community.

Regarding marital roles, the colonial family was *patriarchal*, with wives being expected to be submissive and obedient to their husbands. The English concept of *coverture* was evoked whereby a wife's legal status was subsumed in that of her husband.

Childhood differed in colonial times compared to today. Survival to adulthood was less likely. Child rearing practices were designed to break down a child's willful nature. Many wealthy families had wet nurses breast-feed and care for infants. Finally, childhood was quite short. By age six or seven boys and girls assumed productive roles.

African American Families Under Slavery

Andrew Billingsley has pointed out three important elements that distinguish the experience of African Americans from that of other groups in the United States, including:

        (1)   African Americans came from Africa
                not Europe,
        (2)   they were uprooted from their cultural
                and family moorings and brought here
                as slaves, and
        (3)   they have systematically been excluded
                from participation in the major
                institutions of U.S. society.

Three general areas of family life among African American families under slavery, include slave marriages, childhood, and kinship patterns. Southern laws prohibited slaves from contracting legal marriages, though many slaves went through a religious ceremony to wed. While many slave marriages were stable, slave couples lived under the constant fear of forced separation. While slave parents had no legal rights over their own children, evidence shows that both men and women had ongoing involvement with their families and that both sexes participated in child rearing.

Before and after slavery most African Americans lived in two-parent families. About one-third of the babies born to slave women died before age ten. Strong kinship feelings among slaves are evident. Kinship networks helped slaves adapt to family breakup. *Table 1.1* (p. 15) shows that slave parents frequently named their children after close kin.

Free African American Families

Prior to the Civil War there were approximately 250,000 free African Americans in the United States. About 150,000 lived in the south. Most free African American families were structured around two-parent families, but like today, inadequate income, unemployment, and poor health put considerable strain on these families. Employment opportunities were better for women than men in urban areas. More women slaves were freed than male slaves.

Native American Families

No one description adequately covers all Native American families. Native American peoples were widely dispersed geographically. The Algonquin and Iroquois cultures of the Northeast Woodlands are discussed. Information on the *wigwam* and *longhouse* is reviewed.

Three general areas of Native American life are discussed, including:

(1) rules of marriage,
(2) childhood
(3) consequences of European contact

A wide variety of marriage rules existed among Native American cultures. However, some generalizations are made in the text. First, most cultures practiced monogamy, though some were polygamous. Unhappy marriages were easily dissolved, with either spouse able to divorce the other. In some societies, rules involving widowhood included the **sororate**, or *a widower marrying the sister of his deceased wife*, and the **levirate**, or *a widow marrying one of her dead husband's brothers*. Finally, Native American women married relatively young, many between the ages of twelve to fifteen.

Both the **patrilineal** system, or *a rule of descent and inheritance whereby kinship come through the father and his blood relatives*, and the **matrilineal** system, or *a rule of descent and inheritance whereby kinship comes through the mother and her blood relatives* existed among Native American cultures. Families were generally small. Infant and childhood mortality were high. Parents rarely used physical punishment with their children.

Consequences of European contact were devastating for Native Americans and their cultures. Examples are reviewed.

FAMILIES IN THE NINETEENTH CENTURY

Major changes in the beginning of this century transformed family life in the United States. New technology, factories, wage labor and the separation of work and the family created a social context for smaller nuclear families and a greater division of labor by sex in the family.

Emergence of the Good Provider Role

According to sociologist Jesse Bernard, a special male role known as the *good provider* emerged as early as 1830. A man's status, as well as that of his family, depended on his occupation. Physical and emotional separation of husbands and fathers from their families increased.

The Cult of Domesticity

The *cult of domesticity* was the counterpart of the good provider role for men. The Industrial Revolution advanced this ideology, which argued that women were expected to stay at home.

Changing Views of Childhood

The economic transformation of the early nineteenth century altered marital and children's roles. Childhood became identified as a distinct period, a time of innocence and play.

The Impact of Class and Ethnicity

Family lifestyles for middle and upper-class families were different than they were for working-class families. Among African Americans and many immigrant working-class families, men were typically unable to support their families economically. Family boundaries were more fluid for these groups, with extended families being common. Further, many working-class men would cook, clean, and care for children while their wives worked outside the home.

Immigration and Family Life

Between 1830 and 1930 over thirty million immigrants came to the United States. The first waves of immigrants came from Northern and Western Europe. During the 1880s, emigration patterns shifted, with large numbers of people leaving Southern and Eastern Europe. Common problems faced by immigrants, such as unemployment, are discussed.

The Economic Roles of Women and Children

Women and children in the working-class contributed to the material support of the family in a variety of ways. Many wives whose husbands were unemployed or whose husbands were earning low wags worked outside the home. Other women took in boarders or did laundry or sewing in their homes. Many children were employed in factories.

Ethnic and Racial Family Patterns

Racism and discrimination dramatically affected work and family roles. For example, the Chinese Exclusion Act of 1882 restricted immigration from China and thus limited the number of women who could join the men already in the United States who were building the railroads. For African Americans, even after slavery, many women worked outside the home because African American males earned so little money.

Mexican American Families

After the Mexican-American War in 1848, the U.S. annexed a considerable amount of Mexico's territory. The Mexicans were granted citizenship and the right to retain ownership of their land, but exploitation by Anglos was widespread.

Three areas of family life are addressed, including:

      (1)   family and kinship
      (2)   marital roles
      (3)   signs of change

A distinguishing characteristic of Chicano (Mexican American) families was an emphasis on *familism* or *a constellation of values which give overriding importance to the family and the needs of the collective as opposed to individual and personal needs.* The ritual kinship of *compadrazgo*, which linked two families together, and the inclusion of godparents--*madrinas* and *padrinos*, created a network of people tying families together.

Families tended to be large, with a fairly rigid division of labor. The traditional male role of *machismo* was very important. Families became displaced when white settlers bought large tracts of land in the Southwest, thus disrupting the patriarchal kinship system.

FAMILIES IN THE EARLY TWENTIETH CENTURY

The idealized image of men as providers and women as homemakers, though only applicable to certain groups, dominated popular thought into the early twentieth century. Technological and political changes dramatically affected every aspect of social life.

The emergence of the Companionate Family

The *companionate family* refers to a model for *heterosexual relationships based on mutual affection, sexual fulfillment, and sharing of domestic tasks and child rearing.* Many cultural difference between families began to disappear with the spread of this new understanding about family life. Issues raised by this model are discussed.

The Great Depression

Consequences of joblessness were far reaching and severe during this period in our nation's history. Marriage and family stability suffered given the widespread economic instability. The myth of the self-reliant family could no longer be maintained.

World War II and its Aftermath

Dramatic demographic consequences resulted from World War II for the United States-- marriage rates, birth rates, changing family roles and functions, and for some groups, geographic dislocation.

New Immigration in the Latter Half of the Twentieth Century

Political and economic turmoil around the world in recent years has again created an increase in immigration rate into the United States, especially from Asian and Latin American countries.

CONTEMPORARY PATTERNS IN MARRIAGES AND FAMILIES

A thorough historical analysis reveals much continuity in family patterns across the generations. *Figure 1.2* and *Table 1.2* (p. 22) provide some demographic information on actual and projected family patterns between 1970 and 2000.

Lessons From History

Diverse marriage and family patterns and structures are revealed by carefully studying history. General patterns observed include:

(1) Families have continuously been changing, but not in any significant direction.
(2) We cannot say for certain which change is good or bad.
(3) Historically there has never been a perfect family form.
(4) Understanding our idealistic view of the past can help us develop a more realistic sense about families today.
(5) It is likely that change will continue.

THE SOCIOLOGICAL IMAGINATION

The *sociological imagination* allows us to distinguish between what C.W. Mills called "personal troubles of milieu" and the "public issues of social structure." Mills suggested that we can understand our own life chances by becoming aware of all those individuals in our same circumstances.

Applying this sociological perspective offers many benefits, including

(1) It allows us to take a new and critical look at what we have always taken for granted or assumed to be true;

(2) It allows us to see the vast range of human diversity;

(3) It allows us to understand the constraints and opportunities that affect our lives and those of other people; and

(4) It enables us to participate more actively in society.

WRITING YOUR OWN SCRIPT

Writing your own script is an exercise that utilizes an everyday-life approach to the study of marriages and families. It encourages you to become directly involved in the learning process by using your own personal experiences. Each chapter will conclude with a Writing Your Own Script exercise. The first one (p. 24) is entitled "Define It, and Knowledge Follows." For each of these exercises you should consider the following:

(1) the factual information presented in each chapter,

(2) the key life events and activities around which the exercises are built,

(3) the options available to you in each area of decision-making,

(4) the larger social forces that may affect the range of options available to you,

(5) the possible positive and negative consequences of each option, and

(6) how social forces and your own personal values may interact to influence your choices and those of others.

PART IV. KEY TERMS

Define each of the following terms in the space provided or on separate paper. Check the accuracy of your answers by referring to the text. Do the same for each chapter in the text as each is assigned in class.

companionate family   family of orientation

modified extended family   family of procreation

nuclear family   family

cenogamy   marriage

monogamy   polygamy

polygyny   polyandry

serial monogamy   extended family

modified extended family   patriarchal family

sororate   levirate

kinship   patrilineal

matrilineal   household

institution   status

role   social structure

institutional racism   myth

socialization   sociological imagination

wigwam   longhouse

familism   coverture

PART V. KEY RESEARCHERS

    Go back through the chapter and find references to the following people and their work on marriages and families. In the space provided below briefly write down key points about each person's work. Also, jot down any questions or comments you may have about the research presented. These people and their work may be mentioned more than once in the chapter. Subsequent chapters in this study guide will ask you to review key researchers discussed in the text.

Stephanie Coontz   Christopher Lasch

Andrew Billingsley   C.Wright Mills

Jesse Bernard   John Demos

Steven Mintz and Susan Kellog

VI. STUDY QUESTIONS

True-False

1. T F Our authors suggest that we need to develop *a more precise and narrow definition of marriage* than is currently being used in our society.
2. T F The *family of orientation* is the family into which a person is born and raised.
3. T F Our authors suggest that the *family mosaic* in the United States is limited to *nuclear* and *extended families*.
4. T F Until the post World War II baby boom generation, the family was largely exempt from *public intervention*.
5. T F Every known society has some form of *incest taboo*.
6. T F Although the United States has one of the highest *divorce rates* in the world, the overwhelming majority of divorced people *remarry*.
7. T F Approximately two-thirds of *African Americans* are officially classified by the government as being *poor*.
8. T F Most people in colonial America lived in *extended families*.
9. T F Nineteenth century census data show that before and after slavery most African Americans lived in *two-parent families*.
10. T F Most freed slaves prior to the Civil War lived in the North.
11. T F Industrialization advanced the *ideology of domesticity* for women.
12. T F The first major wave of people coming to America who emigrated from Europe primarily came from Southern and Eastern European countries.

Multiple Choice

1. Our text uses a very comprehensive and reality-based definition for _____, or a union between people (whether widely or legally recognized or not) that unites partners sexually, socially, and economically; that is relatively consistent over time; and that accords each member certain agreed-upon rights.

   (a) marriage   (d) community
   (b) family   (e) society
   (c) kinship

2. *Cenogamy* refers to:

   (a) sibling marriages
   (b) group marriage
   (c) same-sex marriages
   (d) one woman being married to two or more men

3. A family in which the male (husband or father) is the head of the family and exercises authority and decision-making power over his wife and child(ren) is termed:

   (a) the extended family
   (b) the affinal family
   (c) the nuclear family
   (d) the patriarchal family
   (e) the consanguine family

4. According to our authors, which of the following characterized colonial families in America?

   (a) the nuclear family structure was the dominate form
   (b) the family formed the basic economic unit of society
   (c) functions of the family were interwoven within the larger community
   (d) all of the above
   (e) none of the above

5. The English concept of *coverture* related to:

   (a) assimilation of African Americans into white society after the Civil War
   (b) nonfamily household servants during America's colonial period
   (c) a wife's legal identity
   (d) the working status of young children in colonial America

6. The *levirate* involves:

   (a) a widower marrying his deceased wife's sister
   (b) a lineage in which kinship is traced through the female blood line
   (c) a lineage in which kinship is traced through the male blood line
   (d) the removal of the husband/father from the family unit during early industrialization
   (e) a widow marrying her deceased husband's brother

7. During most of the 19th century, *earnings for women* in the United States:

   (a) was only one-third to one-half that of the prevailing earnings for men
   (b) were about the same as the earnings for men
   (c) were slightly higher than earnings for men
   (d) were considerably higher than the earnings for men
   (e) were about three-quarters of the earnings for men

8. The *companionate family* emerged in the United States:

    (a) during the early colonial period
    (b) just prior to the civil War
    (c) after World War II
    (d) during the early 20th century
    (e) during the 1970s

9. Which of the following is identified in the text as a *lesson of history* we should learn?

    (a) changes in family life will likely not be very significant during the next generation as compared to the previous generation
    (b) keeping a sense of a family nostalgia will help create a context in which policies and programs can more effectively help current family problems
    (c) although families have changed continuously over time, this change has not been in any single direction
    (d) none of the above
    (e) a, b, and c are all accurate

10. What percentage of U.S. *households* in the U.S. in 1994 were classified as *nonfamily households*?

    (a) 3.4   (b) 8.5   (c) 12.5   (d) 18.9   (e) 29.5

Fill-In

1. _____ is a broad category that refers generally to one person of one sex married to several people of the other sex.

2. *Polygamy* can take two forms, _____, in which one male has two or more wives, and _____, in which one female has two or more husbands.

3. _____ is the legally recognized marriage structure in the U.S. However, because approximately one-half of all marriages end in divorce and the vast majority of divorced people remarry the U.S. marriage pattern is more accurately classed as _____ _____.

4. The *family of* _____ is the family into which a person is born and raised.

5. Several *functions* of the family are identified and illustrated in the text, including: _____ of sexual behavior, _____, social _____, _____, economic _____, and caring, protection, and _____.

6. *Christopher Lasch* contends that the encroachment of outside institutions, especially the state, has left modern families with too few _____.

7. Public opinion polls during the 1950s suggested that _____ *percent* of couples considered themselves in *unhappy marriages*.

8. Northeastern woodlands peoples prior to European arrival lived in diverse cultures. The social and economic unit of the *Algonquins* was the _____, whereas for the *Iroquois* it was the _____.

9. The rule of marriage where a widower marries a sister of his deceased wife is referred to as the _____.

10. According to sociologist *Jesse Bernard* a specialized male role emerged in the U.S. around 1830. She labeled this the _____.

11. During the early twentieth century the idea of a more personal and _____ model for heterosexual relationships based on mutual affection, sexual fulfillment, and sharing of domestic tasks and child rearing emerged.

12. In 1995, 36.2 percent of families in the U.S. were composed of a married couple with children. What was this percentage in 1970? _____

Short-Answer

1. How is *marriage* typically defined in our society? What concerns do our authors have about this definition? What definition are they proposing we use? What are your opinions about this definition?

2. What is the connection between *power relationships* and the definition of the family? How does the definition of the family relate to *family policy* issues? Can you provide an example to illustrate this connection?

3. Identify and define the five family arrangements (structures) other than the traditional nuclear family or extended family that exist in our society.

4. What are the six *social functions* served by families as identified in the text? Provide an illustration for each function served by families in contemporary U.S. society.

5. Provide three statistics (facts) from our society's history that support *Stephanie Coontz's* argument that we have an *idealized* vision of the past that never actually existed.

6. What historical factors can you think of that may have influenced the median age at first marriage in the U.S. over this century? Please refer to *Figure 1.1* (p. 11).

7. *Andrew Billingsley* points out three important elements that distinguishes the experiences of *African Americans* from that of other groups in the U.S. What are these elements? To what extent do you agree with his conclusions?

8. Describe *childhood* among Native American peoples.

9. Differentiate between the *good provider role* and the *ideology of domesticity*.

10. What are the major characteristics of the *companionate family*? What historical factors helped create a context within which it could emerge?

11. What are the five *lessons from history* our authors suggest we need to observe? What is one other lesson you think should be observed from history concerning marriage and family patterns?

12. What is the *sociological imagination*? What are the types of questions being asked using this perspective? Provide an illustration for each type of question.
13. What are four *benefits* of using the sociological perspective?
14. What do the authors mean by *writing your own script*?

VII. ANSWERS TO STUDY QUESTIONS

True-False

1.	F	(p. 2)	8.	F	(p. 12)
2.	T	(p. 3)	9.	T	(p. 14)
3.	F	(p. 3)	10.	F	(p. 15)
4.	F	(p. 4)	11.	T	(p. 17)
5.	T	(p. 4)	12.	F	(p. 17)
6.	T	(p. 7)			
7.	F	(p. 10)			

Multiple-Choice

1.	a	(p. 2)	7.	a	(p. 18)
2.	b	(p. 2)	8.	d	(p. 20)
3.	d	(p. 3)	9.	c	(p. 22)
4.	d	(p. 12)	10.	e	(p. 22)
5.	c	(p. 13)			
6.	e	(p. 17)			

Fill-In

1. Polygamy (p.2)
2. polygyny, polyandry (p. 2)
3. monogamy, serial monogamy (p. 2)
4. orientation (p. 3)
5. regulation, reproduction, placement, socialization, cooperation, intimacy (pp. 4-6)
6. functions (p. 7)
7. 20 (p. 11)
8. wigwam, longhouse (p. 15)
9. sororate (p. 16)
10. good provider role (p. 17)
11. companionate (p. 20)
12. 49.6 (p. 22)

VIII. COMMENT AND ANALYSIS

Global Perspectives

"In India, Father of the Bride Puts Honor First, Cost Last"

    Key Points:

    Questions you have?

Personal Reflection

"How Well Do You Know U.S. Family History?"

    Key Points:

    Questions you have?

"Define It, And Knowledge Follows"

Ways of Studying and Explaining Marriages and Families

2

PART I. CHAPTER OUTLINE

PART II. LEARNING OBJECTIVES

1. To begin to develop an appreciation of how the sociological perspective can help us better understand issues relating to marriages and families.
2. To begin to develop an understanding about the relationship between theory and research in the study of marriages and families.
3. To gain basic knowledge about the scientific method, including the major research techniques used by social scientists for the study of marriages and families.
4. To recognize the biases in social science research in terms of stereotypical approaches to the study of women, lower-class families, and racial and ethnic minorities.
5. To become aware of the need for new scholarship on marriages and families, and to begin to think about alternatives to traditional research methods typically used for the study of white middle-class families.
6. To identify and describe the major theoretical perspective used by sociologists for the study of marriages and families.
7. To become aware of gender issues related to research on marriages and families.

PART III. CHAPTER REVIEW--KEY POINTS

THE SOCIOLOGY OF MARRIAGES AND FAMILIES

Why do people act, think, and feel the way they do? The sociological perspective provides a unique framework for understanding human behavior. For example, how do we explain teen suicide? Be sure to read the vignette at the beginning of this chapter and think about this question. Our answer probably is framed in terms of certain personal characteristics of the young people themselves. In the late nineteenth century, sociologist Emile Durkheim found that suicides are not purely individual or isolated events but reveal a number of patterns. Some demographic patterns are discussed in the text to illustrate.

STUDYING MARRIAGES AND FAMILIES: THE LINK BETWEEN RESEARCH AND THEORY

A *theory* is *an explanation of some phenomenon*. *Scientific research* *provides us with empirical evidence as a basis for knowledge or theories*. *Empirical evidence* refers to *data that can be confirmed by the use of one or more of the human senses*.

Scientific research allows us to test *hypotheses*, or *statements of relationships between two or more variables*. All scientific research is guided by the *scientific method*, or *a set of procedures intended to ensure accuracy and honesty throughout the research process*. Generally, the scientific method involves the procedures science uses to:

(1) select or formulate research questions and
     operationalize (state in concrete terms)
     concepts,
(2) select an appropriate research design,
(3) collect data,
(4) analyze the data, and
(5) draw conclusions and report the findings.

Theory provides the insights into the nature of individuals and society, while research provides the objective observation upon which theories are verified. However, it is important to stress that no theory or research is totally unbiased.

METHODOLOGICAL TECHNIQUES IN THE STUDY OF MARRIAGES AND FAMILIES

A potential problem for all scientific research is the compromising of *objectivity*. Researchers bring biases to theory and research. Two other critical issues in scientific research include reliability and validity. **Reliability** refers to *the degree to which the research yields the same results when repeated by the same researcher or other researchers*. **Validity** refers to *the degree to which the study measures exactly what it claims to be measuring*.

Surveys

Surveys *enable us to gather information by asking people questions*. They are the most widely used method for studying marriages and families. Surveys are particularly useful when what we want to know about people is not easily observable, such as the private lives of married or cohabiting couples. The two basic types of surveys include interviews and questionnaires. The **interview** *usually involves one person, the interviewer, asking another person questions, with the interviewer recording the answers*. The **questionnaire** *is typically a set of printed questions that people read on their own and then record their answers*. Phillip Blumstein and Pepper Schwartz's large-scale survey on married couples is reviewed to illustrate this approach.

Observation

Observational studies are useful when researchers have only a vague idea of the behavior they want to study, when subjects are not readily accessible, or when there is no other way to get the information. **Participant observation** refers to observational research in which *the researcher participates in or becomes a part of the activity being studied*.

There are limitations with this method. One problem involves the phenomenon of the **Hawthorne Effect**, or *people modifying their behavior because they are ware of being observed*. Other drawbacks include the fact that observational studies take a long time, can be expensive, generally involve few subjects, and have little control over situations.

Case Studies

Case studies involve *the in-depth and detailed study of a particular category of people or a particular situation*. Tony McCormick's study of six families in which one family member had suffered a head injury in an accident is discussed as an example of the case study method.

Ethnography

The *ethnography* is *a research technique describing a social group from the group's point of view*. It is a method for examining the many different versions of reality from the point of view or through the eyes of the researched. As a qualitative method there are methodological biases which limit the reliability and validity of the data gathered. Robin Jarrett's study of low-income African American family life is discussed as an example of this technique.

Scientific Methodologies Used by Feminist Researchers

No method of research is in itself a feminist method. However *feminist researchers* are concerned with several issues, including who researchers study, how they study them, how conclusions are drawn, and what evidence those conclusions are based on. Gender is at the forefront of this type of analysis, with attention given to how race, class, and gender interact. Qualitative data are collected as much as possible. A basic goal of feminist research is to present information that has been previously ignored or suppressed.

A CRITICAL LOOK AT TRADITIONAL RESEARCH ON MARRIAGES AND FAMILIES

Historically, sociology has claimed as one of its goals, to improve social life by affecting social policy. However, critics say a biased understanding of society has been generated by a focus on issues most pertinent to white, middle-class males.

Who Does and Does Not Get Studied

When women have been studied in traditional marriage and family research it has usually been in terms of a one-dimensional stereotypical model of women as nurturant caregiver and caretaker confined to the home. Also, little relevant research has been done on African American women. Few studies have been done on nonwhite middle-class or upper-class families. Virtually nothing is known about gay family life styles.

Specific examples of research biased along gender or racial lines discussed in the text include Peter Blau and Otis Duncan's study of social mobility which focused only on males, and Daniel Moynihan's study on African American families which labeled the African American family as a "matriarchy."

The Need for a New Scholarship on Marriages and Families

Scientific research on marriages and families reflects the structures and values of U.S. society. Social research must be evaluated by:

(1)   who is or is not the researcher,
(2)   who does and does not get studied,
(3)   which theoretical paradigms and
        underlying assumptions are accepted,
(4)   which methods are used and how, and
(5)   what the research actually says and
        does not say about the subjects.

The emergence of such scholarship has indeed begun. There is a growing recognition among family researchers for race, class, and gender diversity in marriage and family lifestyles.

THEORETICAL PERSPECTIVES

A *theoretical perspective* refers to *a broad explanation of social reality from a particular point of view which provides us with a basic image of society and human behavior.* Sociologists approach the study of society and human behavior with a particular set of theoretical assumptions, though there is no single theory of marriages and families.

Structural Functionalism

Structural functionalism is *a theoretical perspective that views society as an organized and stable system, analogous to the human system, that is made up of a variety of interrelated parts or structures.* The structures, or subsystems, are the major social institutions in society and include the family, economy, government, education, and religion. Each of these structures has a function for maintaining society.

The family from a functionalist perspective is regarded as a system which provide functions for the society and individual members. Historically these functions have been divided along gender and age lines. Functionalists are interested in studying both *manifest*, or *intended, overt functions*, and *latent*, or *unintended, unrecognized functions*. They also recognize that families may be dysfunctional.

Talcott Parsons argued that the nuclear family has declined as many of its functions have been taken over and performed by other social institutions. According to Parsons, the two major functions of the modern family are now socialization of the young and personality stabilization of adults.

The nuclear family model places great emphasis on the isolation of the nuclear family from the extended family. It also emphasizes that a differentiation of gender roles within the family is a functional necessity. Two types of roles are needed. The *instrumental traits*, *encourage self-confidence, rationality, competition, and coolness--qualities that facilitate male success in the world of work.* In contrast, the **expressive traits**, encourage nurturance, emotionality, sensitivity, and warmth--qualities that help women succeed in caring for a husband, children, and a home.

A critique of structural functionalism reveals it has a conservative bias, implies functional imperatives for institutions and commodities, and fails to clearly identify all functions.

Conflict Theory

Karl Marx was an economist, political agitator, and social theorist who revolutionized social and philosophical thinking about society. According to Marx every aspect of social life is based on economic relationships. He believed that all industrialized societies are characterized by competition and conflict between two main groups: the *capitalists* (owners) and the *proletariat* (workers). These groups have fundamentally opposing interests. From a Marxian viewpoint, economic power is seen as explaining the structure of societies and social relationships.

The themes of conflict theory revolve around the basic assumption that conflict is natural and inevitable in all human interaction. Of major concern is the unequal distribution of power and scarce resources in society. Three central themes of **conflict theory** are identified:

(1)   humans have basic interests or things they
      want and attempt to acquire,
(2)   power is at the base of all social relationships,
      and it is always scarce, unequally distributed,
      and coercive, and
(3)   values and ideas are weapons used by different
      groups to advance their own ends rather than
      to define society's identity and goals.

The family from a conflict perspective is seen as a set of relationships that benefit some members more than others. Marriages and families can be viewed as smaller versions of the larger class system, where the well-being of one class (men) is the result of the exploitation and oppression of another class (women). In essence, then, the basic source of male dominance and women's subordination is the home and family.

A critique of conflict theory indicates a concern that the underlying assumptions are too narrow and limited. It is also criticized for explicitly advocating social change, thereby giving up some of its claim to scientific objectivity.

Symbolic Interactionism

While functionalism and the conflict perspective both concern themselves with macro-patterns (large-scale patterns) that characterize society or groups, **symbolic interactionism** focuses on micropatterns (small-scale patterns) of face-to-face interactions among people in specific settings. Communication through the use of shared symbols, primarily language, is a major focus of this perspective.

The family from a symbolic-interaction perspective, according to Ernest Burgess, is understood as representing a unified set of interacting individuals. The reality of marriage and family life is socially constructed by participating individuals. ***The social construction of reality** is the process whereby people assign meanings to social phenomena--objects, events, and characteristics--that almost always cause those who draw upon the meanings to emphasize some aspect of the phenomenon and to ignore others*. Taking this perspective, sociologist Jesse Bernard, for example, argued that men and women are likely to experience their marriage differently.

A critique of the symbolic-interaction perspective asks us to see how it focuses on the subjective and ignores the objective realities of inequality, racism, sexism, and the differential distribution of wealth, power, and status.

Social-Exchange Theory

The ***social-exchange** theory adopts an economic model of human behavior based on costs, benefits, and the expectation of reciprocity*. Two of the best-known proponents of this theory are George Homans and Peter Blau. Homans focused on actual behavior that is rewarded or punished by the behavior of others. Blau was more concerned with explaining large-scale social structures.

The family from a social-exchange perspective is seen as being characterized by an exchange of goods and services. Cost and benefits are counter-balanced.

A critique of social-exchange theory concerns it emphasis on humans as rational, calculating beings who consciously weigh the costs versus the benefits of their social relationships.

The Developmental Family Life Cycle Model

***The developmental family life cycle model** pays close attention to changes in families over time and attempts to explain family life in terms of a process that unfolds over the life course of families*. Sociologist Paul Glick identified a series of stages as representing the family life cycle, including:

(1)   family formation
(2)   start of childbearing
(3)   end of childbearing
(4)   empty nest
(5)   family dissolution

One of the most widely used developmental theories in family sociology was developed by Evelyn Duvall. Her stages include:

(1)   beginning families
(2)   childbearing families
(3)   families with preschool children
(4)   families with school children
(5)   families with teenagers
(6)   families as launching centers
(7)   families in the middle-years
(8)   aging families

A critique of the developmental family life cycle model includes a concern that a "typical" family life cycle is difficult, if not impossible to distinguish. Also, life cycle theories, while giving us important insights into the complexities of family life, a shortcoming is that they assume most families are nuclear families with children.

Further, families within various racial and ethnic groups develop through stages that are not recognized in these models. Yet another issue concerns assumed developmental tasks within the family, particularly those involving gender differences. Examples are discussed in the text.

Microstructuralism

Microstructuralism is *an approach that combines symbolic-interactionism and structural-functionalist approaches to explain gendered relationships.* Individuals are seen as being re-created during the life cycle by the opportunities available to them and by their interaction with others. It offers a critical framework within which to analyze marriages and intimate relationships and therefore has direct implications for social change.

The family from microstructural perspective, at its logical extreme, predicts that women and men would behave exactly the same way if they were given identical expectations and positions in society. Illustrations involving parenthood are discussed in the text.

A critique of microstructural theory includes the concern that it blames the system of society for gender inequality while downplaying the role of individuals in creating and maintaining these structured relationships.

Social-Constructionist Perspective

The **social-constructionist perspective** basically *focuses on the process by which human beings give meaning to their own behavior and the behavior of others.* This perspective is based on the idea that human experience is not uniform and universally generalizable to all people. according to this view, the important facts of human social life are not inherent in human biology but are developed through a complex process of human interaction.

Some fundamental assumptions of this perspective are:

(1) reality is invented, constructed largely out of the meanings and values of the observer.
(2) language is a mediating influence on all constructions; we bring forth realities through our interactions with other human beings.
(3) we cannot know an objective reality apart from our (subjective) views of it.
(4) culture, history, politics, and economic conditions all influence individual experiences of social reality.

Social constructionism and the family: There are many applications of this perspective for marriages and families. For example, gender is a socially constructed system for classifying people as girl or boy, woman or man, feminine or masculine. How these constructions relate to the statuses of wife and husband, mother and father and their respective roles is of great interest to social constructionists. This perspective is both historical and comparative.

A critique of this perspective raises concern that it springs from a particular set of political and moral values or biases, and that it is simply an exercise in debunking previously held truths.

Feminist Theory

Feminist theory, while not presenting a single unified view, *presents a generalized set of ideas about the basic features of society and human experience from a woman-centered perspective.* It is woman-centered in three ways:

(1) the starting point of all its investigations is the situations and experiences of women;
(2) it treats women as the main subjects in the research process, that is, it attempts to view the world from the distinctive vantage points of women; and
(3) it is critical and activist on behalf of women.

Not all theories that deal with women or gender issues are feminist theories. To be considered feminist, a theory should adopt three basic philosophical principles:

(1) gender is the central focus,
(2) status quo gender relations are viewed as problematic in that women are defined as subordinant to men, and
(3) gender relations are viewed as the result of social, not natural, factors.

The **For Your Information** box (p. 46) discusses the different types of feminists, including *liberal, socialist, Marxist, radical, lesbian, and women-of-color*. Each one is briefly defined and discussed.

The family from a feminist perspective is investigated asking both macro and micro-level questions. For example, how does society (macro) maintain gender inequality in marriage, and what social and interpersonal (micro) processes occur in families to generate gender inequality?

A critique of feminism focuses on biases toward women and the exclusion of male experiences and perspectives. Further, class and race inequalities are not fully addressed relative to gender inequalities. Finally, feminism has tended to be biased toward white, middle-class, heterosexual women.

MEN'S STUDIES RELATIVE TO MARRIAGES AND FAMILIES

Several diverse perspectives offer insight into the disadvantages of patriarchy for men. Such studies begin with the basic premise that there is no hierarchy of oppression. Men like women are oppressed.

Men in Families

The major issue being addressed in this section of the text concerns the increasing isolation of men from their families. The role of primary provider has been eroded given the changing conditions of work and career and the tragedies of divorce.

A critique of this perspective is that it views men as victims. Another concern is that although many of these analyses focus on the structural and institutional nature of men's exploitation and oppression, they have not clearly identified the alleged oppression or oppressors.

PART IV. KEY TERMS

theory

scientific research

empirical evidence

scientific method

variables

hypotheses

reliability

validity

survey

interview

questionnaire

Hawthorne effect

case study

ethnography

qualitative methods

quantitative methods

ideologies

theory model

structural functionalism

manifest functions

latent functions

functional

dysfunctional   instrumental traits

expressive traits   conflict theory

symbolic interactionism   symbols

social construction of reality   social-exchange theory

developmental family life cycle theory microstructuralism

sexism   social constructionism

feminism (variations: liberal, socialist, radical, Marxist, lesbian, women-of-color)

V. KEY RESEARCHERS

Phillip Blumstein and Pepper Schwartz

Daniel Moynihan

Ellen Annandale

Bruce Brown and Tony McCormick

Robin Jarrett

Peter Blau and Otis Duncan

Talcott Parsons

Paul Glick

Karl Marx

Jesse Bernard

George Homans and Peter Blau

Evelyn Duvall

Emile Durkheim

Tony McCormick

VI. STUDY QUESTIONS

True-False

1. T   F   *Theories* relate ideas and observations to each other as well as help explain them.
2. T   F   A potential problem for all scientific research is a lack of *objectivity*.
3. T   F   The *survey* is the most widely used research method used by sociologists for the study of marriages and families.
4. T   F   *Ethnographies* tend to produce more reliable, valid, and objective data than any other research method.
5. T   F   More is known from survey data about gay and lesbian couples than is known about African American couples or poor couples.
6. T   F   Basically, *structural functionalism* views society as an organized and stable system, analogous to the human system, that is made up of a variety of interrelated parts or structures.
7. T   F   *Talcott Parsons*, a structural functionalist, argued that in modern society the functional importance of the nuclear family has declined as many of its functions have been taken over and performed by other social institutions.
8. T   F   *Symbolic interactionism* tends to focus on *macropatterns* that characterize society.
9. T   F   *Microstructuralism* is a perspective that combines the social-conflict and structural-functionalist approaches to explain relationships within marriages and families.
10. T   F   According to *social-constructionist* thinking, the important facts of human social life are not inherent in human biology but are developed through a complex process of human interaction.

Multiple-Choice

1. In the late 19th century, sociologist *Emile Durkheim* found:

    (a) the nuclear family was weakening as industrialization advanced
    (b) the birth rate was closely correlated with economic conditions
    (c) that family violence was more common in rural, as opposed to urban areas
    (d) that suicides are not purely individual or isolated events but reveal a number of patterns
    (e) that romantic love was less important in modern society as compared to more traditional societies

2. Which of the following statements about theories is *not* accurate?

   (a) a theory is an explanation of some phenomenon
   (b) theories relate ideas and observations to each other
   (c) theories make certain assumptions about the world
   (d) theories do not include unstated or stated value judgments

3. Scientific research provides us with _____ evidence as a basis for knowledge or theories.

   (a) ideological
   (b) real
   (c) empirical
   (d) subjective
   (e) truthful

4. The degree to which a study *measures exactly what it claims to be measuring* is known as:

   (a) validity
   (b) consistency
   (c) ethnography
   (d) reliability
   (e) falsification

5. What is the *most widely used method* of studying marriages and families?

   (a) case studies
   (b) experiments
   (c) participant observation
   (d) ethnographies
   (e) surveys

6. When a researcher becomes a member of the group she or he is studying this is known as:

   (a) researcher bias
   (b) the Hawthorne Effect
   (c) participant observation
   (d) quantitative research
   (e) validity

7. When people become aware that they are being studied they frequently modify their behavior. This is known as:

   (a) subject bias
   (b) participant bias
   (c) the reliability crisis
   (d) the Hawthorne effect
   (e) validity crisis

8. *Bruce Brown* and *Tony McCormick* conducted a case study of six families in which one family member had:

    (a) died
    (b) suffered a head injury
    (c) been born blind
    (d) become pregnant
    (e) been a drug addict

9. *Feminist researchers* are concerned about:

    (a) who researchers study
    (b) how researchers study people
    (c) how researchers draw conclusions
    (d) what evidence conclusions are drawn on
    (e) all of the above

10. A major weakness of most research on *occupational mobility* in the United States, as evidenced by a study done by Peter Blau and Otis Duncan, has been:

    (a) a focus on whites
    (b) a focus on the very wealthy
    (c) a focus on families and not individuals
    (d) a focus on men and not women
    (e) none of the above

11. The *Moynihan Report* of 1965 focused on:

    (a) African American families
    (b) homosexual marriages
    (c) education and social mobility
    (d) religious practices and family solidarity
    (e) cohabitation and marital stability

12. Which of the following theories views society as an organized, stable system, analogous to the human system, that is made up of a variety of interrelated parts?

    (a) humanism
    (b) structural functionalism
    (c) social-conflict
    (d) social constructionism
    (e) symbolic interactionism

13. According to structural-functionalist *Talcott Parsons*, the two major functions of the modern nuclear family are:

   (a) recreation and retreat
   (b) economic stability and affection
   (c) socialization of the young and personality stabilization of adults
   (d) procreation and education

14. _____ theorists focus on society as an arena where individuals and groups compete over limited resources.

   (a) symbolic-interactionist   (d) social-conflict
   (b) structural-functionalist   (e) social constructionist
   (c) developmental

15. Which theory is also known as the *rational-choice* perspective?

   (a) structural-functionalism   (d) social-conflict
   (b) symbolic-interactionism   (e) social-exchange
   (c) social-constructionist

Fill-In

1. Every year more than _____ thousand people in the U.S. commit *suicide*.
2. A _____ is an explanation of some phenomenon.
3. By _____ *evidence* we mean data or evidence that can be confirmed by the use of one or more of the human senses.
4. _____ is the degree to which the research yields the same results when repeated by the same researcher or other researchers.
5. In general, the _____ is a research technique for describing a social group from the group's point of view.
6. According to researchers *Peter Blau* and *Otis Duncan*, social mobility was simply a function of _____ and _____ and that no other conditions affect chances for mobility in the U.S.
7. Research on African American families has primarily focused on _____ and _____-_____ families.
8. *Functionalists* are not only interested in the intended, overt, or _____ *functions* of social institutions, but also the unintended, unrecognized, or _____ *functions* as well.
9. *Talcott Parsons*, a structural-functionalist, emphasized that a differentiation of gender roles within a family is a functional necessity for the solidarity of the marriage relationship. He described the male role as _____ and the female role as _____.

37

10. *Karl Marx* believed that two classes with fundamentally opposing interests as well as unequal power existed in modern industrial society which he called the _____ and the _____.

11. According to proponents of the *conflict perspective*, the source of male dominance and women's subordination is the _____ and _____.

12. The _____ is the process whereby people assign meanings to social phenomena--objects, events, and characteristics--that almost always cause those who draw upon these meanings to emphasize some aspect of the phenomenon and to ignore others.

13. Using the *symbolic-interactionist perspective*, sociologist *Jesse Bernard* argued that men and women are likely to view and experience marriage _____.

14. _____ *theory* assumes that humans are rational, calculating beings who consciously weigh the costs versus the benefits of their relationships.

15. Although *life cycle theories* give us important insights into the complexities of family life, a shortcoming is that they assume that most families are _____ families with _____.

16. Taken to its extreme, the _____ *perspective* predicts that women and men would behave exactly the same way if they were given identical expectations and positions in society.

17. *Liberal feminists theory* assumes that at the basis of women's inequality is _____.

18. In general, the _____ *perspective* begins with the basic premise that there is no hierarchy of oppression. Men, like women, are oppressed by a social conditioning that makes them incapable of developing and expressing a wide range of personality traits or skills and limits their experiences.

Short-Answer and Definition

1. What were the general conclusions made by sociologist *Emile Durkheim* concerning *suicide*?

2. Define the concepts of *theory* and *hypothesis*. Develop an hypothesis and operationalize the variables you identify.

3. What are the five procedures identified in the text that represent the *scientific method*?

4. What are the major *research methods* used by sociologists for the study of marriages and families? What are the relative advantages and disadvantages for each of these research methods for studying marriages and families?

5. Briefly describe the scientific methodologies used by *feminist researchers*?

6. What are the issues being raised in this chapter concerning weaknesses in tradition research on marriages and families?

7. Briefly describe the conclusions by Peter Blau and Otis Duncan concerning *social mobility patterns* in the United States? What were the weaknesses in their methodology?

8. Briefly describe and critique the *Moynihan Report*.

9. Scientific research does not exist in a vacuum. Its theory and practice reflect the structure and values of U.S. society. Given this reality, what are the qualities of research that must be evaluated to properly interpret research results and conclusions.

10. The authors of the text focus on several *theoretical perspectives*, including structural functionalism, conflict theory, symbolic interactionism, social-exchange theory, the developmental family life cycle model, microstructuralism, the social-constructionist perspective, and feminist theory. Select two of these perspectives and discuss how each orients researchers to the study of marriages and families. Identify basic assumptions, key concepts, and general arguments being used by proponents of each perspective.

VII. ANSWERS TO STUDY QUESTIONS

True-False

1.	T	(p. 29)	6.	T	(p. 36)
2.	T	(p. 30)	7.	T	(p. 37)
3.	T	(p. 30)	8.	F	(p. 40)
4.	F	(p. 32)	9.	F	(p. 43)
5.	F	(p. 35)	10.	T	(p. 44)

Multiple-Choice

1.	d	(p. 27)	9.	e	(p. 32)
2.	d	(p. 29)	10.	a	(p. 34)
3.	c	(p. 30)	11.	a	(p. 34)
4.	a	(p. 30)	12.	b	(p. 36)
5.	e	(p. 30)	13.	c	(p. 37)
6.	c	(p. 31)	14.	d	(p. 38)
7.	d	(p. 31)	15	e	(p. 41)
8.	b	(p. 31)			

Fill-In

1.	30 (p. 27)	10.	capitalists, proletariat (p. 38)
2.	theory (p. 29)	11.	home, family (p. 39)
3.	empirical (p. 29)	12.	social construction of reality (p. 40)
4.	reliability (p. 29)	13.	differently (p. 40)
5.	ethnography (p. 32)	14.	social-exchange (p. 41)
6.	education, social origins (p. 34)	15.	nuclear, children (p. 42)
7.	lower, working class (p. 35)	16.	microstructuralism (p. 43)
8.	manifest, latent (p. 36)	17.	sexism (p. 46)
9.	instrumental, affective (p. 337)	18.	men's study (p. 47)

VIII. COMMENT AND ANALYSIS

For Your Information

"Feminist theory"

    Key Points:

    Questions you have?

Applying the Sociological Imagination

"Developing a Minitheory"

    Key Points:

    Questions you have?

<u>Writing Your Own Script</u>

"The Family Life Cycle: Locating Your Family"

Gender 3 Roles

PART I: CHAPTER OUTLINE

I. Distinguishing Sex and Gender Roles
    A. Sex Differences
    B. Gender Differences: The Nature-Nurture Debate
II. Traditional Meanings of Femininity and Masculinity
    A. Traditional Gender Roles: Female and Male
    B. Gender Variations: Race, Class, and Culture
III. Gender Roles in Transition
IV. Theories of Gender Role Socialization
    A. Psychoanalytic/Identification Theory
    B. Social-Learning Theory
    C. Cognitive-Development Theory
    D. Enculturated-Lens Theory
V. Agents of Socialization
    A. Parents
    B. Language
    C. Peers and Play Activities
    D. Teachers
    E. The Mass Media
VI. Consequences of Gender Stereotyping
    A. Lifestyle Choices
    B. Self-Esteem
    C. Self-Confidence
    D. Mental Illness
    E. Women, Men, and Friends
    F. Patterns of Communication
VII. Changing Realities, Changing Roles
VIII. Summary
IX. Questions for Study and Reflection
X. Further Reading

PART II. LEARNING OBJECTIVES

1. To distinguish between sex and gender.
2. To see the connection between ascribed and achieved statuses and role expectations for females and males.
3. To review the nature-nurture debate concerning gender differences
4. To evaluate the effects of gender stereotyping.
5. To describe traditional gender roles and traditional meanings of femininity and masculinity.
6. To consider ways in which gender roles are changing in our society.
7. To review and evaluate four theories of gender-role socialization.
8. To identify the agents of socialization and describe how they provide gender-role socialization.

PART III. CHAPTER REVIEW--KEY POINTS

DISTINGUISHING SEX AND GENDER ROLES

This chapter begins with the story of Shannon Faulkner and her attempt to break the gender barrier at the Citadel, a publicly supported institution of higher education in South Carolina. What do you think about this case?

Sociologists use the term *role* to refer to *a set of expected behaviors associated with a specific status, the position we hold in society.* Statuses into which we are born are known as *ascribed statuses.* Statuses which we acquire via our own efforts are known as *achieved statuses.* *Role expectations* are defined and structured around *the privileges and obligations associated with a status.* Shared role expectations are functional as they make our behavior fairly predictable, thus making social order possible. However, rigid role definitions often lead to the development of stereotypes, in which certain qualities are assigned to an individual solely on the basis of his or her social category. *Gender role stereotypes are oversimplified expectations of what it means to be a woman or a man.*

The status of being a female or male is considered a *master (key) status.* *Sex* refers to *biological aspects of a person* and *gender* refers to *the socially learned behaviors, attitudes, and expectations associated with being female or male.* *Gender identity* is *a person's awareness of being female or male.*

Sex Differences

Our biological sex is established at the moment of conception, when each parent contributes 23 chromosomes to the fertilized egg. The father's genetic contribution, either an X or Y chromosome, determines the child's sex. The process of sexual differentiation does not actually begin until the sixth week of embryonic development.

Gender Differences: The Nature-Nurture Debate

While biological factors create physical, behavioral, and personality differences between females and males, these differences within each sex are often greater than the differences between the two sexes. *Figure 3-1* illustrates this pattern. Social factors greatly influence observed differences between females and males.

The interconnectedness between biology and culture can be seen by examining a few sex/gender variations that exist in the human population--*hermaphrodites, transsexuals,* and *multiple genders.* **Hermaphrodites**, *are people born with a sexual anatomy that cannot be clearly differentiated.* Surgery can sometimes be used change the anatomy of the infant to either female or male. Parents then socialize their child "appropriately" as either female or male.

Another variation of the sex/gender linkage occurs in the case of **transsexuals**, or *persons who believe that they were born with the body of the wrong sex.* These individuals cannot accept their assigned gender even though it is congruent with their biological sex. Surgery or hormone treatments can help some to achieve a body that fits their sense of gender identity.

A third variation occurs in societies with multiple genders. **Berdache** are *individuals who adopt the gender ascribed to members of the other sex.* Among the Mohave, a Native American people who lived in California, women and men were allowed to cross genders.

TRADITIONAL MEANINGS OF FEMININITY AND MASCULINITY

The assignment of *expressive* or *instrumental* roles traditionally has been based on the assumption that females and males are fundamentally different from one another and that the content of these roles reflects the biological differences between the sexes. Certain traits are associated by people in our society as being representative of males or female. There are patterns also found cross-culturally. Examples are discussed in the text.

Traditional Gender Roles: Female and Male

Historically, women were expected to cluster their roles around the family and to be nurturing and emotional while men were supposed to be providers and achievement oriented.

Gender Variations: Race, Class, and Culture

Gender stereotypes--*the overgeneralized beliefs about the characteristics associated with being female or male*--are widely shared within a society. Variation does exist between groups within our society. The **Global Perspectives** (p. 56) discusses the issue of gender equality. Maria Lepowsky studied a society in New Guinea, the Vanatinai, and found evidence for the existence of gender equality. Other cultures are briefly reviewed to illustrate the variety gender role patterns around the world.

GENDER ROLES IN TRANSITION

Demographic changes and social movements during the 1960s and 1970s have challenged and changed traditional gender roles. Women today have more control at work and in their private lives than in generations past. Controversy over these changes remains, though most people in our society prefer a marriage in which housework and child care are shared. Also, some people may support the movement toward gender equality in theory but have trouble implementing the ideas in their everyday lives.

THEORIES OF GENDER ROLE SOCIALIZATION

Psychoanalytic/Identification Theory

Psychoanalytic/identification theory was originated by Sigmund Freud (1856-1939), the founder of modern psychoanalysis. Freud believed children learned gender-appropriate behaviors by unconsciously identifying with their same-sex parent and that they pass through a series of stages in their development. According to Freud, it is during the third stage (phallic stage) that gender identification occurs. Freud called the boy's development the *Oedipus complex* and the girl's development the *Electra complex.*

There are several criticisms of Freud's theory. Critics state that it is impossible to verify the theory empirically, and that it contains anti-female bias. Karen Horney has challenged the notion that women view their bodies as inferior to men. Nancy Chodorow sees the "asymmetrical organization of parenting" as the basis for gender inequality and the source of identification problems for boys.

Social-Learning Theory

Social-learning theory has its roots in behaviorism. Social-learning theory asserts that gender roles and gender identity are learned directly through a system of positive reinforcement (rewards) and negative reinforcements (punishments) and indirectly through observation and *modeling*, learning through imitation. Social-learning theory maintains that behavior that is regularly followed by a reward is more likely to be repeated.

A considerable amount of research supports social-learning theory. However, modeling is more complex than the theory suggests. Children do not always model themselves after same-sex individuals. Also, subcultural differences as well as differences in family structures may affect the variety of choice of available role models. Finally, this theory treats children as passive learners.

Cognitive-Development Theory

Cognitive-development theory is based on the belief that the child's mind matures through interaction with their surrounding environment, and that children take an active role in organizing their world. According to this theory, children create schemas, or mental categories, that emerge through interaction with their social environment. These schemas are fluid. Lawrence Kohlberg adapted cognitive-development theory to explain the emergence of children's gender identities. Children label themselves as girl or boy based on superficial characteristics. Once gender identity is developed, children are able to organize their behavior around it.

A considerable amount of research gives support for cognitive-development theory. However, there are criticisms of this theory. John Money and Anke Ehrhardt question the timing of gender identity as posed by cognitive-development theory. The most serious criticism of this theory is that it overemphasizes gender learning as something children do themselves and minimizes the role of culture plays in gender socialization.

Enculturated-Lens Theory

Enculturated-lens theory argues that hidden cultural assumptions about how social members should look, behave, and feel are so deeply embedded in social institutions and cultural discourse. Using this theory, Sandra Bem argues that gender acquisition is a special case of socialization, or what she calls *enculturation*.

Empirical testing is needed to determine the validity of this theory. The examination of the various *agents of socialization--individuals, groups, and organizations that help form an individual's attitudes, behaviors, and self-concept*--does provide some insight into the content of gender messages and how they are communicated in our society.

AGENTS OF SOCIALIZATION

Parents

Parents provide children with their first exposure to gender learning and play a key role in helping children develop a sense of themselves as females and males. Parents treat and communicate with their sons and daughters differently. Illustrations are provided referencing an extensive body of research. *Clothing, toys and games,* and *chores* are discussed as examples of how parents treat and communicate with their children differently.

Language

As children learn language, they also learn a great deal about how their culture defines females and males. The English language contains a number of gender biases. Masculine pronouns are discussed to illustrate such bias.

Peers and Play Activities

Research suggests that girls and boys both prefer same-sex groups. Janet Lever believes boys' activities better prepare them to succeed in modern industrial societies, because boys' games have more complex rules and involve a variety of roles.

Teachers

From elementary grades through college, researchers have observed differential treatment of females and males. Examples of how teachers structure classroom activities along sex-segregated lines are discussed in the text. The **Personal Reflection** box (p. 64) presents four examples of sexist and nonsexist wording in nursery rhymes.

The Mass Media

The mass media play an important part in shaping the values, beliefs, and behaviors of modern societies. The television is certainly one example. More than 98 percent of U.S. households have at least one television set, almost 79 percent have videocassette recorders, and 62 percent subscribe to cable television. The average school-aged child watches approximately 27 hours of television every week.

Content analysis of *children's shows* reveals that they are predominately white-male-oriented, featuring more than twice as many male as female roles. Further, females are more likely to be found in minor roles with little responsibility for the outcome of the story and are rarely shown working outside the home. Children, especially girls, are aware of the narrowness of television's portrayal of girls lives.

Prime-time television continues to portray traditional gender roles. Female characters are generally thin and physically attractive, which has led some researchers to suspect a relationship between television images and eating disorders. *Table 3.1* (p. 66) shows data concerning the percentage of children with eating disorders, by sex, for 1992. The eating disorders of anorexia nervosa and bulimia are discussed.

News programs reveal similar trends in terms of news reports of real people. Although more women than men graduate with degrees in journalism, women account for less than 2 percent of newspaper corporate management, 5 percent of publishers and general managers, and 13 percent of directing editors.

CONSEQUENCES OF GENDER STEREOTYPING

Studies show that each gender role has its advantage, but both women and men perceive the female role as having more disadvantages.

Lifestyle choices

Current gender expectations continue to limit women's lifestyle choices. Women who choose nontraditional lifestyles often must do so without much societal support. Men too have found their lifestyle choices limited.

Self-Esteem

Self-esteem refers to *the overall feelings--positive and negative--that a person has about herself or himself.* At least two factors seem to play a crucial role in the relationship between gender and self-esteem: *age* and the degree of *sex typing*. Regarding age, boys have higher self-esteem in elementary school than girls, and that the gap between them widens in high school. Latino and white females show the largest decline in self-esteem. In terms of sex typing, researchers report that the highest levels of self-esteem are found among both females and males who are high in masculine traits or who are androgynous.

The **Critical Issues** box (p. 68) provides some examples of new roles for men and women for your consideration, including dual earner families and child care arrangements, and women in law enforcement and military combat positions.

Self-Confidence

As with self-esteem, girls and boys differ in levels of self-confidence, and the gap widens with age. Females tend to underestimate their abilities, whereas males tend to overestimate theirs.

Mental Illness

Gender differences in mental illness has long been observed. For example, higher rates of depression are found among women. Historically, the mental health field has frequently reflected gender-related stereotypes. Women and men who adhere to traditional gender roles are likely to be seen as healthier than those who deviate from these roles. However, rigid adherence to these roles may interfere with the development of good mental health for both women and men. Marital status and level of marital power are also related to feelings of depression.

Women, Men, and Friends

Overall, women's friendships tend to be characterized by intimacy, self-disclosure, nurturance, and emotional support. Men's friendships, in contrast, focus more on shared activities, such as sports, politics, and business.

Cross-sex friendships, from early on in the life of a person, have many societal barriers. Cross-sex friendships tend to increase during adolescence and early adulthood.

Patterns of communication

Researchers have identified gendered patterns of communication. Deborah Tannen suggests women and men speak different languages. She calls women's conversational style "rapport talk," the goal of which is to signal support, to confirm solidarity, or to indicate they are following the conversation. In contrast, men's communication style is referred to as "report talk," intended to preserve independence and to negotiate and maintain status in a hierarchial order. The **Applying the Sociological Imagination** box (p. 72) provides examples of gendered communication.

CHANGING REALITIES, CHANGING ROLES

The world we live in today is very different from generations past. Many of the old patterns of socialization are not sufficient to provide solutions to the psychological and economic strains experienced by many people today.

We must seek new ways to socialize our children to enable them to make satisfying personal choices and to live full and satisfying human lives. Sandra Bem offers two strategies to achieve this goal. First, parents need to be encouraged to teach their children that the only definitive gender differences are anatomical and reproductive. Second, parents should help children substitute the "gender differences" schema with an "individual differences" schema.

PART IV. KEY TERMS

status

role

master status

gender

sex typing

androgynous

berdache

ascribed status

achieved status

stereotype

gender identity

hermaphroditism

gender-role socialization

self-esteem

transsexuals   content analysis

modeling   Oedipus complex

Electra complex

Theories:

social-learning

cognitive-development

enculturated-lens

psychoanalytic/identification

PART V. KEY RESEARCHERS

Sigmund Freud

Erik Erikson

Lawrence Kohlberg

Karen Horney

Nancy Chodorow

Sandra Bem

Deborah Tannen

John Money and Anke Ehrhardt

Maria Lepowski

Janet Lever

VI. STUDY QUESTIONS

True-False

1.   T   F   Rigid role definitions lead to the development of stereotypes.
2.   T   F   *Gender* refers to the physiological characteristics that differentiate between females and males.
3.   T   F   Cross-cultural research on gender roles reveals little if any consistency in traits typically defined as masculine or feminine.
4.   T   F   Approximately three-quarters of adults under the age of thirty think *shared responsibility in marriage* is more satisfying than traditional gender role patterns.
5.   T   F   According to Sigmund Freud's *psychoanalytic theory*, it is during the phallic stage of personality development that boys and girls development proceeds in different directions.
6.   T   F   *social-learning theory* (behaviorism) focuses on the significant impact of genes and gender behavior.
7.   T   F   According to *cognitive-development theory*, a child's mind matures through interaction with the surrounding environment, with the child taking an active role in their world.
8.   T   F   *Enculturated-lens theory* focuses on how anatomical and physiological differences between females and males determines gender role patterns.
9.   T   F   Janet Lever's research suggests that girls activities have *more complicated rules* than boys' activities.
10.   T   F   Children's T.V. shows tend to have more male than female characters.
11.   T   F   *Self-esteem* refers to the overall feelings--positive or negative--that a person has about herself or himself.
12.   T   F   Men have higher rates of *depression* than women.

Multiple-choice

1. Sociologists use the term _____ to refer to a set of expected behaviors associated with a specific _____.

   (a)   status, role   (c)   role, status
   (b)   status, model   (d)   model, role

2. Which of the following would be an example of an *ascribed status*?

   (a)   teacher   (d)   spouse
   (b)   parent   (e)   male
   (c)   student

3. _____ refers to the socially learned behavior associated with being either male or female.

   (a) Sex   (c) Gender
   (b) Status   (d) Gender identity

4. Anthropologists have described a *third gender*, found in several other cultures, known as:

   (a) hermaphrodites   (d) ahila
   (b) androgens   (e) bagonza
   (c) berdache

5. Among the Vanatinai people who live on an island of the coast of Papua New Guinea, anthropologist Maria Lepowsky found:

   (a) a third gender
   (b) gender equality
   (c) a gender hierarchy in which feminine traits are seen as superior to masculine traits
   (d) evidence among a primitive stone age people to support Freud's psychoanalytic theory
   (e) none of the above

6. Who among the following believed that children learn gender appropriate behavior by unconsciously identifying with the same sex parent as they pass through the phallic stage of development?

   (a) Erik Erikson   (d) Sigmund Freud
   (b) Charles Horton Cooley   (e) Karen Horney
   (c) Lawrence Kohlberg

7. Which of the theories of gender-role socialization would be most likely to use the term *modeling*?

   (a) identification   (d) social-learning
   (b) cognitive development   (e) Freudian
   (c) enculturation-lens

8. According to Lawrence Kohlberg's adaptation of *cognitive-development* theory:

   (a) about age 2-3 children become aware that two sexes exist
   (b) gender identity does not develop until children are 6-7 years old and have the mental ability to grasp the concept of constancy or permanency
   (c) once gender identity is developed, children are able to organize their behavior around it
   (d) the emergence of children's gender identity can be explained
   (e) all of the above

9. According to Sandra Bem's *enculturated-lens theory*, what gender issues need to be focused upon?

   (a) gender polarization
   (b) androcentrism
   (c) biological essentialism
   (d) all of the above

10. According to *Janet Lever*, why do boys' games provide more training for leadership than girls' games?

    (a) they are based on competition
    (b) they have complex rules
    (c) their play groups are larger
    (d) all of the above

11. Content analysis of *children's shows* reveals:

    (a) they feature more than twice as many male as female roles
    (b) females are more likely to be found in minor roles with little responsibility for the outcome of the story and are rarely shown working outside the home
    (c) male characters are depicted in a variety of occupations to which many boys realistically can aspire
    (d) children, especially girls, are aware of the narrowness of television's portrayal of girl's lives
    (e) all of the above

12. Rigid adherence to *traditional-gender norms* may interfere with the development of good mental health for:

    (a) men
    (b) women
    (c) both men and women

13. According to *Deborah Tannen* women are more likely to use a _____ *talk style* of conversation.

    (a) rapport   (c) report
    (b) response   (d) reflective

14. *Sandra Bem* suggests that in order to reach greater gender equality:

    (a) parents need to teach children that the only definitive gender differences are anatomical and reproductive
    (b) parents need to help children substitute and "individual differences" schema for the "gender" schema that currently exists
    (c) both (a) and (b)
    (d) none of the above

Fill-In

1. _____ refers to a person's awareness of being female or male.

2. Sociologists use the term _____ to refer to a set of expected behaviors associated with a specific status.

3. Positions we are born into and other which we have little control are referred to _____ statuses.

4. Our biological sex is established at the moment of conception. The father's genetic contribution determines the child's sex, in that he provides either an _____ or a _____ chromosome, whereas the mother always provides an _____ chromosome.

5. People born with incomplete or ambiguous genitalia are called _____.

6. A research methodology that allowed respondents to rate the degree to which traits characterize both the typical man and the typical woman found several interesting patterns. One pattern was that two sets of *adjectives* become evident. The *prototypical woman* was described as _____ and _____, and the *prototypical man* was described as _____ and _____.

7. _____--the overgeneralized beliefs about characteristics associated with being female or male--are widely shared within a society.

8. _____ *theory* maintains that behavior that is regularly followed by a reward is more likely to be repeated.

9. *Lawrence Kohlberg* adopted _____ *theory* to explain the emergence of childrens' gender identities.

10. *Sandra Bem*, using *enculturated-lens theory* focuses on three issues, including gender _____, _____, and _____ essentialism.

11. Parents, the mass media, peers, and teachers are identified in the text as _____.

12. *Janet Lever* found many differences between girls and boys *activities*. She believes boys activities better prepare them to succeed in modern industrial society because the rules for these activities are _____.

13. The average school-aged child in the U.S. watches approximately _____ *hours of television every week*.

14. Eighty-six percent of *commercials* advertising products to enhance personal appearance are aimed at _____.

15. The authors suggest at least two factors seem to play a crucial role in the relationship between *gender and self-esteem*: _____ and _____.

16. According to researcher cited in the text, _____ is a central part of *women's friendship*. *Men's friendships*, in contrast, focus more on shared _____.

17. According to *Deborah Tannen*, women speak and hear a *language of* _____ and _____, whereas men speak and hear a *language of* _____ and _____.

18. Psychologist *Sandra Bem* suggests that parents tell children that the only definitive *gender differences* are _____ and _____, and that they use "individual differences" rather than "gender differences" schema for organizing and processing information.

Short-Answer

1. Differentiate between the terms *sex* and *gender*.
2. What examples in your own life can be used to illustrate *gender stereotyping*?
3. What does the information in *Figure 3.1* (p. 54) suggest about the nature-nurture debate?
4. What patterns have been found in cross-cultural research on traditional meanings of *femininity* and *masculinity*.
5. What is the cross-cultural evidence concerning the universality of certain *gender role traits*?
6. What evidence is there in our society that gender roles are in *transition*?
7. Four *theories* of *gender role socialization* are reviewed in the text. Briefly describe each theory, identifying one strength and one weakness for each theory.
8. What are the major *agents of socialization* as reviewed in the text? Using your own experiences to illustrate, discuss how each agent has influenced your gender identity.
9. Four *consequences of gender stereotyping* are discussed in the book. What are these? what is the evidence provided in the text for each of the four? What are your opinions on this matter?
10. Women and men seem to have different kinds of relationships with *friends*. What are the findings on this subject as reported in the text? Do you agree with these findings and interpretations? Why?

VII. ANSWERS TO STUDY QUESTIONS

True-False

1.	T	(p. 53)	7.	T	(p. 60)
2.	F	(p. 53)	8.	F	(p. 61)
3.	F	(p. 55)	9.	F	(p. 63)
4.	T	(p. 58)	10.	T	(p. 65)
5.	T	(p. 59)	11.	T	(p. 67)
6.	F	(p. 59)	12.	F	(p. 70)

Multiple-Choice

1.	c	(p. 53)	8.	e	(p. 60)
2.	e	(p. 53)	9.	d	(p. 61)
3.	c	(p. 53)	10.	d	(p. 63)
4.	c	(p. 55)	11.	e	(p. 65)
5.	b	(p. 56)	12.	c	(p. 70)
6.	d	(pp. 58-59)	13.	a	(p. 72)
7.	d	(p. 59)	14.	c	(p. 73)

Fill-In

1. Gender identity (p. 53)
2. role (p. 53)
3. ascribed (p. 53)
4. X, Y, X (pp. 53-54)
5. hermaphrodites (p. 54)
6. nice, nurturant, potent, powerful (p. 55)
7. gender stereotypes (p. 56)
8. social-learning (p. 59)
9. cognitive-development (p. 60)
10. polarization, androcentrism, biological (p. 61)
11. agents of socialization (p. 61)
12. more complex (p. 63)
13. 27 (p. 65)
14. girls (. 66)
15. age, sex typing (p. 67)
16. conversation, activities (p. 71)
17. intimacy, connectedness, status, independence (p. 72)
18. anatomical, reproductive (p. 73)

PART VIII. COMMENT AND ANALYSIS

Global Perspective

"Is Gender Equality Possible?"

    Key Points:

    Questions you have?

Personal Reflection

"Nonsexist Nursery Rhymes"

    Key Points:

    Questions you have?

Critical Issues

"New Roles for Men and Women"

    Key Points:

    Questions you have?

Applying the Sociological Imagination

"Gendered Communication"

    Key Points:

    Questions you have?

Writing Your Own Script

"Reflections on Gender"

The Many Faces of Love

4

PART I. CHAPTER OUTLINE

I. What Is This Thing Called Love?
  A. Love as a Social Construction
  B. How Does Romantic Love Develop in Contemporary Society?
  C. Love In Western Society: A Historical Perspective
  D. The Importance of Love
II. How Do People Express Love?
  A. Lee's Six Styles of Loving
III. Love Versus Friendship, Infatuation, and Liking
  A. Close Friendship Versus Love
  B. Infatuation Versus Love
  C. Liking Versus Love
IV. Some Theories of Love
  A. The Wheel Theory of Love
  B. Love As Limerence
  C. Love As a Social Exchange
V. Love Across Gender and Race
  A. Gender Differences in Love Relationships
  B. Lesbian and Gay Love Relationships
  C. Female-Male Relationships Among African Americans
VI. Obstacles to Love and Loving Relationships
  A. Traditional Gender Role Socialization
  B. Patriarchy as an Obstacle to Lesbian Love
  C. Lack of Trust
  D. Jealousy and Envy
VII. Romantic Love in the 1990s and Beyond
VIII. Summary
IX. Key Terms
X. Questions for Study and Reflection
XI. Further Reading

PART II. LEARNING OBJECTIVES

1. To recognize the complex nature of the concept love.
2. To understand the concept of romantic love from a historical perspective.
3. To be able to identify and describe the different ways in which people express love.
4. To be able to differentiate between love, friendship, infatuation, and liking.
5. To gain insight into the nature of love through the application of three explanations of love today--the wheel theory, Limerence theory, and the social-exchange theory.
6. To be able to describe the gender differences in love relationships, compare lesbian and gay love relationships, and heterosexual relationships among African Americans.
7. To identify and understand some of the obstacles to love and loving relationships, including traditional gender role socialization, patriarchy, lack of trust, jealousy, and envy .
8. To consider how romantic love will be influenced by social forces into the next century.

PART III. CHAPTER REVIEW--KEY POINTS

Love is a central feature of life in the modern world. Much time and effort is devoted in our society to love and intimate relationships. There are many types of love. Love encompasses a wide variety of feelings and behaviors. The focus of this chapter is on romantic or erotic love.

WHAT IS THIS THING CALLED LOVE?

Love is an elusive emotion and very difficult to explain. Love is surrounded by myths and metaphors. each person experiences love differently. Most definitions of love describe it in terms of anyone of several of the following characteristics: deep emotional attachment, openness, self-disclosure, physical attraction, and personal growth. William Goode's widely cited definition of love is "a strong emotional attachment, a cathexis, between adolescents or adults of opposite sexes, with a least the component of sex, desire, and tenderness."

How do you define love? How do you know when you are in love? The opening vignette about Brad and Courtney's relationship provides an illustration of love's complexity.

Love as a Social Construction

It is not possible to come up with a single definition of love. However, the criteria that individuals use to arrive at the conclusion that they are in love are social in origin. According to a social-constructionist point of view, love can only be understood as symbolic or social construction that by itself has no meaning.

Feelings of romantic love have a physiological component, but is not only based on body reactions. Romantic love is also based upon the way in which we interpret and label our feelings and reactions. What we define as love or romantic love is rooted in societal and cultural values.

How Does Romantic Love Develop in Contemporary Society?

Love develops within the context of popular culture. The typical development sequence of heterosexual love in the 20th century seems to be: girl meets boy, they interact, they discover that they have common interests, values, and backgrounds, and at some point they define their feelings as love. Sex may or may not be part of the relationships. Variations to this sequence are of course numerous.

Love In Western Society: Historical Perspective

Today romantic love is almost always linked to sex and marriage. The linking of love with sex and marriage is a unique feature of romantic love, a type of love that is relatively new in human history. Its roots are traced back to ancient Greece and Rome.

Love in Ancient Greece: Notions of romantic love are traced back to Greek society of the fifth century B.C., and the writings of the philosopher Plato. Plato identified three kinds of love: *Agape* is selfless love; it is spontaneous and altruistic and requires nothing in return. *Eros* is selfish love; with an emphasis on physical pleasure. *Philos* is a deep friendship or brotherly love.

In ancient Greece, love was not associated with marriage. Love has more to do with the beauty and goodness of a person. Marriages were arranged by families. The primary role of women was to bear and care for children. Greeks believed that high status made people attractive. Since women did not hold high statuses they were not considered attractive. Greeks therefore downplayed the significance of heterosexual love.

Love in Ancient Rome: Upper-class Roman women were more educated and worldly, and more socially and intellectually equal to men, than were their counterparts in Greece. Thus, love in Roman society was oriented primarily toward heterosexual love. Love was still not connected to marriage. The most important par of the love relationship was the seduction of a desirable person. Love in this context was secretive.

The Early Christian Idea of Love: The early Christian idea of love was one of a nonsexual, nonerotic relationship. Sexual relations were even frowned upon for married couples.

Courtly Love: Among the powerful nobility between 1000 and 1300 A.D. *courtly love* emerged, combining to basic ideas of the period: male chivalry and the idealization of women. This idea of love was first heard in the romantic poetry of the French troubadours. Courtly love emphasized the sensuous.

Researcher Morton Hunt noted the emergence and development of romantic love was greatly influenced by three general features of heterosexual relations that became widespread during this period:

(1) the elevation of women in terms of social status and
      thus a greater emotional relationship with men,
(2) sexual fidelity to one person, and
(3) the notion that love should be reciprocal or mutual.

The Institutionalization of Love in Marriage: As society became more industrialized, the roles and functions of individuals and societal institutions changed. The family was seen as the institution responsible for providing emotional strength and support to its members. Love was seen as being a part of marriage. Love and sex were not yet blended. Romantic love was thought to be tender and warm, while sex was thought of as crude and vulgar. The blending of sex and love emerged during the sexual revolution of the 1920s.

The Importance of Love

Researchers have found love to be important both in terms of physical as well as our emotional health and well-being. Research findings concerning the relationship between love, sex, and well-being are discussed in the text.

Research indicates that the ability to love, to express it, and to accept it from others are learned behaviors, acquired through our early experiences in infancy and childhood. Attachment theory is discussed in this context.

HOW DO PEOPLE EXPRESS LOVE?

People express love in a variety of ways. Psychoanalyst Erich Fromm popularized the notion that there are many different kinds of love, romantic, brotherly, maternal, paternal, infantile, immature, and mature. According to Fromm, love has four components: care, responsibility, respect, and knowledge.

Social scientist Robert Sternberg has defined love in terms of a triangle-like relationship formed among three interlocking components: the emotional, or intimacy, the cognitive, or commitment, and the motivational, or passion. *Figure 4.1* (p. 81) diagrams the eight types of love that result from the combination of the interlocking components. The types of love include: nonlove, empty love, liking, infatuated love, compassionate love, fatuous love, romantic love, and consummate love.

Lee's Six Styles of Loving

Sociologist John Allen Lee proposed six based styles of loving. Using an analogy of a color wheel, he identified three primary styles of love relationships (red, yellow, and blue) eros, ludus, and storge.

Primary Styles of Love: Eros (physical attraction), *ludus* (playful, nonpossessive, challenging, without deep commitment), and *storge* (unexciting and uneventful).

Derived Styles of Love: Mania (combines eros and ludus), *pragma* (combines ludus and storge), and *agape* (combines eros and storge).

According to Lee, although people generally prefer one particular style of loving, they often express more than one style. The greater the difference between a couple in their style of loving, the harder it is for them to relate to each other.

Extensive research by Susan and Clyde Hendrick found a number of gender differences in styles of loving. While women and men do not differ significantly on eros and agape, gender differences on other love attitudes or styles consistently show up. Examples are discussed. The **Personal Reflection** box (p. 84) presents the Love Attitude Scale developed by the Hendricks to help identify your type of loving.

LOVE VERSUS FRIENDSHIP, INFATUATION, AND LIKING

Close Friendship Versus Love

Researchers Keith Davis and Michael Todd compared close friendship love and found that while the two are alike in many ways, there are crucial differences between them that make love relationships more rewarding, and, at the same time, more volatile. Their prototype *friendship* includes the following characteristics:

(1)	enjoyment	(5)	mutual assistance
(2)	acceptance	(6)	confiding
(3)	trust	(7)	understanding
(4)	respect	(8)	spontaneity

Love, in contrast is friendship and more: It is passion and caring. But it is also instability and mutual criticism. *Figure 4.2* (p. 85) presents a diagram of the connection between love and friendship.

Infatuation Versus Love

Infatuation involves a strong attraction based on an idealized picture of the other person. It is usually superficial and of short duration. It tends to focus on a single characteristic of the other person and has a physical element.

Liking Versus Love

Liking is more logical and rational, less emotional and possessive, than love. According to Zick Rubin, both liking and love consist of the same basic elements. What sets them apart is their differential emphasis on these components. According to Elaine Hatfield and William Walster contend that the difference between love and liking has to do with the depth of our feelings and the degree to which we are involved with the other people.

SOME THEORIES OF LOVE

The Wheel Theory of Love

While some people fall in love at first sight, many researchers suggest love is not necessarily haphazard or sudden. Ira Reiss's *wheel theory of love* focuses on love as a developmental process. It involves four major interpersonal processes: *rapport*--a feeling of ease or relaxed with one another, *self-revelation*--the disclosure of intimate and personal feelings, *mutual dependence*--a reliance on each other for fulfillment, and *fulfillment of personal needs*--the ability of each partner to satisfy the needs of the other.
This theory is diagramed in *Figure 4.3* (p. 87). All four processes are seen as interdependent.

Love as Limerence

Psychologist Dorothy Tennov used the term *limerence* to describe being in love. Limerence refers to extreme attraction, complete absorption or obsessive preoccupation with another person. Limerence may be characterized by its speed of occurrence, intensity, reciprocation, and time it lasts.

Love as a Social Exchange

Sociologist John Scanzoni uses some basic principles of economics to explain why we are attracted to and fall in love with some people and not with others and why we pursue and remain in some relationships and avoid or break off others.

LOVE ACROSS GENDER AND RACE

Gender Differences in Love Relationships

Much research has shown that females and males construct their realities of love generally in very difference terms. For example, Zick Rubin found that females distinguish much more sharply between liking and loving than males do. Men have also been found to fall in love sooner and harder and to remain in love longer than women. Once a relationship develops, however, women tend to be more expressive than men, more intense and more likely to idealize the love object, and they tend to prefer emotional closeness, whereas men prefer giving instrumental help and sex. The different emphasis women and men put on love and sex carries over into marriage.
The femininization of love: Fancesca Cancian argues that only women's style of loving is recognized, and there is a myth that women both need love more than men do and that

women are more skilled at loving than men. She argues that love should be androgynous. The **Applying the Sociological Imagination** box (p. 90) focuses on the question: How do the media portray love?

Lesbian and Gay Love Relationships

Many lesbian and gay couples often feel compelled to hide their feelings because many people do not approve of such relationships. Because of the societal disapproval, intimacy between people of the same sex is more inclusive, intense, and possessive. Gay love is often very physical and very emotional. In general, however, lesbian and gay love is very similar to heterosexual love. The **Family Profile** box (p. 91) provides perspectives on issues relevant to a particular lesbian couple.

There are major differences between gay and lesbian couples, including the manner in which the relationship develops and in its duration. Gender identity and gender roles are discussed as critical factors affecting the organization of lesbian and gay love.

Female-Male Relationships Among African Americans

Popular literature, which may not be particularly systematic and accurate, has reported a crisis in African American female-male love relationships over the last several decades. There has been difficulty reported in developing and maintaining meaningful love relationships. According to an article in Ebony, romantic entanglements have often become a one-on-one battle for control. The improving economic status of females relative to males among African Americans is an important factor.

The novel *Waiting to Exhale* (there is also a movie version) represents very well the media version of romance and intimate relationships among African Americans. Much of this story focuses on four lovelorn women who are looking for "Mr. Right."

There is some evidence that there is a difference in the way blacks and whites view love. This research indicates, for example, that blacks tend to have a more romantic view of love.

OBSTACLES TO LOVE AND LOVING RELATIONSHIPS

Traditional Gender Role Socialization

Traditional gender-role socialization creates different priorities for males and females in relationships. Researchers have found evidence of an emotional division of labor within heterosexual love relationships. Women tend to be more oriented toward the relationship. Another orientation between the sexes concerns who gets and who gives in a relationship. Researcher Robert Karen has found data that suggest women give more and men get more in heterosexual relationships.

Patriarchy as an Obstacle to Lesbian Love

Some research indicates that men are threatened by romantic love between women. The issue of the dependency of women on men within patriarchal societies is discussed.

Lack of Trust

Trust is seen as one of the most important and necessary aspects of any close or intimate relationship. *Trust* refers to *the degree of confidence a person feels when he or she thinks about a relationship.* John Rempel and John Holmes identified three basic elements of trust: *predictability, dependability,* and *faith.* Each of these elements is discussed and illustrated.

Jealousy and Envy

Jealousy refers to *the thoughts and feelings that emerge when an actual or desired relationship is believed to be threatened.* Many interrelated emotions are involved with jealousy. *Envy* refers to *unhappiness or discontent with ourselves that arises from the belief that something about ourselves does not measure up to someone else's level.* Jealousy, like love, is a social construction, an emotion that is shaped by a person's culture.

The Nature and Pattern of Jealousy: Internally and externally induced factors are involved in causing jealousy. Examples of each are discussed in the text. There is much variation in how jealousy is experienced by individuals and within different relationships. Ralph Hupka has found consistent differences across cultures in both the degree to which jealousy is present in a society and the ways in which it is expressed. The **Global Perspectives** box (p. 96) provides a brief discussion concerning "high" and "low" jealousy societies. Other historical and global examples are reviewed in the text.

In summary, the cultural basis of jealousy is well illustrated in the facts that: (1) the basis for jealousy and the types of behavior appropriate to the expression of jealousy can and often do change over time, and (2) the same behavior can provoke different feelings and actions in different cultures, and (3) within the same culture, the same behavior stimulates feelings and expressions of jealousy under one set of circumstances and does not under another set of circumstances.

Gender differences in jealousy: Research suggests women and men may experience this emotion differently. Some of the more prevalent findings are: (1) women feel jealousy more intensely than men do, (2) jealousy causes women greater suffering and distress than it does men, (3) men are less likely than women to stay in a relationship that makes them jealous, (4) women are more likely than men to fight to win back a lost lover rather than give up the relationship, (5) women's feelings of personal inadequacy lead to jealousy, whereas the reverse is true for men, (6) men are more likely to express their jealousy in the form of violence, and (7) women more often consciously attempt to make their partner jealous as a way of testing the relationship.

Destructive Jealousy: This form of jealousy can be physically damaging and life-threatening. It can also take a toll in the form of depression, fear, anxiety, self-doubt,

67

and low self-esteem. Researchers Lynn Smith and Gordon Clayton suggest four options for dealing with jealousy, these include:

(1) getting out of the relationship
(2) ignore or tolerate those behaviors that make you jealous
(3) attempt to change your partner's behavior
(4) work on your own jealousy

ROMANTIC LOVE IN THE 1990s AND BEYOND

Romantic love in the 1990s reflects the changes that have been evident in the roles of women and men in general. The traditional power relationship characterized by male dominance and female submission is significantly changing. Yet, many traditional aspects of love, dating, intimacy, and mate selection remain entrenched in U.S. society. The result is a great deal of anxiety and uncertainty as couples try to balance traditional norms with current developments in the absence of clear-cut rules and guidelines. The **Writing Your Own Script** box (p. 98) asks you to consider the issue of the social construction of love.

PART IV. KEY TERMS

romantic love   courtly love

wheel theory of love   limerence

androgynous   infatuation

femininization of love   trust

envy   jealousy

68

PART V. KEY RESEARCHERS

Erich Fromm

Robert Sternberg

John Allen Lee

Plato

Morton Hunt

Ira Reiss

Dorothy Tennov

Zick Rubin

Robert Karen

John Rempel and John Holmes

Ralph Hupka

Lynn Smith and Gordon Clayton

PART VI. STUDY QUESTIONS

True-False

1. T F The major difference between *romantic love* and other types of love is the element of *eroticism*.
2. T F *Homosexuality* was viewed with disgust in ancient Greek society.
3. T F The notion of *courtly love* had little influence on Western thought or romantic behavior.
4. T F The concept *storge* is used to depict a style of loving that is unexciting and uneventful.
5. T F According to Ira Reiss' *wheel theory of love*, most people fall in love at first sight.
6. T F Ira Reiss suggests in his *wheel theory of love* that a key factor in the interpersonal processes of rapport is social background.
7. T F *Limerence theory* uses basic economic principles in explaining why people fall in love.
8. T F Research has found that females distinguish much more sharply between *liking* and *loving* than males do.
9. T F Research has found that men fall in *love* sooner and harder and to remain in love longer than women.
10. T F *Envy* refers to unhappiness or discontent with ourselves that arises from the belief that something about ourselves does not measure up to someone else's level.

Multiple-Choice

1. Which of the following is *not* a type of love as identified by Plato?

   (a) eros
   (b) agape
   (c) philos
   (d) thanatos

2. According to the text, what led to the belief that love should occur before, not after marriage?

   (a) industrialization
   (b) ideals of Ancient Rome
   (c) ideals of Ancient Greece
   (d) early Christian notions

3. According to Erich Fromm, the essential *components of love* are:

   (a) care, responsibility, respect, and knowledge
   (b) sex, identity, security
   (c) passion, intimacy, attachment
   (d) companionship, friendship, concern, faith

4. Who defined love in terms of a *triangle-like* relationship among three components: commitment, passion, and intimacy?

   (a) Erich Fromm   (d) Ernie Davis
   (b) Plato   (e) Robert Sternberg
   (c) Jesse Bernard

5. According to John Allen Lee, *manic love* is characterized by obsession and is a combination of:

   (a) eros and storge   (d) eros and ludus
   (b) ludus and storge   (e) pragma and agape
   (c) friendship and infatuation

6. According to Keith Davis and Michael Todd spontaneity, enjoyment, and trust are all characteristics of:

   (a) love   (c) friendship
   (b) liking   (d) infatuation

7. Which of the following is *not* true of *infatuation*?

   (a) it has a strong sexual element
   (b) it focuses on a specific characteristic of the person
   (c) it is long lasting
   (d) it is superficial

8. Ira Reiss's _____ *theory of love* proposes that love involves four major interpersonal processes: rapport, self-revelation, mutual dependence, and need fulfillment.

   (a) wheel   (c) ladder
   (b) color   (d) limerence

9. Dorothy Tennov uses the term _____ to refer to a style of love characterized by an extreme attraction, a complete absorption or obsessive preoccupation of one person with another.

   (a) agape   (d) eros
   (b) rapport   (e) limerence
   (c) mania

10. Researcher Francesca Cancian described he gender differences in love relationships in terms of:

   (a)   an emasculation of males   (c)   the dominance of women
   (b)   a romanticizing of sex   (d)   the feminization of love

11. According to Robert Karen:

   (a)   men get much more out of love relationships than they give
   (b)   women get much more out of love relationships than they give
   (c)   men and women share equally in relationships
   (d)   gay and lesbian couples experience love differently than heterosexual couples
   (e)   patriarchy inhibits the development of love in marriage

12. John Rempel and John Holmes identified three basic elements of _____: *predictability, dependability,* and *faith.*

   (a)   love   (d)   limerence
   (b)   trust   (e)   envy
   (c)   jealousy

Fill-In

1. Although a common thread of caring is woven through all love relationships, the major difference between these feelings of love and *romantic love* is the element of _____.

2. According to a _____ point of view, love can only be understood as symbolic or a social construction that by itself has no intrinsic meaning.

3. _____ *love* combined two basic ideas of the time period (1000-1300 A.D.) male chivalry and the idealization of women.

4. According to Erich Fromm, the four essential *components of love* include _____, _____, _____, and _____.

5. According to Lee's analysis, the *derived styles* of love include _____, _____, and _____.

6. Zick Rubin found that *females* distinguish much more sharply between _____ and _____ than males do.

7. Because of societal disapproval, gay lovers frequently look to each other to satisfy all their needs. Thus, *gay love* is often more _____ and sometimes _____.

8. A major difference between heterosexual and gay or lesbian couples seems to be in the manner in which the love relationship _____ and in its _____.

9. Some evidence suggests that there is a difference in the way blacks and whites view love. Some research indicates that blacks tend to have a more _____ view of love.

10. _____ refers to the thoughts and feelings that emerge when an actual or desired relationship is believed to be threatened.

11. According to researchers John Rempel and John Holmes, the three elements of *trust* include: _____, _____, and _____.

Short-Answer

1. Briefly recount the historical development of *romantic love* in Western society.
2. Differentiate between how love was understood in *ancient Greek* and *ancient Roman* societies.
3. What was *courtly love*? What is its connection to our modern understanding of romantic love?
4. How did *industrialization* affect there development of love in Western societies?
5. Differentiate between *Erich Fromm's* and *Robert Sternberg's* perspectives on love. What are the *types* and *styles* of love being identified by these researchers.
6. Provide illustrations of the *primary* and *derived* styles of love using John Allen Lee's *color wheel theory*.
7. Differentiate between *friendship*, *infatuation*, and *liking*.
8. What does Dorothy Tennov mean by *love as limerence*?
9. Identify the major differences between love relationships as experienced and understood by females and males.
10. How do African American and whites generally differ in the experience of love?
11. What are Ralph Hupka's points about *jealousy*? How is jealousy experienced differently by females and males?
12. How does *jealousy* differ from *envy*?
13. What points are being made by our authors concerning *love* in the 1990s? What are the issues being raised today concerning gender and love?

PART VII. ANSWERS TO STUDY QUESTIONS

True-False

1.	T	(p. 76)	6.	T	(p. 87)
2.	F	(p. 78)	7.	F	(p. 88)
3.	F	(p. 78)	8.	T	(p. 89)
4.	T	(p. 81)	9.	T	(p. 89)
5.	F	(p. 86)	10.	T	(p. 95)

Multiple-Choice

1.	d	(p. 78)	7.	c	(p. 85)
2.	a	(p. 79)	8.	a	(p. 86)
3.	a	(p. 81)	9.	e	(p. 89)
4.	e	(p. 81)	10.	d	(p. 90)
5.	d	(p. 81)	11.	a	(p. 93)
6.	c	(pp. 83-85)	12.	b	(p. 94)

Fill-In

1. eroticism   (p. 76)
2. social-constructionist (p. 76)
3. Courtly (p. 78)
4. care, responsibility, respect, knowledge (p. 81)
5. mania, pragma, agape (p. 81)
6. liking, loving (p. 89)
7. intense, possessive (p. 90)
8. develops, duration (p. 91)
9. romantic (p. 93)
10. jealousy (p. 94)
11. predictability, confidence, faith (p. 94)

PART VIII. COMMENT AND ANALYSIS

Personal Reflection

"Abbreviated Form of the Love Attitude Scale"

Comments and reactions to Scale:

Applying the Sociological Imagination

"How Do the Media Portray Love?"

Key Points:

Questions you have?

Family Profile

"Pamela Outlar and Betty Crum"

Key Points:

Questions you have?

Global Perspectives

"High-and Low-Jealousy Cultures"

Key Points:

Questions you have?

Writing Your Own Script

"The Social Construction of Love"

Dating, Coupling, and Mate Selection

PART I. CHAPTER OUTLINE

I. Mate Selection In Cross-Cultural and Historical Perspective
   A. Mate Selection Cross-Culturally
   B. Mate Selection in the United States: A Historical Perspective
   C. Functions of Dating: Past and Present
II. The Intersections of Race, Gender, Class, and Sexual Orientation
   A. Dating Patterns Among African Americans
   B. The Impact of Gender
   C. The Impact of Social Class on the Dating Process
   D. Lesbian and Gay Dating
III. Theories of Mate Selection
   A. Exchange Theories
   B. Filter Theories
III. Mate Selection: Finding and Meeting Partners
   A. The Marriage Market and the Pool of Eligibles
   B. Freedom Versus Constraint in Mate Selection
   C. Other Factors That Affect Mate Selection
   D. Personal Qualities and Mate Selection
   E. The Life Cycle and Mate Selection
IV. Meeting Partners: Where and How
   A. School, Church, and Work
   B. Singles' Bars and Gay Bars
   C. Self-Advertising: Personal Ads
   D. Dating Clubs and Dating Services
   E. Video Dating
   F. Computer Dating
   G. Dating in Cyberspace
V. The Future of Dating
VI. Violence In Dating and Intimate Relationships
   A. Physical Abuse
   B. Date and Acquaintance Rape
VII. Breaking Up

PART II. LEARNING OBJECTIVES

1. To understand mate selection from a historical and cross-cultural perspective.
2. To describe the functions of dating, both past and present.
3. To discuss the impact of dating behavior of race, gender, and social class.
4. To describe the dating patterns of lesbians and gays.
5. To describe four theories of mate selection.
6. To evaluate the influence of physical attraction and companionship on mate selection.
7. To discuss how people meet potential mates in the 1990s, both traditional and modern.
8. To discuss violence and abuse in dating relationships.

MATE SELECTION IN CROSS-CULTURAL AND HISTORICAL PERSPECTIVE

Dating is not a common practice in most countries. It is rare in China, India, South America, and most countries in Africa, and forbidden in most Muslim countries. Only in Western countries like the United States, Great Britain, Canada, and Australia is dating a common form of mate selection.

Sociologists use the term *mate selection* to refer loosely to *the wide range of behaviors and social relationships individuals engage in prior to marriage and that lead to long- or short-term pairing or coupling.*

Mate Selection Cross-Culturally

Mate selection varies across a continuum of practices around the world. These customs range from *arranged marriages* by village shamans or contractual agreements between families to the seemingly *free choice* of individuals based on criteria varying from love to physical attractiveness to economic considerations. As the opening vignette illustrates, many people who participate in a system of arranged mate selection find it preferable to free-choice mate selection.

Political, social, and/or economic change especially industrialization, in cultures around the world has brought about some significant changes in mate selection customs cross-culturally. According to Philip Shennon the sex ratio of single men to single women is 3:1. There is a great bias in China for male children. Partly as a result of this demographic condition, traditional means of mate selection are changing. The uses of technology to assist in the search for a mate are discussed. Further, discussion focuses on the improving social status of women relative to men given the sex ratio.

A transformation of the nature of the mate selection process as a result of the glut of single men is occurring in other nations as well. In India the sex ratio among the single population is 133 men to every 100 women. However, nonindustrialized nations and often in rural areas within industrial nations, mate selection continues to be predominately arranged.

Mate Selection in the United States: A Historical Perspective

Mate selection in the United States is based on notions of romantic love, a sentiment shared by both women and men. Dating has been described by some researchers as a "courtship game" that has its own set of rules, strategies, and goals.

Early U.S. Courtship and the Development of Dating: As in many societies around the world, mate selection in the U.S. has focused on heterosexual couples. In colonial days marriage was considered to be important in bringing order and stability to life. Demographic considerations as well as very precise cultural norms often dictated the ways in which couples came together.

The process of mate selection eventually assumed a more formal pattern referred to as *calling* and later *keeping company.* This latter custom evolved in *going steady.* In New England states the practice of *bundling*--in which a couple keeping company spent the night together separated by a board in the middle of the bed or wrapped in blankets on the bed-- was common. Some research estimates that one-third of all 18th century brides were pregnant at the time of their wedding.

Industrialization had a significant influence on dating patterns. Mass production of the automobile probably had the greatest impact.

Dating in the United States: The 1920s Through the 1980s: By the 1920s, amid the increased affluence and leisure of the white middle classes, dating became a major method of mate selection. The history of the idea of dating in the U.S. is discussed. It was competitive, and involved rating prospective partners on clear standards of popularity.

During the 1940s and 1950s, dating spread from college campuses to most cultural groups in the United States. Ersel LeMasters described going steady as an important dating pattern of this period. According to LeMasters, dating involved six stages of progressively deeper commitment, including casual dating, random dating, going steady, dating each other exclusively, engagement, and marriage.

Like other cultural patterns, dating partners incorporate many of the values of the larger society. The sexual double standard is discussed. Factors during the 1960s changed sexual norms in significant ways. During the 1980s, dating started at an earlier age and lasted longer than it had in previous generations.

Contemporary Trends in Dating: The 1990s and Beyond: Sociologists agree that dating today is different than it was a generation ago. Even the term *dating* is out of style now. Dating today is based far more on mutuality and sharing than on traditional gender roles.

Functions of Dating: Past and Present

G.N. Ramu summarizes the functions of dating in terms of *socialization, recreation, status Grading and Achievement,* and *mate Selection.* Regarding this last function, Americans are still highly committed to marriage. Given he longer dating period today, dating continues to fulfill the function of **anticipatory socialization**--*socialization that is directed toward learning roles.*

THE INTERSECTIONS OF RACE, GENDER, CLASS, AND SEXUAL ORIENTATION

Dating, like all other social behaviors, is rooted in social as well as historical conditions of life. The literature on dating and mate selection for some groups, while providing some insight, is limited.

Dating Patterns Among African Americans

The practice of dating among African Americans varies by region, historical period, social class, and age. Robert Staples' research concerning changing dating patterns among African Americans as they moved from small Southern communities to large urban areas outside the South is discussed by the author. According to Staples, the historically low *sex ratio--the number of men to every one hundred women*--in the African American community has traditionally limited the dating and mate selection options of African American women. As African American women age, the already small pool of eligible males available to date sinks even further.

A noticeable characteristic of contemporary African American dating patterns is the significant increase in interracial dating, especially on college campuses. Rates of interracial marriage continue to be very low--less than five percent.

The Impact of Gender

Dating scripts are still basically gender specific. Susan Basow, using social-learning theory contends that men's scripts focus on planning and paying for the date as well as initiating sexual behavior, whereas women's scripts focus on enhancing their appearance, making conversation, and controlling sexual behavior.

The Impact of Social Class on the Dating Process

As with race, there is a paucity of research specifically focused on dating across class. What is known is that individuals from similar social class backgrounds share similar interests and goals which are the basis for dating and mate selection choices. Most people in the U.S. date and marry within their social class.

Upper Class: Dating with this class tends to be much more regulated than in other social classes. The young are socialized to focus on education and career rather than romance and sex. Many activities of young people are closely supervised by parents.

Middle Class: Going steady remains common among the middle-class and usually leads to engagement. Contemporary dating in the middle-class includes more freedom from parents' supervision. *Cruising--where a group of teenagers (usually males) pack into a car and drive around the neighborhood looking for females to pick up*--is a popular pattern in the mate selection process.

Lower Class: Most research on dating suggests that lower-class families tend to exercise the least control over mate selection. Dating in the lower-class tends to be more informal, with the engagement stage often being skipped.

Lesbian and Gay Dating

Very little is known about dating behavior among lesbians and gays. Because society continues to stigmatize homosexual behavior, much mate selection behavior is carried out in privacy. Like heterosexual couples, most lesbians and gays date for recreational and entertainment purposes, but the development of love relationships is also an important goal. In our society there are many obstacles to homosexuals in finding a permanent partner.

As with heterosexuals, there appear to be some fundamental gender differences in the dating and mate selection behaviors of lesbians and gays.

African American Lesbian and Gay Dating: A study of middle-class lesbians showed that although two-thirds were in a serious relationship, only one-third lived with their partner. The average age at which women reported first being attracted to a woman was about 16, but the first lesbian experience did not occur until approximately age 19. Two-thirds had had at least one lesbian relationship with some other woman and 39 percent with some other woman of color. The median number of sexual partners was nine. This is similar to white lesbians.

Dating and mate selection among gays may be influenced by sociocultural factors. African American gays tend to be more bisexual than white gays and have fewer brief, anonymous partners. Over two-thirds reported that half of their partners were white men.

THEORIES OF MATE SELECTION

Exchange Theories

Exchange theories revolve around the notion that individuals attempt to maximize their rewards and minimize their costs to achieve the most favorable outcome.

J. N. Edwards refers to this principle as the *exchange theory of homogamous mating* in which people with equivalent resources develop relationships. The one who is least interested has an advantage and is in a position to dominate. This is described as the *principle of least interest.*

Stimulus-Value-Role Theory: According to this theory of interpersonal attraction by Bernard Murstein, in a situation of relatively free choice, attraction and interaction depend on the exchange value of the assets and liabilities that each person brings to the situation.

Equity Theory: Equity theory proposes that a person is attracted to another by a fair deal rather than by a profitable exchange.

Filter Theories

David Klimek suggests that people use a filtering system which reduces the field of eligibles. Filtering theories, or *process theories* as they are also known, suggest that many factors are involved in the marital choice. *Figure 5.1* (p. 114) diagrams the basic idea of the filter theory of mate selection. The *filters* include variables such as age propinquity, age, race and ethnicity, social class, physical attraction, and family and peer pressure.

MATE SELECTION: FINDING AND MEETING PARTNERS

The Marriage Market and the Pool of Eligibles

Sociological research reveals that meeting prospective mates, choosing partners, developing a dating relationship, and falling in love are not random activities but are predictable and are structured by a number of social and demographic factors. This section of the text defines these principles and describes how they apply to mate selection in the United States.

Marriage Market: The marriage market concept implies that we enter the mate selection process with certain resources and we trade these resources for the best offer we can get. In some countries a **dowry**--or *sums of money or property brought to the marriage by females*--is used in the marriage market.

Pool of Eligibles: Sociologists refer to a **pool of eligibles** as *people whom our society has defined as acceptable marriage partners for us.* With amazing consistency, we are very much alike the people we meet, fall in love with, and marry. This phenomenon is referred to as **homogamy**--*the tendency to meet, date, and marry someone very similar to ourselves in terms of important or desirable characteristics.* Two of the most common sets of rules governing mate selection and the pool of eligibles are *exogamy* and *endogamy*. *Exogamy* refers to *marriage outside a particular group.* *Endogamy* refers to *marriage within a particular group.* In *Figure 5.2* (p. 116), the norms of endogamy and exogamy and how they help create our pool of eligibles is described.

Freedom Versus Constraint in Mate Selection

Two of the most important factors that constrain us in the mate selection process are the marriage squeeze and the marriage gradient.

The Marriage Squeeze: Demographic data reveal that at any given time in the United States since World War II, there has been a greater number of women than men who are eligible for marriage and looking for a partner. This imbalance in the sex ratio of marriage-aged women as the **marriage squeeze**, whereby *one sex has a more limited pool of eligibles than the other does.* Recent demographic data indicate that this pattern is reversing. *Table 5.1* (p. 117) show the percentage of married women and men by selected age categories.

The Marriage Gradient: Informal norms require women to marry men of equal or higher social status. Because women marry upward and men marry downward, men at the top have a much larger field of eligibles than men do at the bottom. Women at the top have a very small pool of eligibles, whereas women at the bottom have a much wider range of men to choose from. **Hypergamy** refers to *the tendency to marry upward in social class*, whereas **hypogamy** refers to *the tendency to marry downward in social class*. This marriage gradient has a greater impact on African Americans than on whites.

Race: Dating, mate selection, and marriage are probably most endogamous and homogamous in terms of race. About 98 percent of marriages in the U.S. occur within the same racial group. However, recent surveys have revealed that about one-half of all Americans would be willing to date someone of another race if they were single.

Interracial couples are having a particularly hard time in the midst of rising racial and ethnic tensions in this country. Examples of bigotry in contemporary U.S. society are presented--some may astound you.

Social Class: Sociologists typically measure social class using a composite scale consisting of level of educational attainment, occupation, and level of income. People in the U.S. tend to mate with people from their own socioeconomic class.

Age: Informal norms operate to keep mate election fairly homogamous in terms of age. Most people date and marry someone within two to five years of their own age.

Religion: Religious homogamy limits choices. Some studies show that 90 percent of people in the U.S. who marry select partners who are religiously similar to themselves.

Sex and Gender: Exogamous norms regulating behavior have been encoded into law to ensure that people mate heterosexually. There is great stigma to same-sex relationships in our society.

Other Factors hat Affect Mate Selection

Propinquity: **Propinquity** is used by sociologists to *denote proximity or closeness in place and space*. Traditionally, residential propinquity has been a major part of mate selection in the United States, and has been closely tied to other factors such as race, social class, etc.

Family and Peer Pressure: The pressures of family and friends on mate selection can be significant. Direct and indirect influences are involved.

Personal Qualities and Mate Selection

Attraction: One key point is that we tend to think we are better looking than other people do. Furthermore, men are more likely than women to exaggerate their appearance. Dating and marriage relationships tend to be endogamous for physical appearance. The greater our level of attractiveness the greater our bargaining ability in the marriage market.

Companionship: Communication and sexual adjustment are identified as two crucial attributes that contribute to companionship in an intimate relationship.

The Life Cycle and Mate Selection

The desire to date or participate generally in the mate selection process does not begin and end with youth. The fact that many people are delaying marriage, a high divorce rate, better health, and increasing life expectancy means that an increasing number of older adults will enter or reenter dating relationships across the life course.

MEETING PARTNERS: WHERE AND HOW

School, Church, and Work

The high school and college campus are traditional places where pairing and dating take place. Today places of religious worship less frequently serve the purpose of bringing people together in the mate selection process compared with times past. The work place also plays a role in providing opportunities for mate selection, though it often offers only limited contact with eligible mates.

Singles' Bars and Gay Bars

Bars provide a space where people can feel comfortable and meet other single people. Companionship is a major reason why people go to singles' bars. Gay bars are rejected by some lesbians and gays as meat markets.

Self-Advertising: Personal Ads

Personal ads are becoming a popular way to meet people for mate selection purposes. This form of finding prospective mates is no longer considered either perverted or desperate. There are some interesting gender differences in the personal ads. For example, women defined or offered themselves as attractive more often than men, and men sought attractive partners and requested photographs far more often than women do. Men offered financial security much more than women did.

Dating Clubs and Dating Services

Dating clubs and services can be very popular because they cater to a specific clientele. Examples are discussed in the text.

Video Dating

Many singles now use videos to help in mate selection. There are several companies that prepare and store audiotape and videotape files for clients. Costs can be very high.

Computer Dating

Computer dating services have clients complete a comprehensive questionnaire. This information is fed into a computer that matches it with other clients who have similar profiles. Other people who want more control over the mate selection process use their personal computer to get in touch with prospective partners through dating networks.

Dating in Cyberspace

Modern life for the unmarried professional today is increasingly complicated and full, making finding a partner difficult. According to researcher Pamela Cytrynbaum, many singles today treat their romantic life just as they do their career. The dating industry is changing dramatically as a result of new and increasing computer technology.

Some of the advantages of computer dating services include providing a place for people to meet; saving time and expenses. It also allows people to research and meet people with similar interests, goals, and lifestyles. One of the risks is meeting someone who may later prove to be disappointing, or even worse, violent. Cyberspace *stalkers* are a major concern for people using this avenue in the dating and mate selection processes.

THE FUTURE OF DATING

Dating in some form or another will probably be around for some time to come. The threats of AIDS, physical and sexual abuse, and dangerous drinking habits have complicated traditional dating practices, so new ways of dating will likely emerge.

VIOLENCE IN DATING AND INTIMATE RELATIONSHIPS

Physical Abuse

One in four high school students report involvement in abusive or violent relationships. Most victims are females, most remain in the relationship, and many victims and their offenders see the violence as an indication of love. Most females believe that the violence will come after the wedding; this is not the case however. The **Critical Issues** box (p. 126) takes a closer look at violence and abuse in dating relationships.

Date and Acquaintance Rape

Although most rapes are date or acquaintance rapes, most reported rapes are stranger rapes. Many people still believe that a sexual encounter between two people who know each other cannot be a rape. One study found that one-third of the 2,000 college men surveyed admitted forcing a woman to have sex with him.

Much can be done to reduce or eradicate courtship violence. Given that rape is a learned behavior within the context of a masculine self-concept, then it can be unlearned. College campus security and counseling programs are more available today. Much more needs to be done.

BREAKING UP

Breaking up can take many forms. Some research indicates gender differences related to breakups before marriage. Women are more likely to initiate a break up than men, possibly because women must be more practical than men in choosing a mate. Some research indicates that breaking up before marriage is less stressful than doing so after being married, but breaking up is seldom easy.

In the **Writing Your Own Script** box (p. 128) you are asked to consider your own personal biography and social structure in terms of the selection of a mate.

PART IV. KEY CONCEPTS

dating

mate selection

courtship

getting together

bundling

arranged marriage

going steady

anticipatory socialization

dowries

pool of eligibles

homogamy

exogamy

endogamy

sex ratio

cruising

marriage squeeze

hypergamy

hypogamy

marriage gradient

propinquity

rape   acquaintance rape

date rape

PART V. KEY RESEARCHERS

Susan Steinfirst and Barbara Morgan   Pamela Cytrynbaum

G.N. Ramu   Susan Basow

Phillip Shenon   Willard Waller

Bernard Murstein   David Klimek

Ersel LeMasters   Allen Bell and Martin Weinberg

J. N. Edwards

PART VI. STUDY QUESTIONS

True-False

1. T F   In most traditional (nonindustrialized) societies mate selection takes the form of *arranged marriages*.

2. T F   According to research by Phillip Shenon, given recent demographic changes in Chinese society, the *status of women* in the mate selection process has declined.

3. T F   The *Victorian sex ethic* was not replaced by dating as a means of mate selection until the 1960s in the U.S.

4. T F   In the 1990s dating is based far more on *mutuality* and *sharing* than on traditional gender roles.

5. T F   *Dating* has been found by sociologists to be one of the few social phenomena not rooted in social or historical conditions.

6. T F   Research by Allen Bell and Martin Weinberg suggests that black gays tend to be more *bisexual* than white gays.

7. T F   Two examples of *exchange theories* include *stimulus-value-role theory* and *equity theory*.

8. T F   *Exogamy* refers to marriage outside a particular group.

9. T F   The *marriage gradient* refers to the demographic condition of their being more women than men in a particular age range within a given population.

10. T F   Research has found that we tend to think we are better looking than other people do. Furthermore, men are more likely than women to exaggerate their appearance.

11. T F   Most literature on dating continues to focus on *college students*, thus in many ways perpetuating the myth that dating is primarily a white, middle-class, college-aged phenomenon.

12. T F   Although most rapes are date or acquaintance rapes, most *reported* rapes are stranger rapes.

Multiple-Choice

1. The practice of *dating is*:

    (a)   common in most countries today
    (b)   not a common practice in most countries today
    (c)   allowed in most Muslim countries today
    (d)   not a relatively new phenomenon

2. Sociologists use the term_____ to refer loosely to the wide range of behavior and social relationships individuals engage in prior to marriage and that lead to long-term or short-term pairings or coupling.

    (a) dating
    (b) courtship
    (c) mate selection
    (d) anticipatory socialization
    (e) the marriage gradient

3. In China, the *ratio* of single men to single women over the age of 15 is:

    (a) 2:1   (d) 3:1
    (b) 1:2   (e) 1:3
    (c) 6:1

4. In which of the following cultures has the arranged form of marriage given way to more free-choice practices?

    (a) India   (d) all of these cultures
    (b) Turkey   (e) none of these cultures
    (c) Japan

5. Researchers Daniel Smith and Michael Hindus estimated that approximately _____ percent of all 18th century brides were *pregnant* at the time of their wedding.

    (a) 1   (d) 33
    (b) 20   (e) 60
    (c) 12

6. Which of the following researchers developed a *six stage model* of dating?

    (a) Ersel LeMasters   (d) Reuben Hill
    (b) Willard Waller   (e) Robert Staples
    (c) Bernard Murstein

7. Which of the following is *not* a function of dating as summarized by G.N. Ramu?

    (a) recreation   (c) socialization
    (b) status grading   (d) attainment of power

8. Socialization that is directed toward learning future roles is know as _____ *socialization*.

   (a) anticipatory   (c) functional
   (b) experiential   (d) status

9. According to *exchange theory*, who in a relationship has the power?

   (a) the person with the most interest in the relationship
   (b) the person with the least interest in the relationship
   (c) either person, depending on personality
   (d) males always have the power
   (e) females always have the power

10. The *stimulus-value-role theory, equity theory,* and *the principle of least interest* all have their roots in which of the following theories?

    (a) structural-functional   (c) symbolic-interaction
    (b) conflict   (d) exchange

11. People of the same age who marry one another is an example of:

    (a) hypergamy   (d) the mating gradient
    (b) hypogamy   (e) endogamy
    (c) exogamy

12. Sociologists have defined the imbalance in the ratio of marriage-aged woman as:

    (a) endogamy   (d) a marriage squeeze
    (b) exogamy   (e) a marriage gradient
    (c) hypergamy

13. In most cultures, including the U.S, informal norms encourage women to marry men of equal or higher social status, this is referred to as:

    (a) propinquity   (c) the marriage squeeze
    (b) the marriage gradient   (d) endogamy

14. *Propinquity* has to do with:

    (a) age differences   (d) gender roles
    (b) racial and ethnic similarities   (e) religious differences
    (c) closeness in space

15. Which of the following is/are accurate concerning the *personal ads* taken out by women and men?

    (a)   men offered financial security much more than women did
    (b)   women defined or offered themselves as attractive partners more often than men
    (c)   men requested photographs more often than women
    (d)   men are more likely to place an ad seeking a partner
    (e)   all of the above are accurate

Fill-In

1.   Sociologists estimate that _____ percent of marriages in India are still *arranged*.

2.   In colonial New England, unmarried couples practiced _____, in which they spent the night wrapped in blankets or separated only by a wooden board down the middle of the bed.

3.   Four *functions of dating* (past and present) are identified by G.N. Ramu, including: _____, _____, _____, and _____.

4.   _____ *socialization* refers to socialization that is directed toward learning future roles.

5.   According to Susan Basow's application of *social-learning theory* to dating, women's scripts focus on enhancing their _____, making _____, and controlling _____ behavior.

6.   Seldom are both parties equally interested in continuing a dating relationship. Thus, the one who is least interested has an advantage and is in a position to dominate. Some researchers have described this as the _____.

7.   The people whom our society has defined as *acceptable marriage partners* for us form what sociologists call a _____.

8.   _____ are sums of money or property brought to a marriage by the female.

9.   The opposite of *exogamy* is _____, or *marriage within a particular group*.

10.   Several interrelated *factors* are discussed in the text as limiting our pool of eligibles, including the marriage _____, the marriage _____, _____, _____, _____, _____, _____, _____, and _____ pressure.

11.   The pattern of women marrying men of *lower social standing* than themselves is referred to as _____.

12.   Sociologists typically measure *social class* using a composite scale consisting of--level of _____ attainment, _____, and level of _____.

91

13. _____ is used by sociologists to denote *proximity* or *closeness* in place and space.

14. Sociologically speaking, *rape* is a behavior learned by men in the context of _____.

Short-Answer

1. Review the story told in the opening vignette. What does this story tell us about how people, particularly women, understand arranged marriages?
2. Describe the custom of *arranged marriages* in nonindustrialized societies. What are the *social functions* served by arranged marriages?
3. Describe the current mate selection conditions in China given the *gender ratio* of three men to each woman. How is this demographic condition affecting the status of women in Chinese society?
4. Briefly describe the historical mate selection customs of *keeping company* and *calling*.
5. In what ways is *social class* related to dating and mate selection?
6. What are the factors that constrain or limit one's *pool of eligibles*? Describe the patterns for each of these factors as seen in mate selection in the United States.
7. Review the patterns of *traditional* and *modern* ways to look for a dating partner.
8. What are the advantages and risks of *cyberspace* dating?
9. What are the *personal* and *other factors* that affect mate selection processes?
10. What is meant by J. N. Edwards idea of the *exchange theory of homogamous mating*?
11. Review the points being made in the text concerning *violence* in dating and intimate relationships. What are the estimates of violence in dating and intimate relationships?
12. What are the different patterns of *breaking up*, particularly in terms of gender differences?
13. What are the differences in *personal ads* of women and men? What factors do you think influence these differences?
14. What are the dating and mate selection patterns of *lesbians* and *gays*?
15. Differentiate between *stimulus-value-role*, *equity*, and *filter* theories of mate selection. Provide evidence from your own dating experiences to illustrate the arguments being made using these theories.

PART VII. ANSWERS TO STUDY QUESTIONS

True-False

1.	T	(p. 102)	7.	T	(pp. 113-14)
2.	F	(p. 103)	8.	T	(p. 115)
3.	F	(p. 105)	9.	F	(p. 117)
4.	T	(p. 106)	10.	T	(p. 120)
5.	F	(p. 108)	11.	T	(p. 121)
6.	T	(p. 112)	12.	T	(p. 126

Multiple-Choice

1.	b	(p. 102)	9.	b	(p. 113)
2.	c	(p. 102)	10.	d	(p. 113)
3.	d	(p. 103)	11.	e	(p. 115)
4.	c	(p. 104)	12.	d	(p. 116)
5.	d	(p. 105)	13.	b	(p. 117)
6.	a	(p. 106)	14.	c	(p. 119)
7.	d	(p. 107)	15.	e	(p. 123)
8.	a	(p. 108)			

Fill-In

1. 95 (p. 104)
2. bundling (p. 105
3. socialization, recreation, status grading and achievement, mate selection (pp. 107-08)
4. anticipatory (p. 108)
5. appearance, conversation, sexual (p. 109)
6. principle of least interest (p. 113)
7. pool of eligibles (p. 115)
8. Dowries (p. 115)
9. endogamy (p. 115)
10. squeeze, gradient, race, social class, age, religion, sex and gender, propinquity, family and peer (pp. 116-120)
11. hypogamy (p. 117)
12. education, occupation, income (p. 118)
13. Propinquity (p. 119)
14. masculinity (p. 127)

PART VIII. COMMENT AND ANALYSIS

Applying the Sociological Imagination

"Choosing a Mate: A Content Analysis of Personal Ads"

    Key Points:

    Questions you Have?

Critical Issues

"Violence and Abuse in Dating Relationships"

    Key Points:

    Questions you have?

<u>Writing Your Own Script</u>

"Personal Biography and Social Structure: Selecting a Mate"

Sexuality and Intimate Relationships

PART I. CHAPTER OUTLINE

PART II. LEARNING OBJECTIVES

1. To distinguish between sex and human sexuality.
2. To compare Ancient Jewish and early Christian traditions as they relate to human sexuality.
3. To consider historical trends in sexuality in the United States from Puritan times go the 1990s.
4. To discuss the factors that contribute to our sexual identity, including significant other, generalized others, schools, mass media, and sexual scripts.
5. To understand and discuss heterosexuality, homosexuality, and bisexuality.
6. To describe and discuss the physiology of sexuality, particularly the sexual response cycle.
7. To identify and discuss the various forms of autoeroticism.
8. To identify and discuss interpersonal sexual behaviors.
9. To examine sexuality across the life cycle.
10. To identify and discuss the various types of sexual dysfunctions.
11. To discuss AIDS and understand the importance of sexual responsibility.

PART III. CHAPTER REVIEW--KEY POINTS

HUMAN SEXUALITY: PAST AND PRESENT

For purposes of classification the authors use the term *sex* to refer to genetic or biological sex only and *sexual identity* to refer to a wide range of sexual behaviors, including intercourse.

Human sexuality refers to *the feelings, thoughts, and behaviors of humans, who have learned a set of cues that evoke a sexual or an erotic response.* Two points about human sexuality in Western society are being made:

(1) Although historical descriptions emphasize the sexual codes that were most prevalent during a given historical period, it is not the authors' intention to imply that sexual ideas and behavior have progressed directly from very strict and repressive codes to more liberal sexual codes. Rather, cyclical patterns have existed. Also, many different sexual codes, ideas, and behaviors exist at the same time.

(2) Generalizations about human behavior are always risky. Human attitudes and behaviors are very flexible and are never the same for all people in all groups. The historical period in which people live, the political and economic climate, the social organization of race, class, age, gender, religion, and sexual orientation all affect human attitudes and behaviors.

97

For instance, women historically have experienced sexuality in terms of reproduction, oppression, and vulnerability. In contrast, men have experienced sexuality primarily in terms of power and control.

The **Personal Reflection** box (p. 133) provides you with an opportunity to test yourself on how much you know about human sexuality. The test includes twenty-four true-false questions for you to answer.

Jewish Traditions and Human Sexuality

Ancient Jewish tradition placed great value on marriage and reproduction. The norm of premarital chastity was more rigidly applied to women than men. For example, a woman who was not a virgin at marriage could be killed. Male dominance was the rule.

Christian Traditions and Human Sexuality

Although in the Gospel Jesus refers to marriage as a sacred union, values pertaining to women, marriage, and sexuality decreased as Christian ideas of chastity took hold. St. Paul, and his belief that celibacy is superior to marriage, had a great impact during this period. During the fifth century, St. Augustine continued St. Paul's tradition condemning sexuality, and his influence lasted through the Middle Ages. During the thirteenth century, the church, through the writing of St. Thomas Aquinas, renewed its position on sexuality. Sexual intercourse was seen as animalistic, an activity to be avoided.

The Protestant Reformation of the sixteenth century ushered in a diversity of views and attitudes concerning human sexuality. Religious reformer Martin Luther and theologian John Calvin are discussed.

Sexuality in the United States: An Overview

Puritan Sexuality: Puritan sexuality was based on Calvinist sexual transitions, including the idea that sex was a sin outside of marriage. These views continued to dominate sexual norms well into the nineteenth century.

Victorian Sexuality: The Victorian era was characterized by a number of sexual taboos. At the base of the Victorian view of sexuality was the notion that any kind of sexual stimulation, especially orgasm, sapped a person's "vital forces." Sexuality was seen as a male phenomenon. The *sexual double standard*, referring to *differing set of norms based on gender* was very strong during this period.

Sexuality and Slavery: Victorian standards did not apply to all blacks. Males were often used as studs to increase the slave population. Women were often sexually abused by whites and had no legal protection. Legal marriage between blacks was prohibited.

Sexual Attitudes and Behavior in the Twentieth Century

Researcher Carol Darling has divided the century into three major eras in terms of sexual behavior. The first era lasted from 1900 to the early 1950s. This period witnessed an increase in the number of single women and men reporting sexual involvement prior to marriage. The second era, from the 1950s to 1970, was characterized by greater sexual permissiveness. This period is referred to as an "era of permissiveness with affection." The third era began in 1970 as technological advances, job opportunities for women and men, and greater travel resulted in a decreasing emphasis on the nuclear family and an increasing view that sexuality could be recreational as well as an expression of love.

By the mid-1980s, amid growing awareness, concerns, and fears of sexually transmitted diseases, especially AIDS, many people began to rethink the "sexual revolution."

A Sexual Revolution: Do these changes in sexuality in our society represent a revolution? Researcher Morton Hunt has argued that a revolution has occurred only if institutional structures have changed such that traditional attitudes and behaviors have been replaced with a radically new set of attitudes and behaviors.

This section of the text, highlighting the sexual habits and attitudes of Americans in the 1990s, relies on the results of two recent national sex surveys--the *NORC* survey and *Parade Magazine* survey.

Sexual Attitudes and Behaviors in the 1990s: The permissive of the 1980s continues, but people are less likely to engage in casual sex. Sexual acts that were once considered deviant have become widely accepted today. However, remnants of the double standard continue.

Sex by the Numbers, Sexual Partners, Practices, and Fidelity: In the 1990s, Americans are largely monogamous, reporting having fewer sexual partners in a 12 month period than in the past. More than four in five people have one or no sexual partner in a year, while only 3 percent admit to having five or more sexual partners in a year. Over her lifetime, the typical woman has two sexual partners; a man six. Effects of religious affiliation are discussed.

How Often?: On average, Americans have sex once a week, but clearly two-thirds of the population have sex less often. Marital status appears to have an important impact on the frequency with which people have sex.

How do lesbian and gay sexual practices compare? Over the years, most sex research has reported that gays are far more sexually active than are lesbians. Researchers Philip Blumstein and Pepper Schwartz found that lesbian couples have sex less frequently than any other type of couple and they are less "sexual" as couples and as individuals than anyone else.

The sexual reality of the older population is quite different from its younger counterpart. Twenty-two percent of women and 8 percent of men over the age of fifty report having no partnered sex in a year.

Recent studies of sexual behavior show some differences between patterns of sexuality in the U.S. from other Western societies. *Figure 6.1* (p. 138) illustrates some of the comparisons, focusing on the number of sexual partners over the life course for women and men in different societies.

Kinky Sex?: Members of our society seem to actually favor only a few sexual practices. For example, vaginal intercourse is overwhelmingly preferred by heterosexuals. Other preferences are identified, including the identification of gender differences. *Figure 6.2* (p. 139) show data concerning attitudes about sex, focusing on questions of extramarital sex and emotional involvement and sex.

At What Age?: According to responses in the NORC survey, white teens, both females and males, typically begin having sex at age 17; black males typically begin just before 16 and black females, just before 17. Most sexually active teens practice monogamy. Generation X (young adults 18 to 30 years of age) are more conservative than most people think they are in terms of their sexual attitudes and behaviors.

Choosing Partners: Sexual behavior is strongly affected by friends, family, and coworkers.

Sexual Homogamy: Opposites may attract, but according to the NORC data, it is not for long. People are attracted to others who are like them in terms of such variables as age, race, educational level, and religion.

Gender Differences: Men and women think and behave differently about sex. Men think about sex more than women do and are drawn to a wider range of sexual practices. One alarming gender difference found in the NORC survey was the difference in female and male perceptions of consensual sex. In many areas of sexuality, however, women and men are converging. Men have shown more changes in their sexual attitudes than women have. Examples are discussed in this section of the chapter.

SEXUALITY AS SOCIAL LEARNING

Sigmund Freud suggested that the *sex drive*, which he viewed as a biologically determined force, is the motivator for all human behavior. On the other hand, John Gagnon and William Simon suggest sexual behavior is not unlike other behavior, not coming naturally, but being learned.

Sources of Sexual Learning

Children are learning about sexuality as other important norms of society are being learned. A major source of our understanding of sexuality involves **significant others**, or *people such as parents, friends, relatives, and religious figures, who play an important role in our lives*. Later we learn about sexuality through **generalized others**, or *the viewpoint of society at large*.

Learning Sexuality in the Family: Where sexuality is concerned, evidence suggests that children learn very little from their parents. Parents often go to great lengths to desexualize their children. The issue of sexual abuse of children in families is briefly discussed in this section of the chapter.

Gender Differences in Sexual Scripts: Parents tend to communicate the content of sexual behavior to their children differently depending on the sex of the child. For example, parents tend to be more open with daughters than with sons about reproduction and its relationship to sexual activities as well as the morality of sex.

A number of researchers have identified several areas of gender differences in traditional sexual scripting:

--Interest in sex is part of the male sexual script but not the female sexual script.

--Males are expected to be the initiators and to take control of sexual activities; females are expected to be submissive, conform, and give pleasure.

--The sexual script for males emphasizes achievement and frequency of sexual activities; for females the emphasis is on monogamy and exclusiveness.

--Early and unmarried sexual activity carries little stigma for males; for females such activity carries a negative stigma.

--Exposure of the body is far more acceptable for males than females.

Such sex role socialization, it seems, produces some definite differences in the meanings that females and males attach to sex. For females sex is generally connected with love, affection, and commitment, whereas for males sex is connected with achievement, control, and power, or purely in terms of sexual release.

The Mass Media: The television and magazine media are discussed, illustrating the impact on sexual attitudes and behaviors of females and males. Researcher Linda Lindsay suggests that the impact of soap operas on females is very significant. The impact of sexual dysfunctions as portrayed on television talk shows is also discussed in this section of the chapter. The **Applying the Sociological Imagination** box (p. 143) provides some historical insight into the issue of human sexuality in the mass media.

SEXUAL ORIENTATIONS

Sexual orientation *involves not only whom one chooses as a sexual partner, but, more fundamentally, the ways in which people understand and identify themselves.* Sexual orientation is not synonymous with sexual behavior.

Cultural historians and sex researcher Shere Hite believes that we're are born with a natural desire to relate to people of the same as well as the other sex. She believes our culture has espoused ***heterosexism***, or *the belief that heterosexuality is the only right, natural, and acceptable sexual orientation and that any other orientation is pathological.*

Research suggests that sexual orientation forms a continuum with at least four recognizable levels of orientation, at the two extremes are exclusively heterosexual and exclusively homosexual orientation, with bisexuality and asexuality falling somewhere in the middle.

Heterosexuality

Heterosexuality refers to *the preference for sexual activities with a person of the other sex.* Sexuality generally and sexual activities specifically that are associated with a heterosexual orientation are *phallocentric*, male-centered, and are defined almost exclusively in terms of genital intercourse and male orgasm. Feminist scientist Adrienne Rich has argued hat making heterosexuality compulsory stymies or restricts the sexuality of males as well as females. She suggests that both heterosexism and *homophobia--an extreme and irrational fear or hatred of homosexuals*--act to inhibit the possibility of some homosexual women and men.

Homosexuality

Homosexuality refers to *the preference for sexual activities with a person of the same sex and concerns both identity and behavior.* The **For Your Information** box (p. 145) illustrates the anti-homosexual context through an example of a heterosexual questionnaire. What are your reactions to this questionnaire?

The Biological Basis of Homosexuality: Studies of identical twins and autopsied brain tissue support the biological explanation of homosexuality. However, both studies dealt exclusively with males and the findings are to be regarded with caution. In a recent study that focused exclusively on lesbians a researcher has claimed to have found a link between a synthetic estrogen drug (DES) and lesbianism. This research is suggestive, but again, caution is needed. *Figure 6.3* (p. 149) show data concerning sex in America, focusing on frequency of sex for women, men, heterosexual, and homosexuals.

How Widespread Is Homosexuality?: National survey estimates suggest that about 3-4 percent of the U.S. population is exclusively homosexual. More males are homosexual than females. Early survey results produced a figure of 8-10 percent of the population being exclusively homosexual, so questions of reliability and accuracy remain. A simple dichotomy of heterosexual versus homosexual can be misleading in that there may be aspects of both orientations in everyone. Alfred Kinsey's research findings on the heterosexuality-homosexuality continuum are discussed. *Figure 6.4* (p. 149) illustrates the results of his rating scale.

Bisexuality

Bisexuality is difficult to define. On the one hand, it refers to *individuals who do not have an exclusive sexual preference for one sex over the other.* On the other hand, as with other sexual orientations, it also *represents an identity and a lifestyle.* This sexual orientation is stigmatized in our society, even among the homosexual community.

THE PHYSIOLOGY OF SEXUALITY

The Sexual Response Cycle

William Masters and Virginia Johnson classified the physiological process of sexual response in human beings. According to these researchers we go through four stages in erotic arousal:

Excitement Phase: This stage begins the sexual response process and may last anywhere from a few minutes to several hours. In this phase the body responds to sexual stimulation. Most often this response is achieved through tactile stimulation of an ***erogenous zone--an area of the body that is particularly sensitive to sexual stimulation.***

Plateau Phase: In this stage both heart rate and blood pressure intensify. This phase can last only a few minutes or for quite some time.

Orgasmic Phase: In this phase, the sexual emotions and excitement built up in the previous phases reach a peak and are released in an ***orgasm,*** *the involuntary release of pelvic congestion and accumulated muscular tension through rhythmic contractions in the genitals of both sexes and also through ejaculation in males.* According to Masters and Johnson's research, the clitoris, not the vagina, is the central organ of orgasmic response in women. This refutes the widely accepted Freudian notion that a vaginal orgasm is more sexually mature in women than a clitoral orgasm.

Resolution Phase: After orgasm and the cessation of stimulation, the body returns to its preexcitement physiological state. *Figure 6.5* (p. 151) diagrams the sexual-response cycles of both females and males.

HUMAN SEXUAL EXPRESSION

Human sexual expression covers a wide variety of behaviors, including:

Autoeroticism

Masturbation: ***Masturbation*** *involves gaining sexual pleasure from the erotic stimulation of self through caressing or otherwise stimulating the genitals.* This behavior is said to begin in infancy. Boys and men tend to masturbate more often than girls and women. Attitudes toward masturbation also vary by gender. Young people 18 to 24 years of age are less likely to masturbate than people who are 25 to 34 years of age. Masturbation frequently continues after marriage.

Sexual Fantasy and Erotic Dreams: More males than females engage in sexual fantasy and erotic dreaming. Erotic dreaming frequently leads to ***nocturnal emission,*** *or orgasm during sleep.* Men have more "wet dreams" than women. The most common sexual fantasies for females and males in the U.S. are identified in *Table 6.1* (p. 153). Oral sex tops the list for both females and males.

Interpersonal Sexual Behavior

Pleasuring: Pleasuring involves a couple exploring each other's bodies. It involves touching behaviors in nongenital areas that bring sexual pleasure.

Petting and Oral Sex: Petting involves a variety of types of physical contact for the purpose of sexual arousal. **Cunnilingus** refers to *the oral stimulation of the female genitals*, and **fellatio**, refers to *the oral stimulation of the male genitals*. Oral sex has become standard practices among a majority of white people of all social classes, but not so among African Americans to the same degree.

Coitus: **Coitus** refers *only to penile-vaginal intercourse*. Coitus remains the primary method through which heterosexuals seek erotic pleasure.

Sexual Expression Among Lesbians and Gays

There is little difference in homosexual and heterosexual sexual expression and physiological response. Lesbians are more emotionally involved with their partners and are more likely to connect sex with love than are gays. Gays tend to have sex with more partners and in shorter-term relationships.

SEXUALITY ACROSS THE LIFE CYCLE

Nonmarried Sexuality and Pregnancy

The incidence of intercourse among singles has increased considerably over the last several decades. A brief historical review concerning research data on frequencies of premarital intercourse is presented in this section of the chapter. Adolescents are having sex earlier than in generations past.

Pregnancies Among Unmarried Women: Today about one-third of the births in this country involved single women, an almost eight-fold increase since 1940.

Teenage Pregnancy: Approximately 11 percent of unmarried teenaged females--over one million teenaged girls--become pregnant each in the U.S.

It is suggested we take a lesson from the Dutch. They are so unflustered by sex, sexuality, and birth control compared to we here in the U.S. They have a very low teenage pregnancy rate. They promote the *Double Dutch* birth control method, explained in this section of the text. Lack of knowledge and false myths regarding sexuality are discussed as problems which lead to unwanted teenage pregnancies.

Marital Sexuality: Does Good Sex Make Good Marriages?

Most marriages today have moved toward greater variety in sexual behavior, more frequent intercourse, and higher levels of sexual satisfaction. In general, when couples define their sexual activities as satisfying, they also define their overall relationship as satisfying. Results from the surveys previously discussed are reviewed in this section of the chapter.

Extramarital Sexuality

Research indicates that since the 1950s the incidence of extramarital relationships has increased substantially. Demographic factors associated with extramarital sex are reviewed in this section of the chapter. Differences seem to exist as to why wives and husbands seek intimacy outside of their marriages. Wives often are dissatisfied with some aspect of their relationship with their husbands, especially in the expressive areas. Husbands are often looking for excitement.

Postmarital Sexuality

Divorced People: Most divorced people become sexually active within a year following their divorce. The sex is usually more pleasurable and fulfilling than marital sex was for them.

Widows and Widowers: Almost one-half of widowers and widows engage in postmarital coitus. Little or no specific research has focused on this segment of the population, so information on them is speculative.

Sexuality and Aging

The common stereotype of aging women and men is that they are *asexual*. People who are healthy and happy with their lives can continue to be sexually active well into their advanced years.

Women, Aging, and Sexuality

As women age, their reproductive ability declines gradually. Somewhere around age 50, the menstrual cycle stops completely, marking the *menopause*. A common symptom of menopause is the *hot flash*. Many women fear that they will not be able to enjoy sexual activity after menopause. Experts disagree on the impact of menopause on female sexuality.

Men, Aging, and Sexuality: Men do not have a typical pattern of reproductive aging because there is no definite end to male fertility. A very small percentage of men, about 5 percent, experience *male climacteric*, which is similar in some ways to the female menopause.

Most forms of sexual behavior decline significantly for both men and women after age seventy-five.

SEXUAL DYSFUNCTIONS

Masters and Johnson contend that some kind of sexual problem can be found in at least one-half of all marriages in this country. The majority of cases are the result of social-psychological factors that interfere with or impair people's ability to respond as ordinarily expected to sexual stimuli.

SEXUAL RESPONSIBILITY: PROTECTING YOURSELF FROM AIDS AND OTHER STDs

Sexually transmitted diseases (STDs) are *diseases acquired primarily through sexual contact.* They are fairly common in the U.S. They can be cause by viruses (AIDS, herpes, hepatitis B, and genital warts), bacteria (syphilis, gonorrhea, and chlamydial infections), or tiny insects or parasites (pubic lice). Some 13 million people in our country acquire an STD. Two-thirds of these people are under 25 years of age. In this section of the chapter the focus is on AIDS. The other STDs are discussed in detail in Appendix B.

AIDS

Experts estimate that approximately 1.5 million people in the U.S. are infected with the human immunodeficiency virus (HIV), which is believed to be the main cause of AIDS. *Acquired immune deficiency syndrome (AIDS)* is a *viral syndrome, or group of diseases, that destroys the body's immune system, thereby rendering the victim susceptible to all kinds of infections and diseases.* Medical experts suggest that between 10 and 30 percent of people who possess HIV will actually develop AIDS.

People may have the HIV virus without knowing it, given that the incubation period can be as long as 10 years. Some of the major symptoms of AIDS include persistent fever, diarrhea, a dry or heavy cough, night sweats, chills, swollen glands, severe headaches, sore throat, white spots in the mouth, unexplained and excessive fatigue, dramatic weight loss, blurred vision, unexplained bleeding from any orifice, and bruises on the skin.

Currently, there is no cure for AIDS. People with the disease usually die within a few years after diagnosis. Of the approximately 500,000 people in this country diagnosed with AIDS, two-thirds have already died.

The Transmission of AIDS: AIDS is transmitted through blood and body fluids, such as semen, saliva, vaginal and cervical secretions, urine, tears, and breast milk. According to current evidence, HIV cannot be transmitted by casual contact--touching, coughing, sneezing, breathing, handshakes, toilet seats, drinking out of the same glass, etc.

Figure 6.6 (p. 161) shows data concerning AIDS cases and deaths in the United States per year for 1981 through 1995.

AIDS Treatment: Certain treatments are available that can relieve some of the symptoms of AIDS or prolong lives. Among the most common treatments is CD4 (T-cell), AZT, and ddI. Each are explained in this section of the chapter.

Who Gets AIDS: Approximately 86 percent of the AIDS cases in the United States are men. *Table 6.2* (p. 161) shows data concerning AIDS cases by exposure category. For example, homosexual, bisexual, and intravenous drug users account for 90 percent of all male AIDS victims. Forty-seven percent of female AIDS victims are intravenous drug users, while 36 percent are heterosexuals who are not intravenous drug users.

The intersections of age and race are clearly revealed in various AIDS statistics. It is the sixth leading cause of death among young people between the ages of 15 to 24 years of age.

AIDS is the third leading cause of death among young black women. Other statistics concerning race, ethnicity, and age are presented. *Table 6.3* (p. 163) show data on cumulative AIDS cases by gender, race, and age. *Table 6.4* (p. 163) shows the distribution of AIDS cases across the country, focusing on the top ten leading states and cities where victims of AIDS are living.

AIDS and Women: Although men are more likely than women to contact AIDS, women are increasingly at risk. The World Health Organization projects that by the year 2000 most new infections of AIDS will occur in women.

AIDS and Children: Today AIDS is a leading cause of death in children under the age of five. Most contact the disease from their mothers before, during, and after birth.

AIDS as a National and International Issue: The World Health Organization estimates that 13 million people are infected with the HIV virus in more than 74 countries around the world, the vast majority in Asia and Africa. *Figure 6.7* (p. 166) provides information on adult HIV transmission around the globe.

AIDS Prevention and Sexual Responsibility: Given the increase in STDs in our society, focus has been placed on sexuality and sexual responsibility. A campaign for *safe sex*. The concept of safe sex involves four basic components:

(1) Thinking and talking about HIV prevention before having sexual relations.

(2) Being informed of what safe sex is and that it can be pleasurable.

(3) Using barriers to protect yourself from potentially infected blood, semen, or vaginal fluids.

(4) Avoiding drugs and alcohol, that could impair your ability to comply with each of the first three components.

Some evidence does suggest that publicity concerning AIDS has affected behavior. However, some population groups have ignored the safe sex message to some extent. Research results are discussed in this section of the chapter.

In general, there is some evidence that casual sex is on the decrease among both heterosexual and homosexual males. Some of the findings from the *Parade Magazine* are reviewed, indicating the effects of AIDS on sexual attitudes and behaviors throughout society.

In the **Writing Your Own Script** box (p. 168) you are asked to think about your own sexuality and sexual values.

PART IV. KEY TERMS

human sexuality

sexual double standard

sexual script

Victorian sexuality

Puritan sexuality

sexual orientation

heterosexism

heterosexuality

homosexuality

homophobia

bisexuality

phallocentric

significant others

generalized others

orgasm

erotic arousal

erogenous zone

ejaculation

pleasuring

petting

cunnilingus

coitus

fellatio

masturbation

autoeroticism

nocturnal emission

menopause

sexual dysfunction

safe sex

AIDS

sexual homogamy

Generation X

sexual response cycle

climacteric

sexual scripting

PART V. KEY RESEARCHERS

Alfred Kinsey

Morton Hunt

Carol Darling

Sigmund Freud

Linda Lindsay

Simon LeVay

Allen Bell and Martin Weinberg

Philip Blumstein and Pepper Schwartz

Shere Hite

John Gagnon and William Simon

William Masters and Virginia Johnson

Adrienne Rich

PART VI. STUDY QUESTIONS

True-False

1.   T   F   According to *Ancient Jewish tradition*, a woman who was not a virgin at the time of marriage could be put to death.

2.   T   F   As part of the *Christian tradition*, St. Paul believed that celibacy was superior to marriage and that all human should strive for a chaste life.

3.   T   F   At the base of the *Victorian* view of sexuality was the notion that any kind of sexual stimulation, especially orgasm, sapped a person's "vital forces."

4.   T   F   Recent survey results indicate that both women and men are having *more sex partners* today than during any other decade in this century.

5.   T   F   Marital status does not have much impact on the *frequency* with which people have sex.

6.   T   F   According to Sigmund Freud, the *sex drive* is the motivation for all human behavior.

7.   T   F   Regarding gender differences in sexuality, woman think more about sex than men do.

8.   T   F   Research suggests women have shown more change in their *sexual attitudes* over the last decade than men have.

9.   T   F   Parents tend to communicate the content of sexual behavior to their children differently depending on the *sex* of the child.

10.   T   F   *Heterosexism* is very strong in the United States.

11.   T   F   Twin studies and brain autopsies have shown some evidence for the *biological basis of homosexuality*.

12.   T   F   According to Alfred Kinsey, the dichotomy of heterosexual versus homosexual may be *misleading*, arguing few of us are completely and exclusively heterosexual or homosexual.

13.   T   F   According to William Masters and Virginia Johnson's research, the *vagina*, not the clitoris, is the central organ or orgasmic response in women.

14.   T   F   *Masturbation* is more common among young people 18 to 24 years of age than are those who are 25 to 34 years of age.

15.   T   F   National Survey research indicates that *extramarital sex* has increased since 1950.

16.   T   F   Most divorced people do not become *sexually active* for three years following the divorce.

17.   T   F   According to research by William Masters and Virginia Johnson, about 20 percent of married couples in our society experience some kind of *sexual problem (dysfunction)*.

18. T F Approximately 90 percent of males with *AIDS* are homosexual, bisexual, or intravenous drug users.

19. T F The *majority* of AIDS cases in the world are found in Europe and North America.

Multiple-Choice

1. As used in the text, *sex* refers to:

    (a) intercourse
    (b) genetic or biological sexual behavior
    (c) a wide range of sexual behaviors
    (d) all of the above

2. *Human sexuality* refers to:

    (a) the feelings, thoughts, and behaviors of humans
    (b) sexual intercourse and masturbation
    (c) breast-feeding
    (d) giving birth
    (e) all of the above

3. During the *thirteenth century*, the church, through the writing of _____ renewed its position on sexuality as animalistic and an activity to be avoided.

    (a) St. Thomas Aquinas   (d) John Calvin
    (b) St. Paul   (e) Martin Luther
    (c) St. Augustine

4. Researcher Carol Darling divided this century into three major *eras* in terms of sexual behavior. The *second major era*, from the 1950s to 1970, is termed:

    (a) the traditional period
    (b) the marriage context period
    (c) the permissive era
    (d) the era of permissiveness with affection
    (e) the era of Victorian revival

5. The *differing set of norms* based on gender is referred to as the sexual:

    (a) orientation   (c) double standard
    (b) tradition   (d) script

6. The *generalized other* refers to:

   (a) the viewpoint of society at large
   (b) the opinions we have of our family
   (c) the biological side of our self
   (d) the sexual component of our self
   (e) cross-cultural influences on our society's norms and values

7. *Homosexuality* refers to:

   (a) behavior
   (b) identity
   (c) sexual preference
   (d) all of the above

8. Most research indicates that more than _____ *percent* of Americans identify themselves as *exclusively heterosexual*.

   (a) 83
   (b) 96
   (d) 78
   (d) 71
   (e) 88

9. What is the *second phase* in William Masters and Virginia Johnson's sexual response cycle?

   (a) orgasm
   (b) plateau
   (c) resolution
   (d) excitement

10. Which of the following is *not* a form of *autoeroticism*?

    (a) intercourse
    (b) sexual fantasies
    (c) erotic dreams
    (d) masterbation

11. Among men and women, the most common form of *sexual fantasy* involves:

    (a) using sexual devices
    (b) sex in public places
    (c) sex with a famous person
    (d) anal sex
    (e) oral sex

12. *Coitus* refers to:

    (a) using sexual devices
    (b) fellatio
    (c) cunnilingus
    (d) penile-vaginal intercourse only
    (e) all of these

13. What percentage of births in the U.S. are to *unmarried women*?

   (a) 10
   (b) 26
   (c) 42
   (d) 18
   (e) 33

14. A *male climacteric* is most similar to the female:

   (a) menopause
   (b) excitement phase
   (c) plateau phase
   (d) erogenous zones
   (e) clitoris

15. Each year about _____ million people acquire an STD.

   (a) 1
   (b) 5
   (c) 13
   (d) 30
   (e) 50

16. Experts estimate that approximately _____ people in the U.S. are infected with the HIV virus.

   (a) 100,000
   (b) 1.5 million
   (c) 11.3 million
   (d) 600,000
   (e) 5.2 million

Fill-In

1. In general terms _____ _____ refers to feelings, thoughts, and behaviors of humans, who have learned a set of cues that evoke a sexual or an erotic response.

2. Ancient Jewish tradition placed great emphasis on _____ and _____.

3. The Protestant Reformation of the _____ *century* ushered in a diversity of views and attitudes concerning human sexuality.

4. The differing set of norms based on *gender* is referred to as the _____ _____ _____.

5. According to survey research, in the U.S. over her lifetime, a typical woman has _____ *sexual partners*; a man _____.

6. According to Sigmund Freud, the _____ _____, which he viewed as a *biologically determined force*, is the motivator for all human behavior.

7. _____ _____ involves not only whom one chooses as a sexual partner, but more fundamentally, the ways in which people understand and identify themselves. The four recognizable levels of *orientations* include _____, _____, _____, and _____.

114

8. Social scientists, utilizing a *feminist perspective*, maintain that sexuality and sexual activities in the U.S. associated with a heterosexual orientation are _____--or male-centered, and are defined almost exclusively in terms of genital intercourse and male orgasm.

9. According to research by William Masters and Virginia Johnson, the *sexual response cycle* has four phases, including the _____, _____, _____, and _____.

10. _____ refers only to *penile-vaginal intercourse*.

11. Allen Bell and Martin Weinberg have identified five *gay lifestyles*, including: _____, _____, _____, _____, and _____.

12. As women age, their reproductive ability declines gradually. Somewhere around age 50, the *menstrual cycle stops completely*, marking the _____.

13. Approximately _____ percent of *women with AIDS* are heterosexual and do not use intravenous drugs.

14. Most observers of the HIV/AIDS virus agree that certain kinds of behavior place people at greater *risk* of infection than other kinds of behavior. The two most risky behaviors include _____ _____ and _____ _____ _____.

15. The majority of the HIV/AIDS virus cases in the world today are found on the continents of _____ and _____.

Short-Answer

1. Distinguish between the concepts of *sex* and *human sexuality*.
2. Differentiate between *Ancient Jewish* and *early Christian* traditions on human sexuality.
3. What are the two main points being stressed in this chapter about *human sexuality in Western society?*
4. Take the quiz "How much do you know about human sexuality," (p. 133). How did you do? Which types of questions, if any did you miss? What does this quiz tell you about how much you know about human sexuality?
5. Differentiate between *Puritan sexuality* and *Victorian sexuality*.
6. Describe the relationship between slaves and sexuality in the United States prior to emancipation.
7. Identify five important findings from the human sexuality *surveys* reviewed in this chapter (NORC survey and Parade Magazine survey).
8. What are the *sources of sexual learning* identified in this chapter. Identify one important point being made by the authors for each of these sources.
9. Identify and discuss the different forms of *autoeroticism*.
10. What evidence is there that *homosexuality* is biologically determined?
11. Summarize in a paragraph the data presented in *Figure 6.3* "Sex in America" (p. 148).

12. According to Masters and Johnson, what are the four phases of the sex response cycle? Briefly describe each of the phases.

13. What are the similarities and differences between *lesbians* and *gays* in terms of sexual expression?

14. Describe the demographic patterns of *unmarried sexuality and pregnancy* as reviewed in this chapter. In what ways are things different today than in previous generations this century?

15. What does research suggest about the relationship between *marital sexuality* and *happy marriages*?

16. What are the conclusions being made about sexuality among people over the age of fifty? How is sexuality different for women and men during mid-life and old age?

17. What is AIDS? How is it transmitted?

18. What are the demographics of AIDS in the United States? Globally?

19. What recommendations are being made by the authors for *preventing* STDs and promoting *safe sex*?

PART VII. ANSWERS TO STUDY QUESTIONS

True-False

1.	T	(p. 134)	11.	T	(p. 146)
2.	T	(p. 134)	12.	T	(p. 149)
3.	T	(p. 134)	13.	F	(p. 150)
4.	F	(p. 137)	14.	F	(p. 152)
5.	F	(p. 138)	15.	T	(p. 157)
6.	T	(p. 138)	16.	F	(p. 158)
7.	F	(p. 140)	17.	F	(p. 160)
8.	F	(p. 140)	18.	T	(p. 161)
9.	T	(p. 141)	19.	F	(p. 165)
10.	T	(p. 144)			

Multiple-Choice

1.	c	(p. 132)	9.	b	(p. 150)
2.	e	(p. 132)	10.	a	(pp. 152-53)
3.	c	(p. 134)	11.	e	(p. 153)
4.	d	(p. 135)	12.	d	(p. 154)
5.	c	(p. 135)	13.	e	(p. 156)
6.	a	(p. 141)	14.	a	(p. 159)
7.	d	(p. 145)	15.	c	(p. 160)
8.	b	(p. 147)	16.	b	(p. 161)

1. Human sexuality (p. 132)
2. marriage, reproduction (p. 133)
3. sixteenth (p. 134)
4. sexual double standard (p. 135)
5. 2, 6 (p. 137)
6. sex drive (p. 140)
7. sexual orientation, heterosexuality, homosexuality, bisexuality, asexuality (p, 144)
8. phallocentric (p. 145)
9. excitement, plateau, orgasm, resolution (p. 150)
10. Coitus (p. 154)
11. dysfunctional, functional, open-coupled, close-coupled, asexual (p. 155)
12. menopause (p. 159)
13. 36 (p. 161)
14. anal sex, intravenous drug use (p. 163)
15. Africa and Asia (p. 165)

PART VIII. COMMENT AND ANALYSIS

Personal Reflection

"How Much Do You Know About Human Sexuality?"

Key Points:

Questions You Have?:

Applying the Sociological Imagination

"Human Sexuality in the Mass Media, Past and Present"

Key Points:

Questions You Have?:

For Your Information

"Heterosexual Questionnaire"

Key Points:

Questions Your Have?

Writing Your Own Script

"Identifying Sexual Values"

Nonmarital Lifestyles 7

PART I. CHAPTER OUTLINE

I. Historical Perspectives
   A. Singlehood in Early America
   B. Singlehood in the Nineteenth and Early Twentieth Centuries
   C. Singlehood Today: Current Demographic Trends
II. Demystifying Singlehood
   A. Individual Decision Making
   B. The Influence of Social and Economic Forces
   C. Types of Singles
   D. Advantages and Disadvantages of Singlehood
III. Single Lifestyles
   A. Income
   B. Support Networks
   C. Life Satisfaction
   D. The Never-Married in Later Life
IV. Heterosexual Cohabitation
   A. Historical Perspectives
   B. The Meaning of Cohabitation Today
   C. Reasons for Cohabitation
   D. Advantages and Disadvantages of Cohabitation
   E. Cohabitation and the Division of Labor
   F. Cohabitation and Marital Stability
   G. Cohabitation and the Law
V. Lesbian and Gay Relationships
   A. Methodological Issues
   B. Demystifying Lesbian and Gay Relationships
   C. Living Together: Domestic Tasks, Finances, and Decision Making
   D. The Social and Legal Context of Lesbian and Gay Relationships
   E. Life Satisfaction: Elderly Lesbians and Gays
VI. Communal Living and Group Marriage
   A. Advantages and Disadvantages of the Communal Lifestyle
   B. Communes, Shared Housing, and the Future
   C. Group Marriasges

PART II. LEARNING OBJECTIVES

1. To gain historical perspective on singlehood as a lifestyle in the United States.
2. To discuss and critique the stereotypes of singles, both in the past and in the present.
3. To identify and discuss some of the reasons why people remain single.
4. To identify and discuss push and pull factors related to marriage and singlehood.
5. To identify and describe the various types of singles.
6. To discuss the relative advantages and disadvantages of remaining single.
7. To become aware of single lifestyles and issues of importance to this segment of our population across the life cycle.
8. To discuss the historical perspectives and the meaning of cohabitation today, including demographic trends, reasons for cohabitation, types of couples, advantages and disadvantages, and the legal aspects of this household structure.
9. To understand and discuss lesbian and gay relationships.

PART III. CHAPTER REVIEW--KEY POINTS

This chapter examines the lifestyles of people who, for one reason or another, do not marry, as well as the economic and social trends that help or hinder the development of nonmarital lifestyles. The term *single* is used in the chapter to refer only to those people who have never been married.

HISTORICAL PERSPECTIVES

Data on Singlehood in early America is extremely limited. A survey of America's past reveals that for much of this country's history marriage was a cultural ideal and the norm. While single men made up a large proportion of immigrants during colonial America, its was men's economic and political roles rather than their marital status that were emphasized.

Singlehood in Early America

Being single in early America was not easy. Unmarried people often faced personal restrictions. Single people were often *disposed of* to the home of a responsible family. Singles during this period in our history were stigmatized, often seen as defective or incomplete. Ridicule was common. Even today terms like *spinster* and *old maid* convey negative connotations. Marriage was seen as a practical necessity.

Singlehood in the Nineteenth and Early Twentieth Centuries

The percentage of single women began to increase in the last decades of the eighteenth century and continued to do so into the nineteenth century. For example, in 1890 15 percent of women aged 30 to 34 were single. The Industrial Revolution had a significant impact on rates of Singlehood during the eighteenth and nineteenth centuries. Edward Kain's book *The Myth of Family Decline* reveals that the current increase in never-married people represents a return to historically high rates that existed prior to 1940.

Singlehood Today: Current Demographic Trends

Today, approximately 27 percent of all people 18 and over have never married. This compares with a figure of 15.6 percent in 1970. *Table 7.1* (p. 173) compares the percentage of both sexes remaining single beyond the usual ages of marriage at two points in time-1970 and 1993. Two important patterns are revealed by these data--(1) the number of women and men who remain single into their late 30s has increased across racial and ethnic lines, and (2) in every age category the percentage of single men is higher than that of single women.

DEMYSTIFYING SINGLEHOOD

Sociologist Peter Stein has helped dispel the myth that single people are those who "fail to marry." His work has shown that the decision of whether to marry or stay single is conditioned by psychological, social, cultural, and economic factors. He characterizes these factors as a series of *pushes* (negative factors) or *pulls* (positive factors).

Individual Decision Making

On the one hand, people are pushed toward marriage by pressures from parents, cultural expectations, etc. while children etc. pull people toward marriage. While Peter Stein's data represent common patterns of experiences, these are not necessarily experienced in the same way by different people or even by the same person over the life cycle.

The Influence of Social and Economic Forces

The decision of whether to marry is influenced by many factors. Many Americans no longer view marriage as an economic or social necessity. The stigmas attached to Singlehood have lessened in recent years and the perceived benefits associated with marriage have diminished. Expanding economic opportunities, availability of contraceptives, and the liberalization of sexual norms have also influenced decisions.

Types of Singles

Peter Stein has identified four different categories of singles based on the likelihood of their remaining unmarried. These include: *voluntary temporary singles, voluntary stable singles, involuntary temporary singles,* and *involuntary stable singles*.

Sociologist Arthur Shostak also found five patterns corresponding to Stein's typology. His categories are labeled *freefloating singles, singles in an open-couple relationship, singles in a closed-couple relationship, committed singles,* and *accommodationists.*

The heterogeneity of the single state is emphasized in these typologies. Singles have both advantages and disadvantages to their lifestyle.

Advantages and Disadvantages of Singlehood

Among the most frequently cited advantages of singlehood include personal freedom, financial independence, privacy, and greater opportunities to pursue careers. Among the most frequently cited disadvantages include loneliness and lack of companionship, being excluded from couple events, not having children, and social disapproval. The advantages and disadvantages are identified as general categories and do not necessarily apply in every individual case or at all times in the life cycle.

SINGLE LIFESTYLES

A major challenge for single people is that they must build a satisfying life in a society highly geared toward marriage. There are six different lifestyles identified as representing single people, including *supportive, passive, activist, individualistic, social,* and *professional.* It is stressed that there is a diversity among the population of singles in our society. *Table 7.1* (p. 176) data concerning the distribution of single people by living arrangements are presented. The opening vignette to this chapter discusses the common pattern in our society of young adults living with, or moving back in with their parents.

Income

As revealed in *Table 7.2* (p. 177) female householders living alone had a median income of $12,995; the comparable figure for male householders was $21,372. In contrast, married couples with both spouses present had a median income of $43,129. These figures are for 1993. Why the differences? Two factors are particularly significant in this regard. First, many married households have more than one wage earner. Second, these earnings differences may reflect a systematic bias against singles in the workplace.

Support Networks

Singles who live alone confront a greater challenge in meeting their need for intimacy. They respond by establishing strong friendships. Another key intimacy need is the bond that exists between parent and child. Many singles are choosing to experience parenthood.

Life Satisfaction

In the past, studies have shown consistently that married people are happier and more satisfied with their lives than singles. Singlehood has become a more acceptable lifestyle in the United States; hence, in the future this pattern may change.

The Never-Married in Later Life

In 1993, approximately 1.4 million people 65 years of age and over had never married (4.4 percent). Jaber Gubrium reported that they tend to be lifelong isolates, are not lonely, evaluate everyday life in much the same way as married people do, and avoid the desolation of bereavement that follows the death of a spouse.

The "Lifelong Isolate" Reconsidered: Robert Rubenstein felt that this term was ambiguous. Many of the men in his study lived with family members. Many were lonely, and many experienced bereavement when family members or friends died. Pat Keith found that 50 percent of all older singles interact with family, friends, and neighbors, but many of the others could be considered "isolates." Katherine Allen found that most of the never-married women in her study lived with family members or friends.

Implications for Social Policy: Changes in social customs and social policy could alleviate some of the problems encountered by the never married as they grow older.

HETEROSEXUAL COHABITATION

Historical Perspectives

In America's past, the people most likely to live together outside of a legal marriage were the poor or those involved in unpopular relationships. One form of living together that was visible in America's past is **common-law marriage**, or *a cohabitive relationship that is based on the mutual consent of the persons involved, is not solemnized by a ceremony, and is recognized as valid by the state.*

The Meaning of Cohabitation Today

The U.S. Census Bureau first began to collect data on unmarried-couple households in 1960. *Unmarried-couple households* are defined as those households containing two unrelated adults of the opposite sex who share a housing unit with or without children under 15 present.

Cohabitation is similar to marriage in that couples create emotional and physical relationships with each other, and in some cases they also bear and rear children. It differs from marriage, however, in that it lacks formal legal, cultural, and religious support.

Current Demographic Trends: In 1960 there were 439,000 unmarried-couple households in the United States. By 1994 there were 3.6 million such households. *Figure 7.2* (p. 180) traces he growth in numbers of unmarried-couple households since 1960.

Characteristics of Cohabitants: Most are partners in the same age group, most are under the age of thirty-five, most were never-married adults, and about one-third of the households contain children under 15 years of age. Today, cohabitants are to be found among all classes, races, ages, and ethnic groups. However, there are differing patterns. These patterns are discussed in this section of the chapter. The **Global Perspectives** box (p. 181) compares patterns and characteristics of cohabitation in Sweden, France, and the United States.

Reasons for Cohabitation

Push and Pull Factors: Push factors include loneliness, high expenses of living alone, fear of marital commitment, sexual frustration, and education and career demands that preclude early marriage. Pull factors include a strong physical attraction, desire for intimacy, and to test compatibility for marriage.

Types of Cohabiting Couples: Cohabiting couples vary in terms of individual needs and degree of commitment. Examples are discussed in this section of the chapter.

Advantages and Disadvantages of Cohabitation

Among the most common advantages of cohabitation include better understanding of self; greater knowledge of what is involved in living with another person; increased interpersonal skills, especially communication and problem-solving skills; increased emotional maturity, better understanding of marital expectations; companionship; and the sharing of economic and domestic responsibilities.

Cohabitation is not without its problems, however. Among disadvantages reported are lack of social support for their relationship; conflict with partner about domestic tasks; the potential instability of the relationship; loss or curtailment of other relationships; differing expectations with partner; legal ambiguity; and emotional trauma of breaking up. Research indicates that cohabiting couples, especially younger ones, experience more violence in their relationships than married couples. The **applying the Sociological Imagination** box (p. 183) takes a look at a cohabiting relationship that did not work out. The question is asked--What went wrong?

Cohabitation and the Division of Labor

Patterns of housework and the division of labor within the household among cohabiting couples is similar to those found among married couples. Women assume a larger share of the cooking and cleaning tasks even when they work full-time and earn as much as their partners.

Cohabitation and Marital Stability

Is cohabitation a good predictor of marital success? Research is inconclusive. However, the evidence seems to suggest that couples who engage in premarital cohabitation run a greater risk of divorce than couples who do not cohabit prior to marriage. Reasons for this are discussed in this section of the chapter.

Cohabitation and the Law

The average length of cohabitation is 1.5 years, after which couples either marry or break up. Reasons for breakups are reviewed in this section of the chapter.

Palimony: **Palimony** *is a payment similar to alimony based on the existence of a contract (written or implied) between the partners regarding aspects of their relationship.* The high profile case involving actor Lee Marvin and Michelle Triola Marvin is discussed.

Domestic Partnerships: This concept refers to unmarried couples who live together and share housing and financial responsibilities. Insurance benefits for cohabiting couples is reviewed in this section of the chapter

LESBIAN AND GAY RELATIONSHIPS

Homosexuality has existed throughout history and in every known culture. Nevertheless, cultures have varied considerably in their attitudes toward this behavior. In U.S. society, homosexuality historically has been considered a form of deviant behavior.

Methodological Issues

Problems of small, unrepresentative samples limit the study of homosexual relationships. There are many variations in lesbian and gay lifestyles. These are briefly discussed in this section of the chapter.

Demystifying Lesbian and Gay Relationships

The major stereotypes involving same-sex couples assume that these couples imitate heterosexual patterns, with one partner acting as "wife" and the other playing the "husband." Few such partnerships exist. Richard Higginbotham argues that the problem with using the marriage model in studying lesbian and gay relationships is that it brings with it a set of expectations and norms that simply do not correlate with the realities of a same-sex relationship. He suggests the use of a friendship model.

Living Together: Domestic Tasks, Finances, and Decision Making

Research shows that there is considerable discussion and conscious joint decision making among same-sex couples, but decision making, like housework, is often related to income. Research by Philip Blumestein and Pepper Schwartz is discussed illustrating these findings.

The Social and Legal Context of Lesbian and Gay Relationships

Lesbians and gays must deal with the same issues of living together as heterosexual couples. Research has found no significant differences regarding couple adjustment, feelings of attachment, caring, and intimacy. There has been some improvement in the legal status of lesbians and gays (e.g., a surviving life partner may now take over the interest in a rent-controlled apartment in New York City). However, lesbians and gays have experienced a backlash among some voters. Discrimination in the workplace is also discussed in this section of the chapter.

Many lesbians and gays keep their sexual orientation hidden because of the fear of harassment, ridicule, and discrimination. The **Critical Issues** box (p. 188) takes a look at the issue of "coming out."

Life Satisfaction: Elderly Lesbians and Gays

Older homosexuals are usually well adjusted, experience high levels of life satisfaction, and are not isolated.

COMMUNAL LIVING AND GROUP MARRIAGE

A **commune** refers to *a group of people (single or married, with or without children) who live together, sharing many aspects of their lives.* They are likely to develop or expand during periods of political and social unrest. The communal movement in the U.S. originated around the end of the eighteenth century. Most of the early communes were religious in origin. The **For Your Information** box (p. 189) presents information on the Shakers to illustrate life within a communal religious community.

Advantages and Disadvantages of the Communal Lifestyle

Among the advantages reported are close intimate relationships with a variety of people and personal growth, while disadvantages include limitations on privacy and restrictions on personal freedom. Most communes last for only short periods of time.

Communes, Shared Housing, and the Future

Some researchers suggest that if the economy worsens or if new political turmoil develops, the number of communes will grow. If they are to be viable as an option in our society, critical social policy issues must be addressed. Shared housing programs (group homes and matchups) are discussed to illustrate this point. Cooperative forms of living are becoming more important as an issue given the larger proportion of older people in our society.

Group Marriages

Group marriages represent a variation of communal living. A ***group marriage*** is defined as *a marriage of at least four people, two female and two male, in which each partner is married to all partners of the opposite sex*. The Oneida community is discussed as an example of a group that follows this marriage form as the normative pattern.

The **Writing Your Own Script** box (p. 190) asks you to consider what your marriage plans are at this point in time, and to consider some issues relevant to the marital decision.

PART IV. KEY TERMS

push/pull factors

common-law marriage

domestic partnership

group marriage

commune

palimony

cohabitation

PART V. KEY RESEARCHERS

Judy Rollins

Peter Kain

Pat Keith

Jaber Gubrium

Katherine Allen   Richard Higginbotham

Philip Blumestein and Pepper Schwartz   Arthur Shostak

PART VI. STUDY QUESTIONS

True-False

1.	T	F	In this chapter, the term *single* refers only to never-married people.
2.	T	F	The status of *singles* during colonial America was relatively high, especially compared with their status in society.
3.	T	F	The view that marriages should be *happy* rather than merely a duty evolved gradually during the early nineteenth century.
4.	T	F	A higher percentage of *whites*, females and males, remain single past age 30 than is the case for African Americans and Latinos.
5.	T	F	Across all age categories over age 18, the percentage of *single (never-married)* men is higher than that of single women.
6.	T	F	According to the Census Bureau, most young adults between the ages of 18 to 24 live with their parents.
7.	T	F	The population of singles in our society are described by the authors as being very *homogeneous*.
8.	T	F	Historically, studies have shown married people to be *happier* and *more satisfied* with their lives than singles.
9.	T	F	According to the research of Katherine Allen and Pat Keith, aged, never-married singles tend to *live alone* and experience considerable *loneliness*.
10.	T	F	*Unmarried-couple households* are defined as those households containing two unrelated adults of the opposite sex who share a housing unit with or without children under 15 present.
11.	T	F	Research has found more *violence* in cohabiting couples, especially young ones, as compared to married couples.
12.	T	F	There is significantly more *egalitarianism* within cohabiting couples in terms of the division of labor and sharing household tasks than is found among married couples.
13.	T	F	*Homosexual behavior* has existed throughout history and in every known culture.

14.　T　　F　　Lesbians and gays often keep their sexual orientation hidden because of fear of discrimination, ridicule, and harassment. For those who do "come out," typically the first person told is the homosexual's mother.

15.　T　　F　　*Elderly homosexuals* tend to be poorly adjusted, isolated, and experience few life satisfactions compared with other lesbians and gays.

Multiple-Choice

1.　As used in this chapter, the term *single* means:

(a)　never-married
(b)　widowed
(c)　separated

(d)　divorced
(e)　all of these statuses

2.　In 1994, approximately 30 percent of men and 20 percent of women aged thirty to thirty-four were *single*. In 1890, comparable figures were:

(a)　10/5
(b)　27/15
(c)　25/20

(d)　5/10
(e)　30/30

3.　Peter Stein characterized factors which *attract* a person to a potential situation as:

(a)　pushes
(b)　pulls
(c)　assets

(d)　magnets
(e)　draws

4.　What percentage of people over the age of 65 in the United states are *never-married singles*?

(a)　10.3
(b)　15.1
(c)　7.5

(d)　1.2
(e)　4.4

5.　According to Jaber Gubrium, which of the following is *not true* of elderly, never-married singles?

(a)　they tend to be lifelong isolates
(b)　they are lonely
(c)　they are more positive than the widowed or divorced
(d)　they evaluate every day in much the same way as their married peers
(e)　all of the above

6. A cohabitative relationship that is based on the mutual consent of the persons involved, is not solemnized by a ceremony, and is recognized as valid by the state, refers to:

(a) cohabitation
(b) palimony
(c) common-law marriage
(d) marriage

7. Approximately, how many *unmarried-couple households* are there in the U.S. today?

(a) 1.7 million
(b) 489,000
(c) 3.6 million
(d) 10.3 million
(e) 8.6 million

8. Which of the following is *inaccurate* regarding unmarried-couple households?

(a) most adults living in these households are under age thirty-five
(b) most adults living in these households have never been married before
(c) about one-third have children present
(d) the rate of cohabitation for white women is higher than for black women
(e) all of the above are accurate regarding unmarried-couple households

9. Which of the following statements is *not true* of cohabiting women?

(a) they are more educated than noncohabitants
(b) white women are more likely to cohabitative than black women
(c) they become sexually active at an early age than noncohabitants
(d) they tend to be older than noncohabitants
(e) they are less likely to identify with organized religion than noncohabitants

10. Compared to the U.S, *cohabitation* in Sweden and France:

(a) has a longer history
(b) represents a larger percentage of households
(c) lasts longer
(d) all of the above
(e) none of the above

11. What differences exist between married couples and cohabiting couples in the amount of time devoted to *household chores*?

    (a)   cohabiting couples are much more egalitarian
    (b)   females in both groups did more
    (c)   males in cohabiting couples did more than females
    (d)   males in cohabiting couples did more than their male married counterparts

12. On average, cohabiting lasts for _____ *years*.

    (a)   1.5   (d)   2.3
    (b)   5.6   (e)   8.1
    (c)   3.9

13. Robert Higginbotham argues that we use a _____ *model* to study and understand same-sex couples.

    (a)   marriage   (d)   friendship
    (b)   deviant   (e)   wife-husband
    (c)   alternative

14. A _____ refers to a group of people (single or married, with or without children) who live together, sharing many aspects of their lives.

    (a)   palimony   (d)   egalitarianism
    (b)   domestic partnership   (e)   common-law marriage
    (c)   commune

Fill-In

1. *Singles* in early America were often _____ to responsible families.
2. Sociologist Peter Stein has characterized psychological, social, cultural, and economic factors as a series of _____, or *negative factors* and _____, or *attractions* to a potential situation.
3. Although there is some overlapping of activities, six different *lifestyle patterns* have been observed among the single population over the age of thirty, including _____, _____, _____, _____, _____, _____.
4. Referring to singles who live alone, both women and men value friends, but in somewhat different ways. Women concentrate on establishing close _____ bonds, whereas men focus more on sharing their _____ and their _____.

132

5. Two factors are particularly significant in helping to explain why married couple households have a higher *median income* than households of single people. First, many married couple households have more than one _____ _____, and earnings differences many reflect a systematic bias against _____ in the workplace.

6. According to research by Jaber Gubrium, *elderly singles* tend to be lifelong _____, they are not particularly _____, they _____ everyday life in much the same way that their married peers do, and they avoid the desolation of _____.

7. _____ refers to a cohabitative relationship that is based on the mutual consent of the person involved, is not solemnized by a ceremony, and is recognized as valid by the state.

8. There are approximately _____ million *unmarried-couple households* in the U.S. today.

9. Just as many reasons are given for cohabitation, the relationship established by cohabiting couples vary in terms of _____ *needs* and *degree of* _____.

10. _____ is a payment similar to alimony and based on the existence of a contract (written or implied) between the partners regarding aspects of their relationship.

11. Richard Higginbotham suggests that instead of using a *marriage model* for studying *same-sex* relationships we use a _____ *model*.

Short-Answer

1. Describe the status of singles in *early America*.
2. What are three factors that have affected the increasing rates of *singlehood* in the United States over the last century?
3. Briefly review the *demographics* of single people in the United States today. What are two demographic facts that you found particularly interesting or surprising?
4. Differentiate between the different *categories* of singles. Provide an illustration for each category.
5. What are the *advantages* and *disadvantages* of being single in our society today?
6. What are the six different *lifestyle patterns* of singles (over the age of thirty) identified in this chapter?
7. What conclusions has Robert Rubinstein made about *lifelong isolates*?
8. Briefly describe the demographic pattern of *cohabitation* in the U.S. today.
9. What are the *pushes* and *pulls* involved as reasons for cohabiting?
10. Discuss the characteristics of the *never-married in later life*. What generalizations can be made about this category of people in our society?
11. What are the relative *advantages* and *disadvantages* of *cohabitation*?
12. What is the relationship between *cohabitation* and *marital stability*?

13. Briefly review the stereotypes that exist in our society concerning lesbian and gay couples. What are the facts about this segment of our society's population?
14. Describe the *social* and *legal* context of lesbian and gay relationships.
15. Who are the *Shakers*? Describe their lifestyle as reported in this chapter.
16. What was the *Oneida community*?

PART VII. ANSWERS TO STUDY QUESTIONS

True-False

1.	T	(p. 171)	9.	F	(p. 178)
2.	F	(pp. 171-72)	10.	T	(p. 180)
3.	T	(p. 172)	11.	T	(p. 183)
4.	F	(p. 173)	12.	F	(p. 184)
5.	T	(p. 173)	13.	T	(p. 185)
6.	T	(p. 175	14.	T	(p. 187)
7.	F	(p. 176)	15.	F	(p. 188)
8.	T	(p. 177)			

Multiple-Choice

1.	a	(p. 171)	8.	e	(p. 180)
2.	b	(p. 172)	9.	a	(p. 181)
3.	b	(p. 173)	10.	d	(p. 181)
4.	e	(p. 178)	11.	b	(p. 184)
5.	a	(p. 178)	12.	a	(p. 184)
6.	c	(p. 179)	13.	d	(p. 186)
7.	c	(p. 180	14.	c	(p. 188)

Fill-In

1. disposed (p. 171)
2. pushes, pulls (p. 173)
3. supportive, passive, activist, individualistic, social, professional (p. 176)
4. emotional, interests, values (p. 177)
5. wage earner, singles (p. 177)
6. isolates, lonely, evaluate, bereavement (p. 178)
7. Common-law marriage
8. 3.6 (p. 180)
9. individual, commitment (p. 182)
10. Palimony (p. 185)
11. friendship (p. 186)

PART VIII. COMMENT AND ANALYSIS

Global Perspectives

"Cohabitation in Sweden and France"

Key Points:

Questions You Have?

Applying the Sociological Imagination

"What Went Wrong?"

Key Points:

Questions You Have?

Critical Issues

"Coming Out"

      Key Points:

      Questions You Have?

For Your Information

"Would You Like to Join the Shakers"

      Key Points:

      Questions You Have?

Writing Your Own Script

"The Marital Decision"

The Marriage Experience

PART I. CHAPTER OUTLINE

I. Why do People Marry?
    A. Sociological Perspective
II. The Meaning of Marriage
    A. Marriage as a Commitment
    B. Marriage as a Sacrament
    C. Marriage as a Legal Contract
    D. Some Legal Aspects of the Marriage Contract
III. Change and Continuity in the Meaning of Marriage
    A. Provisions of the Modern Marriage Contract
    B. The Marriage Contract Today
    C. The Wedding
IV. Marriage and Gender
    A. "Her" Marriage
    B. "His" Marriage
V. Transitions and Adjustments to Marriages
    A. A Typology of Marital Relationships
VI. Heterogamous Marriages
    A. Interracial Marriages
    B. Interethnic Marriages
    C. Interfaith Marriages
VII. Marital Satisfaction, Communication, and Conflict Resolution in Marriages
VIII. Summary
IX. Key Terms
X. Questions for Study and Reflection
XI. Further Reading

PART II. LEARNING OBJECTIVES

1. To identify the personal and sociological factors that affect a person's decision to marry.
2. To describe the meaning of marriage from both emotional and legal perspectives.
3. To discuss the meaning of marriage from a historical perspective.
4. To explain how gender affects marriage, particularly marital satisfaction.
5. To identify and describe different types of marriages.
6. To identify and analyze the transitions and adjustments to marriage across the family life cycle.
7. To identify and discuss demographic patterns of heterogamous marriages.
8. To discuss the importance of communication and conflict resolution in marriage.

PART III. CHAPTER REVIEW--KEY POINTS

The opening vignette presents an example of a marriage in which the couple is experiencing difficulties in their relationship. Consider the questions at the end of the story. What do you think?

Surveys continually reveal that Americans rank a good marriage at the top of their list of sources of satisfaction. In this chapter, focus is placed on the meaning of marriage in the United states in both traditional and contemporary terms.

WHY DO PEOPLE MARRY?

Love is the single most important reason that people give for getting married. Companionship comes in a distant second as the next most frequent reason. Other reasons include the desire to have children, happiness, money, convenience, dependence, and the fear of contracting AIDS. *Figure 8.1* (p. 193) presents the distribution of responses to the question of why people marry.

Rushworth Kidder identifies commitment and sharing as two key aspects of a durable marriage in the United States. However, these may not be significant aspects around the world. Nicholas Kristof reports that happiness and love are not key aspects of a durable marriage in Japan. The traditional married couple household is still very prominent in Japan. Yet, compatibility among Japanese couples is relatively low compared to other nations, yet the divorce rate in Japan is less than half what it is in the United States. *Figure 8.2* (p. 194) shows cross cultural data on marital compatibility.

In the United States, social, economic, and historical factors influence a person's decision to marry. Gender, race, and social class are also discussed as factors affecting a person's decision to marry.

Sociological Perspective

A dominant point of view concerning why people marry within the field of sociology has been structural-functionalism. This view ignores individual motivation and explains marriage in terms of society's need or demand for the legitimacy of children. The *principle of legitimacy*, or the *notion that all children ought to have a socially and legally recognized father*, was first put forth by anthropologist Bronislaw Malinowski.

In contrast, a feminist perspective challenges the theory as giving more importance to the role of social father. They focus on traditional gender-role socialization as a basis for marriage. Whatever the reason, 95 percent of us decide to marry at some points in our lives.

THE MEANING OF MARRIAGE

Marriage means different things to different people. However, virtually everyone regard marriage as a relatively permanent and committed relationship. Marriage as a sacrament and as a legal contract are discussed in this section of the chapter to illustrate how complex relationships are regulated through this social institution.

Marriage as a Commitment

Commitment is a key factor in any intimate, emotionally satisfying, and meaningful relationship. In a survey of couples with long-term marriages, Jeanette Lauer and Robert Lauer found that a key factor contributing to the longevity of the relationship is the couples belief in marriage as a long-term commitment and sacred institution.

Marriage as a Sacrament

From a religious standpoint, marriage is regarded as a *sacrament--a sacred union or tie*. At least three-fourths of first-time marriages and three-fifths of remarriages among divorced people take place within the context of some type of religious ceremony.

Marriage as a Legal Contract

Legal marriage is *a legally binding agreement or contractual relationship between two people and is defined and regulated by the state.* In contrast, a *social marriage* is *a relationship between people who cohabit and engage in behavior that is essentially the same as that within a legal marriage, but without engaging in a marriage ceremony that is validated by the state.*

Marriage in the United States is a legal and financial contractual agreement that is regulated by certain legal requirements. The most important marriage laws are state laws.

Some Legal Aspects of the Marriage Contract

Sexual Orientation: In no state can people of the same sex legally marry, though such unions are recognized as domestic partnerships. Marriage is a civil right that most heterosexual take for granted. Legal protections and rights involve tax and inheritance laws, pension and health care benefits, etc.

In 1989, Denmark became the first country to legalize same-sex unions. Carl Weiser points out several key ways in which gay marriage has become a prominent part of American culture. Reasons for why people oppose or advocate same-sex marriages are discussed. What do you think? Remember, this is not just a matter of debating about abstract concepts regarding the definitions for marriage, family, and minority group. It is also about mundane matters of taxes, inheritance rights, and medical benefits. *Table 8.1* (p. 199) illustrates the benefits that lesbian and gay partners could share if same-sex marriages were legalized in our society. *Figure 8.3* (p. 199) provides data on state legislation to sanction or bar same-sex marriages.

In addition to requiring *heterosexuality* in marital relationships, marriage law also requires *monogamy*. **Bigamy**, or *marrying one person while still being legally married to another*, is against the law. Also, though seldom enforced, many states have laws that prohibit **adultery**, *extramarital sexual intercourse*.

The Incest Taboo: Laws prohibit sexual relations or marriage between a variety of relatives ranging from parents and siblings, to non-blood-related in-laws. Some states prohibit marriage between **affinal relatives**, or *people related by marriage*, such as a brother- or sister-in-law.

Age Restrictions: In the past, the legal age at which people could marry was tied to puberty. Today, the concern is whether a person is mature enough to marry. The typical age requirement with parental consent is 16, though two states (Mississippi and California) have no age limits. In every state except one, the legal age at which a marriage can take place without parental consent is 18. In Georgia the legal age is 16.

Blood Tests: In every state, when two people wish to marry they must file an application with the state and obtain a marriage license. In approximately two-thirds of the states, blood test is required. This test is to determine the presence of STDs.

CHANGE AND CONTINUITY IN THE MEANING OF MARRIAGE

The most fundamental premises on which U.S. marriage and family laws have been based on the common-law concept of **coverture**, or *the idea that a wife is under the protection and influence of her husband*. The **For Your Information** box (pp. 201-02) discusses the traditional marriage contract as a transference of property among males. Focus is on wedding traditions and rituals.

Provisions of the Modern Marriage Contract

The provisions of the modern marriage contract are similar to those based on the old principle of coverture. Lenore Weitzman has identified four basic provisions of the traditional marriage contract that have been incorporated into marriage laws in this country:

    (1)   the wife is responsible for caring for the home
    (2)   the wife is responsible for caring for any children
    (3)   the husband is head of the household
    (4)   the husband is responsible for providing support
            for the family

The authors examine some specific beliefs and practices from the past in terms of their impact on current marital patterns, noting both continuity and changes where they have occurred.

Residence: Although a wife is no longer required to take her husband's name, a husband retains the legal right to decide where the couple will live. Examples pertaining to a situation in which a wife and husband live in separate residences, particularly if they are not in the same state, are discussed.

Property Rights: Most U.S. states recognize the individual ownership of property. Whoever has proof of ownership of property own it in the eyes of the law. If neither the wife nor husband has proof of ownership, however, most courts determine that the husband is the owner, particularly if the wife has remained in the home as a homemaker. Common-law property states give quite an advantage to husbands. In community property states wives and husbands own all assets jointly and equally.

The Law: According to Virginia Sapiro, a husband's right to his wife's services is basically unenforceable by law in a direct sense. However, because of a husband's **conjugal rights**--*rights pertaining to the marriage relationship*--in about half of U.S. states a wife cannot charge her husband with rape. The marriage contract obligates the wife to perform domestic labor. Although a husband has no legal obligation to compensate his wife for domestic services, if a third party injures the wife he can sue for the value of the domestic services that he lost.

The Marriage Contract Today

Marriage and family law has changed significantly since 1970, however, certain traditions and legal restrictions continue to leave women at a disadvantage. Focus is given to surname changes and wedding rituals to illustrate changes that have occurred. The **Global Perspectives** box (p. 204) provides illustrations of marriage practices around the world.

Marriage Vows: Examples of marriage vows are illustrated for your consideration. As people change their views of marriage, they are also changing or modifying many of the rituals and traditions of weddings.

Prenuptial Agreements: **Prenuptial agreements** are developed and worked out in consultation with an attorney and filed as a legal document. *They negotiate ahead of time the settlement of property, alimony, or other financial matters in the event of death or divorce.*

Personal Contracts: Personal contracts serve primarily as guides to future behavior, but are sometimes legal contracts. Examples over history in our society are provided in this section of the chapter. The **For Your Information** box (p. 207) discusses the case of Lucy Stone and her husband-to-be, who in 1855 wrote their own personal contract in protest against the inequality of women in marriage.

The Wedding

Today's couples tend to prefer traditional weddings, but increasingly they are infusing the wedding ceremony with a touch of personal style. Offbeat examples are identified in the text. Cultural or ethnic weddings are also rising in popularity.

Weddings today are far more expensive than in the past. This is in part due to the fact that people are waiting longer to marry (median age of about 23 for females and 26 for males) and have more money to spend for their weddings. The average cost of a wedding today is approximately $18,000. *Table 8.2* (p. 208) shows the approximate costs for typical items associated with traditional weddings of various sizes. Honeymoons today are averaging between $3,000-5,000.

MARRIAGE AND GENDER

In her now classic book *The Future of Marriage*, sociologist Jessie Bernard detailed the different experiential realities of wives and husbands which she called "his marriage" and "her marriage."

"Her" Marriage

Bernard found that wives were much less happy in their marriages than their husbands. Married women also reported much higher rates of anxiety, phobia, and depression than any other group in society except single men. Wives also had a higher rate of suicide than husbands. Research has found that husbands tend to rate almost everything as better than their wives.

"His" Marriage

Men seem to prefer marriage to being single and when asked if they would marry the same person again, they respond in the affirmative twice as often as do their wives. Married men live longer, have better mental and physical health, are less depressed, have a lower rate of suicide, are less likely to go to prison, earn higher incomes, and are more likely to define themselves as happy than are single men.

TRANSITIONS AND ADJUSTMENTS TO MARRIAGES

Marital adjustment is *the degree to which a couple get along with each other or have a good working relationship and are able to satisfy each other's needs over the marital life course.* It is an ongoing process..

A Typology of Marital Relationships

There is no single model for a successful marriage. In there study of marital adjustment and happiness, researchers John Cuber and Peggy Harrof identified five distinct types of marriages, representing a wide range of communication patterns and interaction styles.

The Conflict-Habituated Relationship: Extensive tension and conflict are managed or controlled. The couple engage in verbal arguments or fights about everything and anything.

The Devitalized Relationship: Involves little conflict but also little passion and attention to each other. The couple were once in love but the excitement and passion is gone, and duty remains.

The Passive-Congenial Relationship: Similar to above, but the passivity in this marriage was always there.

The Vital Relationship: Highly involved couples, who have not lost their individual identities. They enjoy each other when they are together, but do not monopolize each other's time.

The Total Relationship: Constant togetherness with few tensions and conflicts. Total relationships are rare.

HETEROGAMOUS MARRIAGES

Heterogamous marriages are *marriages between people who vary in certain social and demographic characteristics.* Two major types of heterogamous marriage are interracial and interethnic and interfaith marriages.

Interracial Marriages

Although legal restrictions have been removed, the sociocultural norms concerning these marriages remain the most inflexible of all mate selection boundaries. A brief historical review of laws regarding interracial marriage is presented in this section of the chapter. Even though the number of interracial marriages has doubled since the early 1980s, today only about 2 percent of marriages are interracial.

African Americans: African Americans have the highest rate of endogamous marriages and the lowest rate of exogamous marriages. If they do marry interracially, most often their partner is white. Men are twice as likely as women to have a white mate.

Native Americans: Of six racial groups studied by Richard Clayton, Native Americans were the least endogamous. Reasons for these patterns are discussed in this section of the chapter.

Asian Americans: Asian American families are becoming increasingly acculturated, with 33 percent marrying exogamously, primarily with whites. Patterns for different Asian nationalities are reviewed in the text.

Figure 8.4 (p. 211) show the patterns of interracial marriages in the United States for 1992. The **Family Profile** box (p. 212) takes a look at some issues relevant to an interracial couple.

Interethnic Marriages

Latinos: Latinos are a very diverse ethnic group. Although the rates of interracial marriage between Latino groups have increased in recent decades.

Whites: Interethnic marriage among non-Latino whites is now so commonplace that most people do not pay much attention to it. Estimates are that three-fourths of U.S. born whites are married interethnically.

144

Interfaith Marriages

People are more willing to cross religious than racial boundaries in selecting a spouse. Nonetheless, if we take the average of three categories (Catholic, Protestant, and Jewish), about 90 percent of all marriages are to people of the same religion. Defining exactly what an interfaith marriage is can be difficult. While the rate of interfaith marriages are increasing, they do vary according to location and population.

Some studies indicate that racially and religiously heterogamous marriages have somewhat higher divorce rates and slightly lower levels of satisfaction than do homogamous marriages.

MARITAL SATISFACTION, COMMUNICATION, AND CONFLICT RESOLUTION IN MARRIAGES

Research has consistently found that married people, compared with unmarried people, report being happier, healthier, and generally more satisfied with their lives. This section of the text focuses on a variety of terms researchers have developed to help them understand marital quality, including *marital success, marital happiness,* and *marital satisfaction.*

Successful Marriage: Although the divorce rate has leveled off in the 1990s, almost two-thirds of marriages begun today are expected to end in divorce. Some researchers argue that this indicates a decline in marital success.

On the other hand, general survey data repeatedly show that an overwhelming majority of married couples say they are happy or very happy and describe their marriage as satisfying.

Factors related to marital satisfaction/happiness/quality/stability include: being in love, sharing aims, goals, and other important beliefs, sexual compatibility, financial security, having children, the amount of time spent together, family rituals, self-disclosure, open communication, and the ability to resolve conflict in a positive manner.

Effective Communication: Communication is essential to the success of marriages and other intimate relationships. Two key components of communication are *what is said* and *how it is said*.

Self-Disclosure: Susan Hendrick and Clyde Hendrick define self-disclosure as "telling another person about oneself; to honestly offer one's thoughts and feelings for the other's perusal, hoping that truly open communication will follow." Through reciprocal self-disclosure togetherness, closeness, and higher marital satisfaction can be achieved. However, Judy Pearson has found that marital satisfaction increases with self-disclosure to a point, there is a decrease in marital satisfaction at the highest levels of self-disclosure.

As in many other aspects of heterosexual relationships, women and men tend to differ in terms of disclosure, although the research findings are somewhat mixed. For example, some research has found women to be more disclosing than men. Also, the target person to whom disclosure is made varies between women and men, with men tending to disclose more only to romantic partners than women.

In general, successful communication includes a number of conditions and skills. Two basic conditions are a *nonthreatening, noncoercive atmosphere* and *mutual commitment*. John Gottman suggests that the real reason marriages succeed or fail is really very simple: Couples who stay together are *nice* to each other more often than not.

Conflict and Conflict Resolution: Some conflict is inevitable. Good communication alone does not prevent conflict. Several key areas of marriage and family life generally contribute to conflict in marriages: money, sex, children, power, division of marital and family tasks, work, in-laws, substance abuse, etc.

John Gottman believes that the four most destructive behaviors to marital happiness are *criticism, contempt, defensiveness,* and *stonewalling*. Each of these behaviors is described and illustrated in this section of the text.

When conflict arises in a relationship, as it inevitably does, it does not have to be destructive. Researchers have found that some conflict can be constructive. Conflict management is the key.

The **Writing Your Own Script** box (pp. 117-18) provides you with an opportunity to consider your own "relationship contract."

PART IV. KEY TERMS

principle of legitimacy

sacrament

legal marriage

social marriage

bigamy

adultery

coverture

affinal relatives

conjugal rights

heterogamous marriage

prenuptial agreement

marital adjustment

personal marriage agreement

PART V. KEY RESEARCHERS

Rushworth Kidder

Jeanette and Robert Lauer

Virginia Sapiro

Nicholas Kristof

Carl Weiser

John Cuber and Peggy Harrof

Lenore Weitzman

Jessie Bernard

Susan and Clyde Hendrick

Judy Pearson

John Gottman

Bronislaw Malinowski

PART VI. STUDY QUESTIONS

True-False

1.   T   F   The Japanese Research Institute has found that couples in Japan have a relatively low level of *compatibility* compared to other nations around the world.

2.   T   F   *Structural-functional theory* has been a dominant point-of-view in sociology for explaining why people marry while focusing on society's need or demand for the legitimacy of children.

3.   T   F   Most people in the U.S. who marry for the first time do so under the auspices of some religious figure such as a Priest, Rabbi, of Minister.

4.   T   F   Most researchers have found that *commitment* is a key factor in any intimate, emotionally satisfying, and meaningful relationship.

5.   T   F   *Social marriage* is a legally binding agreement or contractual relationship between two people that is defined and regulated by the state.

6.   T   F   The most important marriage laws are *state laws*.

7.   T   F   The U.S. was the first nation to legalize *same-sex marriages*.

8.   T   F   *Blood tests* are required in all 50 states.

9.   T   F   The typical *age requirement* for marriage with parental consent in the U.S. is 16.

10. T   F   *Conjugal rights* pertain to inheritance issues involving siblings.

11. T   F   Research by Jessie Bernard has found very high levels of similarity in how wives and husbands evaluate their marriages.

12. T   F   Studies have shown that wives are twice as likely than husbands to say they *would marry* the same person again.

13. T   F   It is expected that about two-thirds of marriages that begin today will end in *divorce*.

14. T   F   According to John Gottman, the real reason marriages succeed or fail is really very simple: Couples who stay together are *nice* to each other more often than not.

Multiple-Choice

1. Which of the following do Americans rank at the *top* of their list of sources of satisfaction?

    (a)   wealth   (d)   good health
    (b)   fame   (e)   satisfying work
    (c)   good marriage

2. The single most important reason that people give for *getting married* is that they:

   (a) want financial stability
   (b) want a companion
   (c) what to secure their social status
   (d) are in love

3. Rushworth Kidder asked couples why they married or what they thought marriage offered. Their answers most frequently focused on:

   (a) commitment and sharing
   (b) fun and excitement
   (c) having children
   (d) financial security

4. The *principle of legitimacy* was first put forth by:

   (a) Emile Durkheim
   (b) Jessie Bernard
   (c) Nepoleon Chagnon
   (d) Tom Seaver
   (e) Bronislaw Malinowski

5. Almost universally, *marriage* is based on the official control of:

   (a) wealth
   (b) childbearing
   (c) ideas
   (d) society
   (e) sex

6. Approximately _____ *percent* of Americans will marry at least once in their lives.

   (a) 85
   (b) 90
   (c) 95
   (d) 74
   (e) 99

7. According to recent estimates, approximately _____ of *first-time marriages* take place within the context of some type of religious ceremony.

   (a) one-half
   (b) three-fourths
   (c) one-eighth
   (c) two-thirds
   (d) four-fifths

8. According to the text, the most important *marriage laws* are _____ *laws*.

   (a) state
   (b) federal
   (c) local
   (d) international

9. In how many sates in the U.S. can people of the *same sex* marry?

(a) 0
(b) 50
(c) 14
(d) 5
(e) 26

10. In 1989, _____ became the *first country* to legalize same-sex unions.

(a) the United States
(b) Japan
(c) Singapore
(d) Denmark
(e) Australia

11. *Cohabitation* and *common-law marriage* are both examples of:

(a) legal marriage
(b) social marriage
(c) sacred marriage
(d) state marriage
(e) residual marriage

12. In every state except one (Georgia) the legal age at which marriage can be contracted *without parental consent* is:

(a) 14
(b) 16
(c) 12
(d) 15
(e) 18

13. Which of the following have been incorporated into *marriage laws* in the U.S?

(a) the wife is responsible for caring for any children
(b) the husband is the head of the household
(c) the wife is responsible for caring for the home
(d) all of the above
(e) none of the above

14. The average *cost* for a wedding today in the U.S. is:

(a) $1,500
(b) $31,300
(c) $10,000
(d) $7,600
(e) $18,000

15. Which *type* of marriage relationship involves little conflict but also little passion and attention to each other?

(a) total
(b) devitalized
(c) conflict-habituated
(d) passive-congenial

16. Approximately what percentage of marriages today are *interracial*?

   (a) 2
   (b) 6
   (c) less than 1
   (d) 4

17. According to John Gottman, the four most *destructive behaviors* to marital happiness are:

   (a) fear, hatred, avoidance, and rejection
   (b) criticism, contempt, defensiveness, and stonewalling
   (c) withdrawal, violence, jealousy, and envy
   (d) dependence, denial, acceptance, and projection

Fill-In

1. In addition to *love* and *commitment*, particularly in the United States, a number of _____ and _____ reasons motivate people to marry.
2. The _____ of _____ is the notion that all children ought to have a socially and legally *recognized father*.
3. From a *religious* perspective marriage is regarded as a _____.
4. Jeanette and Robert Lauer found that a key factor contributing to the longevity of a relationship is the couples belief in marriage as a long-term _____ and _____ institution.
5. _____ and _____ _____ marriage are examples of *social marriage*.
6. In addition to requiring _____ in marital relationships, *marriage law* also requires _____.
7. *Blood tests* prior to marriage are required in many states to determine _____.
8. The *common-law* concept of _____ is the idea that a wife is under the protection and influence of her husband.
9. _____ relatives are people *related by marriage*.
10. In the past, *age restrictions for marriage* were tied to _____, whereas today the concern is _____.
11. In China the _____ _____ is an *ancient custom* that is being revived. It ensures that everyone may have a partner in the *afterlife*.
12. Among the Tiwi of Australia, there is *no such thing as a* _____ _____.
13. Two key components of *communication* are _____ is said and _____ it is said.
14. Two basic *conditions of successful communication* are a _____, _____ environment and _____ _____.
15. According to John Gottman, the four most *destructive behaviors* to marital happiness are _____, _____, _____, _____, and _____.

1. What are the major reasons given by people in the United States as to why they marry?

2. Cross culturally, how does the United States rank in terms of survey results on *marital compatibility*? What factors are important for marital compatibility in other parts of the world that might be important to consider?

3. How do *structural-functionalists* explain why people marry?

4. Differentiate between the legal, social, and sacred meanings of marriage.

5. What are the important points being made in the text concerning the *legal aspects* of the marriage contract?

6. Review the major legal implications of the fact that *same-sex marriages* are not legal in our society.

7. Review the major points being made about the *legal gender bias* in marriage laws today in the United States.

8. What are the conclusions being made by Jesse Bernard in terms of the relative advantages and disadvantages of marriage for *wives* and *husbands*?

9. Identify and describe the different *types of marriages* as presented by John Cuber and Peggy Haroff.

10. What are the demographic patterns in our society in terms of *heterogamous marriages*?

11. What seem to be the major determinants of *marital satisfaction* in our society?

12. What points are being made in the text concerning *conflict* and *conflict resolution* in the text?

PART VII. ANSWERS TO STUDY QUESTIONS

True-False

1.	T	(p. 194)	8.	F	(p. 200)
2.	T	(p. 195)	9.	T	(p. 200)
3.	T	(p. 196)	10.	F	(p. 203)
4.	F	(p. 196)	11.	F	(p. 208)
5.	F	(pp. 196-97)	12.	F	(p. 209)
6.	T	(pp. 197)	13.	T	(p. 214)
7.	F	(p. 197)	14.	T	(p. 216)

Multiple-Choice

1.	c	(p. 193)	10.	d	(p. 197)
2.	d	(p. 193)	11.	b	(p. 197)
3.	a	(p. 193)	12.	e	(p. 200)
4.	e	(p. 195)	13.	d	(p. 202)
5.	b	(p. 195)	14.	e	(p. 206)
6.	c	(p. 195)	15.	b	(p. 209)
7.	b	(p. 196)	16.	a	(p. 211)
8.	a	(p. 197)	17.	a	(p. 216)
9.	a	(p. 197)			

Fill-In

1. social, economic (p. 194)
2. principle, legitimacy (p. 195)
3. sacrament (p. 196)
4. commitment, sacred (p. 196)
5. Cohabitation, common-law (p. 197)
6. heterosexuality, monogamy (p. 199)
7. the presence of STDs (p. 200)
8. coverture (p. 200)
9. Affinal (p. 200)
10. puberty, maturity (p. 200)
11. spirit wedding (p. 204)
12. unmarried female (p. 204)
13. nonthreatening, noncoercive, mutual, commitment (p. 209)
14. what, how (p. 215)
15. criticism, contempt, defensiveness, stonewalling (p. 216)

PART VIII. COMMENT AND ANALYSIS

For Your Information

"The Marriage Contract: Tradition and Rituals"

Key Points:

Questions you Have?

"The Marriage of Lucy Stone: Under Protest

Key Points:

Questions you Have?

Global Perspectives

"Marriage Practices in Other Places"

Key Points:

Questions you Have?

<u>Writing Your Own Script</u>

"Preparing Your Relationship Contract"

Reproduction and Parenting

9

PART I. CHAPTER OUTLINE

LEARNING OBJECTIVES

1. To define and illustrate important concepts used in the analysis of demographic patterns in society.
2. To consider historical trends in fertility in the United States.
3. To outline the costs and benefits of being a parent.
4. To identify factors affecting the decision by married couples to remain childless.
5. To consider the issue of fertility control, and define contraception and analyze the pattern of contraceptive use in the U.S.
6. To provide a historical overview of the abortion issue.
7. To identify and describe the new technologies available for facilitating the birth of a child.
8. To define and address issues related to conception, pregnancy, and prenatal care.
9. To identify and describe issues related to becoming a parent, differentiating between those most relevant for the father and those relevant for the mother.
10. To identify and discuss the adjustments involved in becoming a parent
11. To review advantages and disadvantages of several different parenting styles.
12. To identify issues related to lesbian and gay parents, single parents, and teenage parents.

CHAPTER REVIEW--KEY POINTS

The opening vignette illustrates a dilemma faced by many families--the balancing of family and career. Regardless of how carefully marriage and family issues may be discussed, there are many contingencies that make life complicated for couples. This is particularly the case when children are involved.

*Fertility--the actual number of live births in a population--*is both a biological and a social phenomenon. This chapter focuses on issues relating to fertility patterns in the United States, conception, pregnancy, and parenthood.

HISTORICAL OVERVIEW: FERTILITY TRENDS IN THE UNITED STATES

Demographers use the term *fertility rate* to refer to *the number of births per thousand women in their childbearing years (ages 15-44) in a given year.* The *total fertility rate* refers to *the average number of children women would have over their lifetime if current birthrates were to remain constant.* In 1790, when the first census was taken, the total fertility rate was estimated to be 7.7. Today it is approximately 2.0.

By 1900 the total fertility rate had declined to half that of a century earlier. Explanations include the transformation of the country from rural-agricultural to urban-industrial, rapid advances in science and technology, and the changing role of women. During the early part of the twentieth century the birth rate continued to decline, particularly during the Great Depression of the 1930s.

Between 1946 and 1965, a period called the *baby boom*, 74 million babies were born in the U.S. Two factors seem to have played a key role in creating the baby boom--the expanding postwar economy and certain government policies. The birth rate fell dramatically during the 1970s, a period known as the *baby bust. Figure 9.1* (p. 222) presents a graph depicting the total fertility rates in the U.S., 1800-1994.

Current Fertility Patterns

Although the total fertility rate is slightly under the population replacement level of 2.1, the rate is not uniform across all racial and ethnic groups. *Figure 9.2* (p. 223) shows the total fertility rate by racial and ethnic groups in the U.S. for 1994. *Table 9.1* (p. 223) presents data on births per 1000 women by age and race/ethnicity for 1994. Significant differences are revealed.

The birthrate in the U.S. has been declining over the last two centuries. Much of the change is the result of the changing economic value of children. Almost two-thirds of women aged 18-34 today plan on having only one or two children.

TO PARENT OR NOT

Parenthood involves both costs and benefits that vary over the family life cycle. People should consider many factors before becoming a parent.

The Costs of Parenthood

Children today are primarily consumers. Demographers estimate that middle-income families spend between 16 to 20 percent of their income on a child from birth to age 17.

Time, Energy, and Economic Costs: Raising children involves more than economic outlay. It requires a great investment of parental time and energy. It also carries a high emotional cost in terms of parental worries.

Lifestyle Disruptions: The birth of a child can disrupt previously satisfying lifestyles. Infants interrupt sleep and lovemaking, change household routines, and alter social life and recreational pursuits.

158

The Benefits of Parenthood

Emotional Bonds: Most parents believe the benefits of parenthood outweigh the costs. Children are not only consumers and takers; they also give love and affection, and are a tangible symbol of love for many parents. Children also enlarge the social interaction network of a family.

Adult Status: Many people see children as a means of achieving adult status, recognition, and personal fulfillment. Children provide parents with a sense of pride and immortality.

Fun and Enjoyment: Having children can be great fun. Through children adults can reexperience some of the delights of their own childhood.

The Social Pressures to Procreate

It is in society's interest to promote a **pronatalist attitude**, *one that encourages childbearing.* Societies vary in their strategies for accomplishing this goal.

The Child-Free Option

Today, about 5 percent of married couples in the U.S. are consciously choosing to be child-free; the rate is almost three times higher among college graduates. The reasons for not having children include: *career and marital considerations, career fulfillment, qualifications for parenthood, and antinatalist forces.* **Antinatalist forces** refer to *policies or practices that discourage people from having children.* An extreme example of this is China's one-child policy. The **Personal Reflection** box (p. 226) discusses the issue of delayed parenting. Delayed parenting is defined as having a first child after the age of 30. Today, 22 percent of women are choosing this option.

CONTROLLING FERTILITY

Throughout history many groups and societies have attempted to control the timing and number of births to ensure an adequate supply of food and other resources for the entire community. Techniques have varied across history and by society--celibacy, abstinence, delayed marriage, abortion, and infanticide.

In contrast to these early methods, today efficient and safe methods of *contraception-- mechanisms for preventing fertilization*--are available. The **For Your Information** box (p. 227) discusses the history of the struggle to legalize birth control in the U.S. The role played by Margaret Sanger during the first half of this century is the focus of this box.

Reasons for Not Using Contraceptives

Jerry Burger and Linda Burns have studied the issue of unprotected sex among young people. They call this pattern of behavior the "illusion of unique invulnerability."

According to these researchers, the reasons for not using contraception include: *symbolism of sexual activity, role of peers, role of parents, contraception is not romantic,* and *the nature of the relationship.*

ABORTION

Abortion refers to *the termination of a pregnancy before the fetus can survive on its own.* This can occur spontaneously (miscarriage) or be induced through a variety of external methods (see Appendix D). In 1992 there were 1.5 million abortions performed in the U.S. (25 percent of all pregnancies).

Historical Perspectives

Until the nineteenth century, American laws concerning abortion reflected the tradition in English common law that abortion was permissible until *quickening*--the time at which a pregnant woman could feel the fetus moving in her womb.

By the middle of the nineteenth century there was one induced abortion out of every four live births, a figure comparable to today. Connecticut was the first state to regulate abortion in 1821--in order to protect women from dangerous poisons. By 1900 abortion was illegal in the U.S. except when a physician judged it necessary to save a woman's life.

Two events in the 1960s became a catalyst for new debate on the abortion issue. One involved the drug thalidomide, and the other an outbreak of rubella. In 1973, the Supreme Court, by a 7 to 2 vote in Roe versus Wade, struck down all antiabortion laws as violations of a woman's right to privacy.

Race, Class, and Age

Although still legal, abortion has become increasingly less accessible. This is especially the case for poor women, women of color, and young women. In 1976, Congress passed the Hyde Amendment, which prohibited using federal Medicaid funds for abortions except in cases where the pregnancy threatens a woman's life. Other Supreme Court decisions are identified that limit access to an abortion. It is further pointed out that the approach to abortion varies cross culturally.

Public Attitudes Toward Abortion

Attitudes about abortion change over time and are affected by many factors--economic, political, technological, etc. Recent national polls show that 60 percent of Americans think abortion should be legal in some cases, 30 percent think it should be legal under all circumstances.

INFERTILITY

The medical profession defines *infertility* as *the inability to conceive after 12 months of unprotected intercourse or the inability to carry a pregnancy to live birth*. At any given time, approximately 15 to 20 percent of all married couples experience some form of infertility. Reproductive impairments are more common among African American and couples with low income.

Causes of Infertility

About 40 percent of fertility problems are traced to the male partner and an equal percentage to the female; the remaining 20 percent involve both partners. The major causes of female infertility are failure to ovulate and blockage of the fallopian tubes. The major cause of male infertility is low sperm production.

Consequences of Infertility

Many infertile couples experience a *crisis of infertility* characterized by a feeling of loss of control over their lives. As a result, a wide range of emotions are experienced. Reactions to infertility vary by gender, with wives being preoccupied with the task of solving their infertility problems, and husbands more likely viewing infertility as an unfortunate circumstance. These different reactions can cause considerable strain in a couple's relationship. Two options are available for couples experiencing infertility--adoption or the new reproductive technologies.

REPRODUCTION WITHOUT SEX: THE NEW TECHNOLOGIES

Artificial Insemination: **Artificial insemination** involves *the injection of semen into the vagina or uterus of an ovulating woman*. This method dates back to the 1890s, and has been quite successful. The cost for this procedure is moderate--about $250 per insemination. There are legal and ethical concerns when sperm from a donor other than the husband is used for insemination.

Embryo Transplant: **Embryo transplant** refers to *a procedure whereby a fertilized egg from a woman donor is implanted into an infertile woman*. Criticism of this technique revolves around two central issues. One issue is the possible exploitation of woman donors. The other issue raises questions of what constitutes biological motherhood.

Surrogacy: In **surrogacy**, *a woman agrees to be artificially inseminated with a man's sperm, carry the fetus to term, and relinquish all rights to the child after it is born*. This is perhaps the most controversial of all the reproductive techniques. Social, ethical, and legal issues surrounding surrogacy are discussed in this section of the chapter.

THE CHOICE TO PARENT

Once the decision to have a child is made, individuals and couples must turn their attention to matters of conception, pregnancy, childbirth, and child rearing.

CONCEPTION

Pregnancy and eventual childbirth begin with *conception*, *the process by which a male sperm cell penetrates the female ovum (egg), creating a fertilized egg, or* **zygote**.

What makes conception possible is the process of *ovulation*, *the release of a mature egg*. The egg is viable for approximately 24 hours. Thus, on average, for conception to occur, a couple must have intercourse during or within 2 days prior to ovulation.

Sex Preferences and Selection

Research on parental sex preferences overwhelmingly show a preference for a male child over a female child. Medical and sociological issues are briefly discussed in this section of the chapter.

PREGNANCY

Prenatal Development and Care

The attitudes and behaviors of a mother during pregnancy greatly influence the health and well-being of the fetus and later of the human infant. Race, class, age, and gender experiences significantly affect maternal attitudes and behaviors during pregnancy. Pregnancy is a multifaceted event for women. During the *first trimester*--the first three months of pregnancy--women can experience a wide array of biological, psychological, and social conditions.

The Health and Well-Being of the Fetus: Two of the most commonly used prenatal tests are amniocentesis and ultrasound. *Amniocentesis* is performed when there is some concern about a hereditary disease. It can also provide information about the sex of the fetus. *Ultrasound* allows a physician and the couple to observe the developing fetus directly by viewing electronically the echoes of sound waves pulsating through the pregnant woman's body.

For many women, the onset of the *second trimester* of a pregnancy signals the end of many of the first-trimester symptoms such as morning sickness and fatigue. The movement of the fetus, *quickening*, can be a joyous event for many women and their partners.
By the end of the second-trimester the fetus has all its essential structures. During the *third-trimester* development consists primarily of gains in weight and length and refinements in the developing fetus.

162

Prenatal Problems and Defects

Most estimates concerning birth defects in the U.S. fall between 2 and 4 percent, though some are as high as 7 percent. Birth defects can usually be traced to one or more of the following factors: (1) the influence of the prenatal environment on the fetus, (2) heredity, and (3) injuries sustained at birth.

Protecting the Prenatal Environment: Only about one-fifth of birth defects can be traced to heredity. Research has shown repeatedly that experiences such as those of age, race, and class have important effects on **morbidity** *(illness)* and **mortality** *(death)*. Examples of these influences are briefly discussed in this section of the chapter.

Protection of the prenatal environment is critical for the proper development of the fetus. Some of the most prevalent prenatal concerns include:

Nutrition: The failure of the mother to eat properly can deprive the fetus of proper nutrition. The probability of malnutrition during pregnancy is highest among teen mothers and poor and working-class women regardless of age.

Smoking: Smoking affects the fetus by lowering the amount of oxygen the fetus receives as well as impairing the circulation of the fetus's blood. Research has found that men who smoke are 60 percent more likely than men who do not smoke to have children that have various cancers.

Alcohol: Alcohol can cause **fetal alcohol syndrome**. This condition is characterized by a number of physical deformities, severe problems with the central nervous system, heart defects, mental retardation, and small birth size.

Drugs and other Substance Abuse: The majority of drugs, whether street drugs, common drugs like caffeine and aspirin, or prescription and over-the-counter medications, contain chemicals that have been found to have some effect on the fetus. Almost all drugs taken or ingested during pregnancy cross the placenta. The fetus is particularly vulnerable during the first-trimester.

AIDS and Pregnancy: The results of the effects of HIV on the health of pregnant women are inconsistent and inconclusive. In addition, little is known about the rates, methods, and risks of transmitting HIV to the fetus. Nonetheless, many health professionals often encourage HIV-positive women to either not to get pregnant or to terminate a pregnancy. The physical appearance of an HIV-positive infant is referred to as **embryopathy**. Appendix B discusses AIDS and other STDs.

EXPECTANT FATHERS

The Cultural Double Bind

Lee Shapiro suggests that the pregnancy of a partner thrusts a man into an alien world. One important issue, suggests Shapiro, is that on the one hand, men are encouraged to participate in the pregnancy and birth of their children; but on the other hand, they are treated as outsiders by everyone concerned. He refers to this as the *cultural double bind*.

Fears and Concerns of Expectant Fathers

Shapiro has also identified seven major fears and concerns expectant fathers typically experienced, including: *queasiness, uncertain paternity, loss of spouse or child, increased responsibility, being replaced, obstetrical-gynecological matters,* and *life and death*. Each of these is defined and briefly discussed in this section of the chapter.

CHILDBIRTH

Childbirth has both physical (physiological changes in a woman's body) and social-emotional (feelings and attitudes) aspects.

Until the nineteenth century, midwives and female family and friends presided over and assisted in most births. Today, a *midwife* is *a professional, most often a woman, who is trained either to deliver a baby or to assist in delivery*.

In most cases today, , physicians routinely define pregnancy and childbirth in terms of a medical model. Alternatives to hospital births are discussed in this section of the chapter.

PARENTAL ADJUSTMENTS, ADAPTATIONS, AND PATTERNS OF CHILD REARING

Parenthood is one of the most demanding roles that individuals and couples face in their lifetime. Research shows that children increase stress in a relationship and lower relationship satisfaction. For some women, these stresses can show up in *postnatal depression, a condition characterized by mood shifts, irritability, and fatigue*. Approximately one-third of mothers experience postnatal depression. About one in ten fathers experience this condition.

Parental Roles

Research has shown that for many people he transition to parenthood means taking on more traditional sex roles.

Motherhood: Traditional notions of motherhood are rooted in a Eurocentric middle-class ideology that emphasizes the centrality of mothering for women. Such traditional ideas of motherhood have been referred to as the *motherhood mystique*. The motherhood mystique proposes that:

(1)   the ultimate achievement and fulfillment of womanhood is through motherhood;

(2)   to be a good mother a woman has to enjoy being a mother and all the work that is defined as part of the mothering role; and

(3)   a woman's attitude about mothering will affect her children.

According to Patricia Hill Collins, the basic assumptions that underlie the traditional view of motherhood apply primarily to white middle-class families and most often do not reflect the realities of black families and other families of color. Collins proposed a model of African American motherhood that consists of our basic themes:

(1) bloodmothers, other mothers, and women-centered networks
(2) providing as part of mothering
(3) community othermothers and social activism
(4) motherhood as a symbol of power

Fatherhood: The traditional notion of fatherhood emphasizes an instrumental role of father as breadwinner and authority figure. According to Nancy Gibbs, the message that fathers continue to receive is that they are not up to the job. She provides a number of examples of how we perpetuate the notion that we not only do not trust men to be parents but also we do not really need them to be. Examples from corporate America, popular culture, and education are given. The **Profiles** box (p. 241) discusses a family represented by a house-husband.

Today, four different views of fatherhood coexist, with some degree of overlap: (1) the aloof and distant father, (2) the father as breadwinner, (3) the father as a gender role model for the couple's children, and (4) the father as an active, nurturant parent.

Gender Differences in the Experience of Parenthood

After a child is born mothers are typically more involved in child-care activities than fathers are. In less than 2 percent of married-coupe families are fathers full-time homemakers, and in less than 15 percent do they equally share child-care and housework responsibilities.

Styles of Parenting

Sociologists have identified some common patterns of parenting among families in the United States, especially within particular social classes. Melvin Kohn has discussed parenting styles in terms of a *traditional,* or *conformity value orientation* (working-class and lower-class) and a *developmental,* or *self-esteem value orientation* (middle-class).

Other researchers have incorporated Kohn's findings into a model that divides parenting styles into three general categories: *authoritarian* (obedience and physical punishment model), *permissive* (autonomy and freedom model), and *authoritative* (autonomy, self-reliance, and positive reinforcement model).

A major issue for many parents is how to change their children's behavior when it is unacceptable. National polls reveal that over two-thirds of adults agree that it is sometimes necessary to discipline a child with a "good hard spanking." According to Murray Strauss, more than 90 percent of American parents hit toddlers and most continue to hit their children for years. Strauss points out several harmful consequences of spanking. For example, spanking is related to greater aggressiveness in children, the erosion of affection between parent and child, abuse of children, and the passing on this behavior to your kids.

Race and Class

African Americans: African American families have historically experienced issues that many families have only recently become attentive to--combining work and family, single parenthood, and extended families relationships.

African American middle-class families have a value orientation characterized by high achievement motivation, social striving, and a high regard for property ownership. The parenting style in working-class families includes an emphasis on respectability, conformity, and obedience. Many poor African American families are disenchanted, disillusioned, and alienated. As a result many of them are generally limited in their ability to guide their children and often have little control over their children's behavior.

African American fathers are often portrayed as uninterested and uninvolved. However, research on noncustodial black fathers have more daily contact with their children than do noncustodial whites.

Native Americans: Native Americans are a very heterogeneous group. However, Native American parents of all backgrounds stress to their children a sense of family unity and tribal identity.

Latinos: Among Puerto Ricans, females are charged with the responsibility of creating and maintaining these values in offspring. The general pattern is one of authoritarianism.

Asian Americans: Parenting styles among Asian Americans vary according to the degree to that parents are acculturated into U.S. society. Newly immigrated or first generation parents stress obedience and conformity are expected, and discipline is strict and involves physical punishment. In contrast, acculturated parents generally are more nurturing and verbal and give their children more autonomy.

Lesbian and Gay Parents

Approximately one million lesbian and gay couples in the U.S. are raising one or more children. Little is known about parenting styles of lesbians and gays. The available research indicated that lesbians tend to form extended networks of support, and tend to be less structured around a gender-specific division of labor. Gays who raise children, like lesbians, tend to be more nurturing and less rigid in terms of gender role socialization. Children raised in lesbian and gay households are as well adjusted as children raised in heterosexual households.

Single Parents

The number of single-parent families has increased dramatically over the past two decades as both the divorce rate and the number of children born outside of legal marriage have increased. Approximately one-third of all births in the U.S. are now to single parents.

166

According to some experts, half of all children born today will live in a single-parent family before they reach adulthood. One in every four white infants is born to a mother who is not legally married, as are two of every three black infants and one in three Latino infants. Eighty-eight percent of children living in single-parent households live with their mothers only. *Figure 9.3* (p. 245) show data on births in the U.S. to single mothers, 1940-1993. The largest percentage of single parents are beyond the teenage years. Economic constraints are significant for single-parent families. *Figure 9.4* (p. 246) shows data concerning single mothers by race, compared with all women age 15-44, 1993.

Single Fathers: About 14 percent of single-parent households are male-headed, though the rate has more than doubled since 1980. Over two million children today are living in single-father families.

All too often the focus on single-parent families is on the problems they face. The impression is given that this structure is inherently problematic. However, this is not the case. Depending on the resources and support systems available to parents, single parents, like other parents, will determine the degree to which parenting will be rewarding or challenging. Studies have identified many benefits of growing up in a single-parent family.

Trends in unmarried births in the United States are very similar to those found in other countries. Although many complex factors account for the differential rates of unmarried births around the world, two important factors are believed to be the differential levels of contraceptive use and rates of teenage pregnancy between countries.

Teenaged Parents

Contrary to popular belief, teenagers account for less than one-third of all unmarried mothers. *Figure 9.5* (p. 247) shows the percentages of births before and after marriage, 1960-1989. The results may surprise you. Latinos account for a large percentage of the increase in teen births over the last decade. However, the typical teenaged mother in the U.S. today is white and in her late teens, and she is more likely to have a child outside of legal marriage than her counterparts in other industrialized countries. The U.S. has the highest rate of unintended childbirth than any other industrialized country: 40 percent among married women and 88 percent among never-married women.

Teenaged Fathers: Research on single fathers, especially teenage fathers, is limited. Stereotypes typically held concerning teenaged fathers are brought into question in this section of the chapter. Contrary to popular belief many young fathers acknowledge paternity of their children and actively seek to be involved in the rearing of their children.

From a sociological perspective, in analyzing teenage births, we must consider structural and institutional factors--racism, sexism, poverty, mass media influences to name a few. Teenage childbirth is deeply rooted in many of our society's social problems and cannot be understood simply on an individual level.

The **Writing Your Own Script** (p. 249) entitled "To parent of not?" asks you to think about parenthood. Questions to consider include: Do you want children? For What reasons? What are the advantages and disadvantages of being child-free?

PART IV. KEY TERMS

fertility

fertility rate

total fertility rate

pronatalist attitude

antinatalist attitude

contraception

abortion

infertility

artificial insemination

in vitro fertilization

embryo transplants

surrogacy

conception

zygote

ovulation

aminiocentisis

ultrasound

sonogram

congenital

morbidity

mortality

embryopathy

midwife

motherhood mystique

fetal alcohol syndrome

couvade

postnatal depression

PART V. KEY RESEARCHERS

Jerry Burger and Linda Burns

Jarrold Shapiro

Margaret Sanger

Joan Huber

Sigmund Freud

Marian Faux

Diane Baumrind

Patricia Hill Collins

Melvin Kohn   Murray Strauss

Nancy Gibbs   Margaret Usdansky

PART VI. STUDY QUESTIONS

True-False

1.	T	F	*Latinos* have higher fertility rates than other women in the U.S.
2.	T	F	China's one-child policy is an example of *antinatalist forces*
3.	T	F	Margaret Sanger coined the term *birth control* as a positive description of family limitations.
4.	T	F	Most pregnancies in the U.S. are *unintended* (the result of accidents).
5.	T	F	The *Hyde Amendment* provided for federal funds for poor women's birth control costs.
6.	T	F	About 75 percent of *infertility* problems is traced solely to the male partner.
7.	T	F	*Amniocentesis* involves a procedure whereby a fertilized egg from a women is surgically implanted into an infertile woman.
8.	T	F	The *cultural double bind* refers to the dilemma faced by women because of the conflicts between the motherhood mystique and the changing gender roles in society.
9.	T	F	Most adults in the U.S. *agree* that it is sometimes necessary to discipline a child with a good hard spanking.
10.	T	F	Most unwed mothers in the U.S. are *teenagers*.
11.	T	F	The typical *teenaged mother* in the U.S. is white, in her late teens, and unmarried.
12.	T	F	The U.S. has a higher rate of *unintended* childbirth than any other industrialized society.

1. The period between *1946 to 1965* has come to be known among demographers as the *baby _____ era*:

   (a) bust
   (b) strain
   (c) bullet
   (d) boom
   (e) echo

2. The *total fertility rate* in the U.S. today is approximately:

   (a) 1.5
   (b) 2.5
   (c) 2.0
   (d) 1.0
   (e) 2.9

3. In comparison to other racial groups _____-Americans have the *lowest fertility rates*.

   (a) Asian
   (b) Latin
   (c) Native
   (d) African

4. According to the U.S. Census Bureau, most American women aged 18 to 34 *expect to have _____ children*.

   (a) no
   (b) one or two
   (c) two or three
   (d) four or more
   (e) three or four

5. Approximately _____ *percent* of all married couples in the U.S. choose to remain *child-free*.

   (a) 1
   (b) 5
   (c) 3
   (d) 10
   (e) 15

6. The battle to make *contraception* legal was ignited by _____, a public-health nurse in the early 1900s.

   (a) Elizabeth Cady Stanton
   (b) Ruth Benedict
   (c) Kristen Luker
   (d) Margaret Mead
   (e) Margaret Sanger

7. In which of the following cases did the Supreme Court hold that the state *cannot deny minors* the access to contraceptives?

    (a) Carey v Population Services International
    (b) Eisenstadt v Baird
    (c) Griswold v Connecticut
    (d) Webster v Reproductive Health Services
    (e) Shriver v Agnew

8. Approximately _____ *million* women become pregnant each year in the United States.

    (a) 2   (d) 8
    (b) 6   (e) 3
    (c) 4

9. Approximately _____ *percent* of all pregnancies in the U.S. are terminated by abortion.

    (a) 10   (d) 25
    (b) 50   (e) 15
    (c) 20

10. The *Hyde amendment* of 1976:

    (a) legalized abortion
    (b) provided tighter regulation of surrogacy
    (c) prohibited federal Medicaid funds to be used for abortions except in cases where the woman's life is threatened
    (d) required minors to get parental permission to get married
    (e) enabled minors to get contraceptives without parental permission

11. At any given time, approximately _____ of all married couples in the U.S. experience some form of *infertility*.

    (a) 15 to 20   (d) 5 to 10
    (b) 30 to 40   (e) 1 to 5
    (c) 25 to 30

12. About _____ *percent* of *fertility problems* are traced directly to the *male* partner.

    (a) 10   (d) 90
    (b) 20   (e) 60
    (c) 40

13. A *zygote* is:

   (a)   a male sperm
   (b)   an infertile male
   (c)   an infertile female

   (d)   an unfertilized egg
   (e)   a fertilized egg

14. *Amniocentesis*:

   (a)   allows parents to see the fetus and any movements it makes
   (b)   is a form of in vitro fertilization
   (c)   is performed when there is some concern about a hereditary disorder
   (d)   produces a zygote
   (e)   is a condition in which a male has a low sperm count due to excessive spitting and pants-hiking

Fill-In

1.   Demographers use the term _____ *rate* to refer to the number of births per thousand women of childbearing years (ages 15-44) in a given year.

2.   _____--the actual number of live births in a population--is both a _____ and a _____ phenomenon.

3.   By 1900, the *total fertility rate* had _____ to _____ that of a century earlier.

4.   According to economists, middle-income families spend between _____ to _____ *percent* of their income on a child from birth to the age of 17.

5.   Benefits of *parenthood* identified in the text include: _____ bonds, _____ status, and _____ and _____.

6.   _____ refers to mechanisms for preventing fertilization.

7.   _____ was the first state to *regulate abortion*. It did so in _____.

8.   Recent polls indicate that _____ percent of Americans think *abortion* should be legal under some circumstances, and _____ percent under all circumstances.

9.   _____ involves surgically removing a woman's eggs, fertilizing them in a petri dish with the partner's sperm, and then implanting one or more of the fertilized eggs in a woman's uterus.

10. In _____, a woman agrees to be artificially inseminated with a man's sperm, carry the fetus to term, and relinquish all rights to the child after it is born.

11. Research has shown repeatedly that experiences such as those of *race, age* and *class* have important effects on _____ (*illness*) and _____ (*death*).

12.	When HIV infested babies are born they generally have prominent physical features--small heads, slanted eyes that sit far apart from each other, a square forehead, a wide flat nose, and loosely shaped lips. This *physical appearance* is referred to as _____.

13.	On the one hand, men are encouraged to participate in the pregnancy and birth of their children; but on the other hand, they are treated as outsiders by everyone concerned. Jerrold Shapiro refers to this situation as the _____ _____ _____.

14.	In most cases, today, physicians routinely define pregnancy and childbirth in terms of a _____ *model*.

15.	In less than _____ percent of married-couple families are fathers *full-time homemakers*, and in less than _____ percent do they *equally share* child-care and housework responsibilities.

16.	The _____ *style of parenting* encourages children to be autonomous and self-reliant and utilizes positive reinforcement to direct behaviors of children.

17.	One in every _____ white infants is born to a mother who is not legally married, as are _____ of every three black infants and one in every _____ Latino infants.

Short-Answer

1.	How has *fertility rates* changed in the U.S. over the last 200 years? What factors influenced these rates?

2.	What are the current *fertility patterns* in the U.S. by race, ethnicity, and age?

3.	What are the relative *costs* and *benefits* of *parenthood*?

4.	Why do married couples choose to remain *child-free*?

5.	What are the major methods of *fertility control*? Describe each.

6.	Why do many sexually active people *not use* contraception?

7.	Discuss *abortion* in historical perspective. How do abortion rates vary by age, race, and class? What events during the 1960s were critical for the abortion issue?

8.	What is *infertility*? What are its causes?

9.	Identify and describe the *new reproductive technologies* reviewed in the text. What are the moral, legal, and social issues involved with these technologies?

10.	What is *conception*? Describe this event physiologically.

11.	Describe a *pregnancy* and *prenatal* development. What are the prenatal care recommendations being made in the text?

12.	What are the major *prenatal problems* (defects)? What are their causes?

13.	What is meant by the term *cultural double bind*?

14.	What are the major concerns of *expectant fathers*?

15.	Describe *childbirth as reviewed in the text*.

16.	What are the major *parental adjustments* and *adaptations* after the birth of a child?

17.	What points are being made in the text concerning *parental roles*? What are the three aspects of the *motherhood mystique*?

18.	Discuss the issue of *gender differences* in the experience of parenthood.

19. What are the various *styles of parenting* as identified in the text. Describe each. Are there other styles you can identify?
20. How does parenting vary by *race* and *class* in the U.S?
21. What are the issues being raised in the text concerning *lesbian* and *gay* parents?
22. What are the issues being raised in the text concerning *single* parents?
23. Describe the demographics of *teenaged* parents in the U.S. today. Why do so many teenagers in the U.S. have unintended pregnancies?

PART VII. ANSWERS TO STUDY QUESTIONS

True-False

1.	T	(p. 223)	7.	F	(p. 234)
2.	T	(p. 225)	8.	F	(p. 237)
3.	T	(p. 227)	9.	T	(p. 243)
4.	T	(p. 228)	10.	F	(p. 246)
5.	F	(p. 229)	11.	T	(p. 248)
6.	F	(p. 230)	12.	T	(p. 248)

Multiple-Choice

1.	d	(p. 222)	8.	b	(p. 228)
2.	c	(p. 223)	9.	d	(p. 228)
3.	a	(p. 223)	10.	c	(p. 229)
4.	b	(p. 223)	11.	a	(p. 229)
5.	c	(p. 225)	12.	c	(p. 230)
6.	e	(p. 227)	13.	e	(p. 233)
7.	a	(p. 227)	14.	c	(p. 234)

Fill-In

1. fertility (p. 222)
2. Fertility, biological, social (p. 222)
3. declined, half (p.222)
4. 16, 20 (p. 224)
5. emotional, adult, fun, enjoyment (p. 225)
6. Contraception (p. 227)
7. Connecticut, 1821 (p. 228)
8. 60, 30 (p. 229)
9. In vitro fertilization (p. 231)
10. Surrogacy (p. 231)
11. morbidity, mortality (p. 235)
12. Embryopathy (p. 236)

13. cultural double bind (p. 237)
14. medical (p. 238)
15. 2, 15 (p. 242)
16. authoritative (p. 242)
17. 4, 3, 3 (p. 245)

PART VIII. COMMENT AND ANALYSIS

Personal Reflection

"Delayed Parenting"

    Key Points:

    Questions you have?

For Your Information

"Margaret Sanger: The Struggle to Legalize Birth Control"

    Key Points:

    Questions you have?

Profile

"The Roberts Family"

    Key Points:

    Questions you have?

Writing Your Own Script

"To Parent or Not?"

Evolving Work and Family Structures

PART I. CHAPTER OUTLINE

1. To be able to describe the changing composition of the U.S. labor force.
2. To consider the transition in U.S. families from the traditional nuclear family to the two-income family.
3. To analyze the impact of work on family relationships.
4. To identify and evaluate strategies for conflict resolution within families.
5. To identify and discuss inequalities in the workplace and their consequences for families.
6. To become aware of some demographic characteristics of unemployment and poverty in the U.S.
7. To discuss the problem of homelessness in the U.S.
8. To consider how the workplace can be restructured to accommodate the changing needs of families in the U.S.

PART III. CHAPTER REVIEW--KEY POINTS

While usually thought of as separate spheres, the worlds of family life and work significantly affect each other. The opening vignette illustrates this fact, demonstrating that changing economic and social conditions means that single income families are no longer sufficient to provide household members with an adequate standard of living. *Spillover effects* of work into the family are discussed.

THE TRANSFORMATION OF WORK AND FAMILY ROLES

The **labor force participation rate** refers to *the percentage of workers in a particular group who are employed or who are actively seeking employment. Figure 10.1* (p. 253) traces the change in women's and men's labor force participation rates from 1900 to 1994. Historically, such rates have been affected by gender, race, and marital status. Today, 58.8 percent of women of the age of fourteen are in the labor force. The comparable figure for men is 75.1 percent. *Figure 10.2* (p. 254) shows data concerning the percentage of married working mothers with children under the age of six for the years 1975-1994. Today, the rate is over 58 percent, with little difference by race or ethnicity. For men, the differences in labor force participation rates are more pronounced across race and ethnicity.

Reasons Women Work

Most women work for the same reasons men do--to support themselves and their families. Women today are better educated, have fewer children, and live longer. In recent decades the U.S. has experienced major changes, which have had a negative impact on family budgets. Many high-paying jobs have disappeared. *Figure 10.3* (p. 255) shows what happened to displaced workers. Less than a third found jobs with earnings the same or higher than what was being earned prior to displacement. Real earnings for most families have remained stagnant or fell.

WORK AND FAMILY STRUCTURES

Traditional Nuclear Families

The traditional nuclear family structure (mother-housewife, father-breadwinner, and one or more children) currently represents only 7 percent of all households in the U.S. The advantages and disadvantages of the role of *home production worker* (housewife or househusband) are discussed.

The Two-Person Career

The *two-person career* is a variation of the traditional nuclear family where the wife assists in her husband's career.

Dual-Earner Families

Dual-earner families are not new, however, today they represent about 70 percent of all married couples and cut across all class and ethnic lines. The *Family Profile* box (p. 256) focuses on issues concerning challenges to the dual earner family.

Commuter Marriages

Today many commuter marriages develop because both spouses pursue careers but cannot find suitable jobs for each spouse in the same geographic location. This type of marriage arrangement is generally more stressful for younger couples. Research suggests commuter marriage couples are more satisfied with their work and the time they have for themselves but are more dissatisfied with family life, their relationship with their partner, and with life as a whole.

THE IMPACT OF WORK ON FAMILY RELATIONSHIPS

The attempts by dual-earner couples to integrate work and family experiences affect many aspects of life: power relationships and decision making, marital happiness, and the household division of labor.

Marital Power and Decision Making

One of the most consistent findings relating to the impact of work on family life deals with the relationship between income and power in decision making. When both spouses work, the traditional pattern of male dominance in the relationship shifts to one of greater equality in terms of more joint decision making. This pattern holds true across

180

racial and ethnic lines. There are exceptions to this pattern. According to research by Karen Pyke, the meanings couples give to women's paid employment or unpaid household labor is key to determining the woman's power in the relationship. Her focus was on second marriages for women.

Marital Happiness

Research findings concerning the relationship between dual-earner families and marital happiness is inconsistent. More important than work per se, however, is the couple's attitude toward work. Also important is the amount of time the couple spends together. Time is also related to two other important aspects of family living: household tasks and the care of children.

Husbands and the Division of Household Labor

Husbands do not make equal contributions to housework. This often leads to role overload for women, and has been referred to as the *second shift* working women. A national survey found "help with household chores" was second to money problems as the biggest cause of resentment among married women. Data reveal that across family types and regardless of women's employment status, women performed 2-3 times more housework than their husbands. Race and ethnicity are also factors in how family work is divided. **Table 10.1** (p. 260) reveals the time men spend on specific household tasks. There seems to be some consensus among both women and men for the need to alter traditional gender roles.

Child Care

Both working and nonworking wives still do the majority of child care. This situation puts working women at a competitive disadvantage with male colleagues who are freed of this responsibility by their wives. Nonpoor families spend an average of 8 percent of their income for child care, while poor families spend 25 percent.

Some couples respond to child care demands through split-shift employment and parents. This enables one parent to work and the other to stay home with the children. Parents rarely see each other and this can cause tension.

For parents who work the same shift, child care is a problem. *Figure 10.4* (p. 261) shows data on primary child-care arrangements of preschool children. Thirty percent of couples who work the same shift use organized day care facilities. High cost and limited availability are critical concerns. The **Global Perspective** box (p. 262) looks at child care cross-culturally. Other industrialized nations invest significant tax dollars on child care.

The Mommy Track: Felice Schwartz suggested that working women be divided into two groups--*career-primary* and *career-and-family*. The first group should be placed on the same career track with talented men, the other group should be provided with considerations for their parental responsibilities. Criticism of this proposal was swift. While fathers say that they want to spend more time with their families, few adjust their work schedules to allow for more family time.

INTEGRATING WORK AND FAMILY LIFE: RESOLVING ROLE CONFLICT

The transition to work, marriage, and parenthood requires taking on multiple roles. These roles frequently conflict with one another. *Role conflict occurs when a person occupies two different roles that involve contradictory expectations of what should be done at a given time.* *The* **Critical Issues** box (p. 263) provides several examples of family-work contexts that produce role conflict.

Strategies for Conflict Resolution

Establishing Priorities: The process of making decisions about which activities are more important and will receive more energy and attention is often complicated by gender, race, and class. Gender role assumptions in society, family structure, and work schedules are discussed.

Role Exit: Role exit can occur in a number of ways, including leaving the workplace or taking a part-time job.

Public Awareness: Making other people aware of how gender inequality at work and in the home adversely affects everyone's well-being is another important strategy to use to help reduce role conflict. People are pressuring the government and employers to introduce or modify policies to help resolve conflicts between work and family responsibilities.

INEQUALITIES IN THE WORKPLACE: CONSEQUENCES FOR FAMILIES

While changes are occurring, women still confront issues of inequality in the labor market. These issues affect a woman's sense of self-worth and her families well-being. The issues of special significance include: occupational distribution, the gender gap in earnings, and sexual harassment.

Occupational Distribution

Occupational distribution refers to *the location of workers in different occupations.* Much work in the U.S. is still gender stratified. Women tend to work in lower-paying jobs even when they are professionals. *Table 10.2* (p. 264) shows the percentage of the work force in selected occupations, by sex, race, and ethnicity. Women comprise 46 percent of the labor force. Illustrating gender differences, women account for 59.6 percent of all service occupation workers and only 9.3 percent of precision production, craft, and repair workers.

More women have been entering traditionally male dominated occupations, however, men have been reluctant to enter "womens" occupations in any significant numbers. This occupational segregation has consequences for the well-being of workers and their families. Women in nontraditional occupations often suffer prejudice, discrimination, and hostility. The issues of the *glass ceiling* and the *glass escalator* are discussed.

The Race-Gender Gap in Earnings: Good News and Bad News

Women's wages are lower than men's, regardless of race or ethnicity. Median incomes for full-time, year-round workers by race, ethnicity, and gender are presented. Women earn on average approximately 74 percent of what men earn. In some occupational categories the differences are not that great. Much research has suggested that along with discriminatory treatment, the major cause of the earnings gap between women and men is the fact that women do more housework than men. The U.S. gender gap in earnings is greater than in most other industrialized societies. The concept of *comparable worth*, *the principle of equal pay for different jobs of equal worth*, is discussed. To put this into practice requires evaluating jobs in terms of education, experience, and skill requirements.

Sexual Harassment

Sexual harassment refers to *unwanted leers, comments, suggestions, or physical contact of a sexual nature that the recipient finds offensive and causes discomfort or interferes with academic or job performance.* Survey research suggests that 30-50 percent of female students and as many as 75 percent of female employees have been sexually harassed. The comparable figures for males approximate 15-20 percent.

Race, socioeconomic status, sexual orientation, age, and marital status affect the experience of sexual harassment. Illustrations are presented. Although sexual harassment violates equal-employment laws, enforcement is difficult.

THE ECONOMICS WELL-BEING OF FAMILIES

Table 10.3 (p. 266) reveals the median weekly earnings of families in 1993. Half of all families had a weekly income above $707. Most families, as previously mentioned are dual-earner families. There are considerable differences though by race and ethnicity and by type of family. Illustrations are provided in the text.

In 1995 the poverty level, as determined by the federal government, was $15,150 for a family of four and $7,470 for an individual.

Who Are the Poor?

Poverty rates vary significantly by race, ethnicity, and family structure. Married couples have the lowest poverty rate. Families headed by women accounted for the largest portion of increase in poor families since 1970. Children under 18 years of age account for 40 percent of the poor.

Although in absolute numbers most of the poor are white, white families have a lower poverty rate overall (about 10 percent) than black families (about 31 percent). The rate for Latino families is about 27 percent.

The majority of people living in poverty live in households where individuals work full-time but make vary low wages. This category of poor families (56 percent of the poor) are known as the working poor.

Unemployment and Underemployment

The economy today is undergoing a number of structural transformations (e.g., new technology, global competition, plant closings that affect the size and composition of the workforce. In 1994, the U.S. unemployment rate was 6.1 percent. Many people are not counted as being unemployed because they have given up looking for work. *Figure 10.5* (p. 268) shows unemployment rates for several other industrialized societies.

Unemployment and Marital Functioning: Joblessness can lead to a disruption in previously agreed-upon family roles, resulting in dissatisfaction for one or both partners.

Variations in Family Responses to Unemployment: Patricia Voydanoff uses family stress theory to explain the conditions under which unemployment contributes to family crisis or disrupts family functioning. The model she uses is Reuban Hill's A,B,C,X model of family crisis. A is the event of unemployment, B is the family's crisis-meeting resources, C is the definition the family gives the event, and X is the crisis--the degree to which family functioning is affected.

Age, Race, Ethnicity, and Unemployment: Unemployment is unevenly distributed throughout our society. *Table 10.4* (p. 269) shows data on unemployment rates by sex, age, race, and ethnicity for 1994. The rate for teenagers is about three times higher than for the society as a whole. Black unemployment is over two times higher than for whites. Latinos have an unemployment rate that is about 40 percent higher than whites.

Additionally, significant numbers of people experience **underemployment**. Examples of this situation include a condition called *involuntary part-time employment*, people who work full-time and make very low wages, and workers with skills higher than those required by their current job. The authors suggest that this discussion of unemployment and underemployment illustrates C.W. Mills distinction between personal troubles and social issues.

Homelessness

Unemployment can trigger many problems, one of which is homelessness. Yet, 20 percent of those who are homeless are employed. Homelessness is not a new phenomenon in our society. Historical responses to homelessess are briefly identified, including *blinding-out, warning out,* and *greyhound relief.*

The Homeless Today: The homeless population today is diverse and encompasses every age, race, religion, and marital status. Peter Rossi distinguishes between two kinds of homelessness, those who are *literally homeless* and those who are *precariously homeless*.

Defining homelessness is also difficult, as is estimating how many homeless people there are in the U.S. Homelessness can often be a temporary condition. Many homeless people move often and also stay out of public view.

Who Are the Homeless: Officials estimate that 46 percent of the homeless are single men, 36 percent are families with children, 14 percent are single women, and about 3 percent are unaccompanied minors. Children account for about 25 percent of the homeless.

Causes and Remedies: There are several causes identified for why homelessness is such a problem in our society, including--a rapid decline in supply of low-income housing, an increase in the number of families living in poverty, mental illness and deinstitutionalization, family violence, adolescent runaways, unemployment and low earnings, substance abuse, budget cuts in public welfare programs, increases in the cost of living, and racism and sexism.

There are no quick and easy solutions for homelessness. However, reducing poverty, increasing the supply of affordable housing, and expanding employment opportunities would significantly reduce the number of homeless people in our society.

The Welfare Debate

Recent concern over the federal budget deficit has made the welfare system a popular target for budget cuts. While welfare is received across income levels, we typically think of it in terms of the poor. Topics discussed in this section of the text include--AFDC, workfare, and the Family Support Act of 1988.

New legislation calls for placing limits on the time recipients can collect benefits so they will be forced to go out and find jobs. Survey research suggests that most Americans seem to favor this move. Researchers Katherine Newman and Chauncy Lennon focused on the question of whether *workfare* really will succeed. They tracked work histories of individuals and found that 73 percent had not found work of any kind in a year, despite considerable effort. These researchers found that the oversupply of job seekers caused a creeping credentialism in low-wage service industries.

RESTRUCTURING THE WORKPLACE

A gap still exists between the current structures of families and the way other institutions continue to relate them. For example, traditional business hours of 9 to 5 are difficult for many people have to work during these hours. Accommodations to dual-earner families are slowly being made.

Workplace Changes

A major problem confronted by working parents concerns *latchkey children*. Government studies estimate about 8 million children return after school to an empty home. Three approaches being taken to deal with conflicts between work and family schedules include job sharing, permanent part-time jobs, and flextime. *Flextime* arrangements which allow employees to choose when they arrive at and leave work--within specified time limits--can relieve some of this strain.

Family Leave

It is being suggested that much of the role conflict experienced by workers could be reduced by adequate family leave, which would include maternity and paternity leaves for

185

the birth or adoption of a child as well as leaves to care for an elderly parent. *Table 10.5* (p. 273) shows information on parental-leave policies for selected Western industrialized countries. Until 1993, the U.S. was one of the few industrialized countries that did not have a national family-leave policy. The *Family and Medical Leave Act* is discussed. It provides for up to three months of unpaid leave for births, adoptions, and family emergencies. Such a policy falls far short of what is offered in most other industrialized societies. Another issue discussed is the *Pregnancy Discrimination Act*, which requires the pregnant employees be treated the same as employees with any temporary disability. *Table 10.6* (p. 274) shows the top ten companies for working mothers in 1995. While more companies are paying attention to the needs of families, many workers are employed by companies that do not.

The **Writing Your Own Script** box (p. 274) asks you to consider a number of questions concerning decisions about work and family relationships.

PART IV. KEY TERMS

labor force participation rate

commuter marriage

role overload

role conflict

occupational distribution

comparable worth

sexual harassment

femininization of poverty

working poor

underemployment

unemployment

Aid to Families with Dependent Children

job sharing

flextime

186

Pregnancy Discrimination Act of 1978   latchkey children

Family and Medical Leave Act of 1993   working poor

poverty level   homelessness

workfare   comaparable worth

PART V. KEY RESEARCHERS

Peter Rossi   Felice Schwartz

Patricia Voydanoff   Katernine Newman and Chauncy Lennon

Ruben Hill   C. Wright Mills

Beth Shelton   Karen Pyke

PART VI. STUDY QUESTIONS

True-False

1. T   F   The *labor-force participation rate* refers to the percentage of workers in a particular group who are employed or who are actively seeking employment.

2. T   F   The rate of participation in the labor force is significantly higher for African American women than for white women.

3. T   F   For men, the difference in participation rates are more pronounced across race and ethnicity than is true for women.

4. T   F   In 1994 African American and white women had approximately the same rates of labor-force participation.

5. T   F   One of the most consistent findings relating to the impact of work on family life deals with the relationship between *income* and *power* in decision making.

6. T   F   Among men who are employed full-time, whites, as compared to African Americans and Latinos, spent the most time in such tasks as cooking, cleaning, and caring for children.

7. T   F   *Felice Schwartz* suggested that employers divide women into two groups based on whether they are *career-primary* or *family-and-career* women, calling this notion the *mommy-track*.

8. T   F   The *median full-time, year-round earnings* for minority women are higher than for white women.

9. T   F   Race, socioeconomic status, sexual orientation, age, and marital status do not seem to affect the experience of sexual harassment.

10. T   F   A majority of Americans seem to believe that there should be limits placed on the time recipients of public welfare should receive benefits, and that most welfare recipients are taking advantage of the system.

11. T   F   Single women and their children represent over two-thirds of *homeless* people.

12. T   F   Until 1993, the U.S. was one of the few industrialized countries that did not have a national family-leave policy.

Multiple-Choice

1. Today, approximately _____ percent of *men* aged 16 years of age and older are in the *labor force*.

    (a) 55   (d) 65
    (b) 85   (e) 94
    (c) 75

2. The highly idealized family structure consisting of a working husband, a wife who is a full-time homemaker, and at least one child under the age of 18, currently represents _____ percent of all *households* in the U.S.

   (a) 14
   (b) 33
   (c) 20
   (d) 7
   (e) less than 1

3. Today's *dual-earner couples* constitute approximately _____ percent of all married couples and cut across all class and ethnic lines.

   (a) 70
   (b) 50
   (c) 20
   (d) 90
   (e) 35

4. When both spouses work there is a tendency for:

   (a) men to have more power in family decision making
   (b) women to have more power in decision making
   (c) more equality between the spouses in family decision making
   (d) there is no difference if both spouses work or not

5. Which of the following, according to census survey data, is the single most important *cause of resentment among married women*?

   (a) money
   (b) pets
   (c) disciplining children
   (d) problems with relatives
   (e) how much her mate helps around the house

6. Today, approximately _____ percent of employed women with a child under the age of five uses *organized day care*.

   (a) 60
   (b) 15
   (c) 21
   (d) 5
   (e) 30

7. Which of the following is/are identified as *strategies* for conflict resolution in families?

   (a) establishing priorities within the home and workplace
   (b) exiting one of the roles
   (c) making the role conflict public and demanding changes either within the family or within the larger society
   (d) all of the above
   (e) none of the above

8. What percentage of the workforce is represented by *women*?

   (a) 20
   (b) 46
   (c) 53
   (d) 35
   (e) 27

9. On average in the U.S. women earn _____ *percent* of what men earn:

   (a) 46
   (b) 74
   (c) 96
   (d) 102
   (e) 87

10. The *median weekly earnings* for all families in the U.S. in 1993 was $707.00. For families with two or more earners it was:

    (a) $1290.00
    (b) $1456.00
    (c) $712.00
    (d) $810.00
    (e) $973.00

11. In 1995, the *poverty level*, as determined by the federal government, was $_____ for a family of four.

    (a) 10,200
    (b) 7,800
    (c) 15,150
    (d) 23,050
    (e) 19,400

12. Which of the following is/are examples of *underemployment*?

    (a) involuntary part-time employment
    (b) full-time workers who make very little money
    (c) worker with skills higher than required by their current job
    (d) all of the above
    (e) none of the above

190

Fill-In

1. Negative _____ involves bringing home the problems and stresses experienced at work.

2. Approximately 75.9 percent of white men are in the *labor force*. This figure compares to _____ percent of Latino men and _____ percent of Black men.

3. Many business, professional, and political wives are often viewed as typical of the _____ career.

4. Some authors are now calling the job of housewife or househusband _____ workers.

5. According to a national opinion poll, next to money, how much my mate _____ is the single biggest cause of resentment among married women or women who are living as if they are married.

6. Regardless of the type of *child-care arrangement* in use, the majority of families who need child care confront two major problems: _____ and _____.

7. *Felice Schwartz* proposed that employers divide women into two groups based on whether they are *career-primary* or *career-and-family* women. This latter category Schwartz called the _____.

8. Three *strategies for conflict resolution* are proposed in the text, including establishing _____, role _____ and public _____.

9. Three issues of special significance in the workplace that point to *inequalities between the sexes* concern occupational _____. the gender gap in _____, and _____.

10. In 1993, the *median full-time, year-round earnings* for white men was $31,832. For black men it was $_____ and for black women it was $_____.

11. _____ refers to unwanted leers, comments, suggestions, or physical contact of a sexual nature that the recipient finds offensive and causes discomfort or interferes with academic or job performance.

12. Children under the age of 18 account for _____ *percent* of the *poor*.

13. Children account for _____ *percent* of the *homeless* population.

14. Peter Rossi distinguishes between two kinds of *homelessness*. The _____ homeless are those who already live on the streets. The _____ homeless are those who are in danger of losing their home.

15. Three approaches to changing the workplace to make it easier for *working parents* to balance family and employment. These include: companies providing permanent _____ *employment* with benefits, *job* _____, and _____ *arrangements*.

Short-Answer

1. What have been the major *transformations* in the workforce during this century?
2. What are the *reasons* why more women are working outside the home?
3. Differentiate between *commuter marriages* and the *two-person career*.
4. What are the relative advantages and disadvantages of the status of *housewife*?
5. What is the impact of work on *marital power* and *decision making*?
6. What is the relationship between dual-earner marriages and *marital happiness*?
7. Briefly review the *family ABCX model* developed by Ruben Hill. Use unemployment or a serious health problem in the family to illustrate the components of this model.
8. Review the research data concerning the *division of household labor* for dual earner families. What are the issues being raised?
9. What are the patterns in *child care* arrangements for dual-earner families? what are some of the problems confronted by such families?
10. Identify three categories or types of *underemployment*.
11. What are the three issues related to *inequalities* in the workplace which are of special significance for women? Provide evidence for each of these.
12. What are the demographics of *homelessness* in the U.S. today? What factors in our society affect rates of homelessness?
13. What is the current *poverty level* in the U.S. for a family of four? Develop a budget for a family of four using this household income level. How adequate is this amount?
14. What are three recommendations being made in the text for *restructuring the workplace*?
15. What are the three *strategies for conflict resolution* as discussed in the text? Briefly describe each of these?

PART VII. ANSWERS TO STUDY QUESTIONS

True-False

1.	T	(p. 253)	7.	T	(p. 262)
2.	F	(p. 254)	8.	F	(p. 265)
3.	T	(p. 254)	9.	F	(p. 266)
4.	T	(p. 254)	10.	T	(p. 267)
5.	T	(p. 258)	11.	F	(p. 270)
6.	F	(p. 260)	12.	T	(p. 273)

Multiple-Choice

1.	c	(p. 253)	7.	d	(pp. 263-64)
2.	d	(p. 255)	8.	b	(p. 264)
3.	a	(p. 257)	9.	b	(p. 265)
4.	c	(p. 258)	10.	e	(p. 266)
5.	a	(p. 260)	11.	c	(p. 267)
6.	e	(p. 261)	12.	d	(p. 269)

Fill-In

1. spillover (p. 253)
2. 79.2, 69.1 (p. 254)
3. two-person (p. 255)
4. home production (p. 255)
5. helps around the house (p. 260)
6. high cost, limited availability (p. 261)
7. mommy-track (pp. 262-63)
8. priorities, exit, awareness (pp. 263-64)
9. distribution, earnings, sexual harassment (p. 264)
10. 23,566, 20,315 (p. 265)
11. sexual harassment (p. 266)
12. 40 (p. 267)
13. 25 (p. 270)
14. literally, precariously (p. 270)
15. part-time, sharing, flex-time (p. 272)

PART VIII. COMMENT AND ANALYSIS

Family Profile

"The Schlichting Family"

   Key Points:

   Questions You Have?

<u>Global Perspective</u>

"Child Care"

    Key Points:

    Questions you have?

<u>Critical Issues</u>

"Role Conflict"

    Key Points:

    Questions you have?

<u>Writing Your Own Script</u>

"Work/Family decisions"

Challenges Confronting Today's Families

PART I: CHAPTER OUTLINE

PART II. LEARNING OBJECTIVES

1. To become aware of the challenges being posed by the world economy today.
2. To become aware of inequalities in wealth and income, both within our society and around the world.

3. To describe the relative health of the U.S. compared to other countries around the world.
4. To address the issues of inequalities in health care with our society and the increasing costs of health care.
5. To identify and describe the different types of drugs used in our society, and to consider their impact on people.
6. To differentiate between drug use and drug abuse.
7. To consider issues in our child welfare system, particularly concerning adoption.
8. To become aware of the challenge of racism and ethnic discrimination in our society and around the world.
9. To describe the problem of street gangs in our society.
10. To define and illustrate terrorism and war.
11. To focus on issues relating to families coping with loss.

PART III, CHAPTER REVIEW--KEY POINTS

Globalization began centuries ago. Today however, the depth and breadth of this process is so much greater than in previous periods in history. In this chapter the challenges of globalization are identified and discussed. The opening vignette discusses two examples, one in the U.S. and one in Columbia, of poor people trying to make a living for their families. The focus is on *global interdependence*, or *a state in which the lives of people around the world are intertwined closely and in which any one nation's problems--unemployment, substance abuse, environmental pollution, etc.--increasingly cut across cultural and geographic boundaries.*

CHALLENGES OF A WORLD ECONOMY

The ongoing desire to be more competitive and profitable had led companies originally started in one country to open branches or production facilities in other countries. These *multinational corporations* are not under the control of any one nation. A "new international division of labor" has been created. Some of the indicators of these changes are:

(1) Today, the wealthiest fifth of the world's population controls 85 percent of total economic activity. The poorest fifth controls about 1 percent of total economic activity.
(2) U.S. corporations have discovered that they can pay some foreign workers owner wages and avoid occupational safety requirements and environmental regulations.
(3) In Third World nations, married women who work are still responsible for domestic labor.
(4) Worldwide there has been an increase in unemployment and underemployment. Thirty percent of the world's labor force of about 2.5 billion people is either unemployed or underemployed.
(5) Governments have begun to cut back on social welfare programs.

INEQUALITIES IN INCOME AND WEALTH

Several recent studies have documented a widening income gap in both the United States and the world at large. *Table 11.1* (p. 279) shows the share of aggregate income received by each fifth of U.S. families between 1980 and 1993. Wealth is even more unevenly distributed in the U.S. than is income. The top .5 percent of households owned 40 percent of the nation's wealth in 1995.

Figure 11.1 (p. 279) provide insight into the income disparities that exist around the globe. The average per capita gross national product of industrial countries in 1990 was $14,580, compared with only $240 in the least developed countries. It is estimated that nearly a quarter of the world's population lives in abject poverty. Women represent 70 percent of the world's poor.

HEALTH AND HEALTH CARE

Health is defined by the World Health Organization as *a state of complete physical, mental, and social well-being.* **Table 11.2** (p. 280) examines two commonly used indicators of well-being--life expectancy and infant mortality.

Death and Disease: Another indication of well-being is access to primary health resources, such as safe drinking water, sanitation facilities, and basic health services. *Table 11.2* (p. 280) reveals the wide gulf between crude death rates in the developing and developed countries. Health services, safe water, and sanitation are three indexes used to differentiate between developed and developing countries.

Disabilities: The emergence of the disability rights movement in the U.S. in the 1970s has drawn public attention to the needs and concerns of this long-neglected segment of the American population. This movement has been successful in making public facilities more accessible.

A **disability** is defined as *a physical or health condition that stigmatizes or causes discrimination.* Attitudes toward the disabled have historically been negative or paternalistic. Contemporary attitudes still tend to involve pity and avoidance. Disabled people tend to adapt to their disabilities in a manner similar to that suggested by Elizabeth Kubler-Ross in adjusting to death and dying: denial and isolation, anger, bargaining, depression, and acceptance. The rate of poverty among the disabled is much higher than it is among the able-bodied.

Health Insurance: Although U.S. per capita health expenditures are high compared to other industrialized societies, it is last in terms of the percentage of its population covered by public health insurance. Over 15 percent of our population, nearly 40 million people, do not have health insurance. The issue of national health insurance is briefly discussed in this section of the chapter.

Drug Use

A **drug** is *any substance that alters the central nervous system and states of consciousness.* The most commonly used and abused drugs include *narcotics, depressants,* *stimulants, hallucinogens,* and *cannabis.*

As *Table 11.3* (p. 283) shows, drug abuse is common in the U.S. Alcohol is the most commonly used legal drug, with cigarettes not far behind. ***Drug use*** is defined as *the taking of a drug for its intended purpose and in an appropriate amount, frequency, strength, and manner.* ***Drug abuse*** is defined as *the deliberate use of a substance for other than its intended purpose, in a manner that can damage health or ability to function.*

Drug Abuse: Economic and Social Consequences: The illegal production, distribution, and use of drugs is a worldwide problem. The consequences of the illegal traffic in drugs are many and varied.

Alcohol

Although the media pay far more attention to illegal drugs such as cocaine and heroin, alcohol abuse affects a much larger percentage of the population. Concern about alcohol has a long history. The earliest known legal code, the Hammurabi Code (circa 1758 B.C. in Babylon), contained laws regulating the operation and management of drinking establishments.

Alcoholism: ***Alcoholism*** is *a chronic behavioral disorder manifested by repeated drinking of alcoholic beverages in excess of dietary and social uses of the community and to an extent that interferes with the drinker's health or social and economic functioning.* It is estimated that the annual costs for alcohol abuse in the U.S. are over $98 billion. These costs are not only economic, but also social. Alcohol is often implicated in antisocial behavior; it can lower inhibitions against violence.

Addiction and the Family

Many people who are or who become addicted to chemicals are married. Also, the problem of parental chemical use and abuse is a significant one. It has been estimated that more than 10 percent of the U.S. population was raised in an alcoholic home.

Alcoholism: A Family Problem: Initially, research on and treatment of alcoholism focused on the drinking alcoholic, particularly men. In the 1950s and 1960s the focus shifted to the "family disease" concept.

When one member becomes chemically addicted, the remaining family members become enmeshed in the addiction process as they attempt to cope with the impact this behavior has on their lives. Children as well as spouses learn how to adapt to meet the demands of the addicted parent. Family roles and responsibilities are restructured as other family members take over the addicted parent's responsibilities.

Just as the onset of alcoholism leads to changes in the stability of the family system, recovery may also disrupt family functioning. Recovery can be a time of great stress.

Children of Alcoholics: It is estimated that approximately seven million children under the age of 18 have an alcoholic parent. For the most part these children grow up in homes where there is considerable family stress and conflict that negatively impact the parent-child relationship. However, despite the difficulties of living in an alcoholic family, many children manage to cope and develop into happy, well-adjusted adults.

THE CHILD WELFARE SYSTEM: FOSTER CARE AND ADOPTION

According to the Children's Defense Fund, five hundred thousand children are currently without permanent homes. By the year 2000 it is estimated that this number may increase to nine hundred thousand. The idea behind foster care is that substitute families will provide short-term care until the children can be adopted or returned to their biological homes.

Problems Within the Child Welfare System

The problems within the child welfare system are many and varied and their solution will require a national commitment to children not currently demonstrated. Some of these problems include:

    (1)   welfare workers continue to turn over at a high rate

    (2)   the pool of foster families is shrinking

    (3)   services to prepare older youths in foster care for independent living are lacking

    (4)   permanent adoptive homes for older, handicapped, and healthy minority children are in short supply

    (5)   the needs of children in care are becoming increasingly complex and specialized, and few resources are available to meet their needs

Only about one-half of all foster children return home and many of the rest are suspended in a legal limbo by parents who make little effort to regain their children, but refuse to relinquish them fully. Estimates are that only about 13 percent of the children currently in foster care ar eligible to be adopted.

Characteristics of Adoptive Parents

Couples who adopt are most commonly white and affluent, with at least come college education. Due to the shortage of healthy infants, prospective parents using an adoption agency face a waiting period of 5 or more years. Privately arranged adoptions with baby brokers, particularly if babies from economically impoverished countries are involved, often includes stolen infants and children. Private adoptions may be closed or open.

Marital Status: According to the National Adoption Center, approximately 25 percent of the adoptions of children with special needs are by single women and men; it is estimated that about 5 percent of all other adoptions are by single people.

Sexual Orientation: Although single heterosexuals have been accepted as adoptive parents for the past two decades, it is only recently that lesbians and gays have been allowed that same right.

International Adoptions

The majority of international adoptions involve infants of color from economically disadvantaged countries. International adoptions can be risky because some children are obtained illegally. Further, there are many bureaucratic obstacles to overcome.

Transracial (Interracial) Adoptions

Forty percent of the children eligible for adoption are African American, but many of them will remain in foster care indefinitely because prospective African American parents cannot meet agency income and housing requirements and because of the curtailment of interracial adoptions.

Over recent years, people of color have become more critical of interracial adoptions, raising concerns about the possible adjustment problems of these children to their original communities. Research show that adopted children raised in interracial homes generally adjust well. Research findings on identity issues are mixed. Current legislation, including the Multiracial Placement Act of 1994, and the recently introduced in Congress (not yet law) Adoption Promotion and Stability Act, are discussed. Until more progress is made in race relations, transracial adoptions are likely to be controversial and one-sided.

THE CHALLENGE OF RACISM AND ETHNIC DISCRIMINATION IN FAMILY LIFE

In the past two decades there has been a resurgence of racist hate groups in the United States. Racism, prejudice, discrimination, violence, and inequality among racial and ethnic groups are deeply interwoven into the fabric of American society. Such patterns can be found all around the world. The connection between racial and ethnic prejudice, discrimination, and violence and immigration into the United States is discussed in this section of the text.

Racism in the United States

Racism continues to be one of the major challenges to the well-being of many families, particularly families of color. *Racism* is *an ideology of domination and a set of social, economic, and political practices by which one or more groups define themselves as superior and other groups as inferior and then systematically deny the latter groups full access and participation in mainstream society.* Examples of racism in the United States of recent years are presented in this section of the chapter. *Individual racism* refers to *personal attitudes and behaviors directed toward certain racial or ethnic groups by individual people. **Institutional racism** occurs when a total community acts against another community.* Institutional racism is less overt and more subtle than individual racism. It exists in the operation of established and respected forces in the society.

The racial attitudes of many whites are consistent with what some researchers have labeled *symbolic racism, the denial of the presence of racial inequality in society and the opposition to any social policy aimed at undoing the effects of racism and discrimination.*

Some social scientists have argued that race has declined as a significant factor in the discriminatory treatment and unequal socioeconomic status of some racial groups, especially African Americans. Researcher Lois Benjamin disagrees with this argument. The view is that racism affects African Americans across socioeconomic levels.

Racism in Global Context

Racism, prejudice, and discrimination are common throughout the world. Racial and ethnic pride and solidarity among some groups are on the rise, and racial and ethnic conflict around the world is increasing. The glut of global racial and ethnic hatred and violence is blatantly exemplified in Bosnia-Herzegovina. Also, in Africa and Asia, the collapse of totalitarian states has been accompanied by a resurgence of sometimes long-standing racial and ethnic hatred and conflict. The impact of this hatred and violence on individuals and families is immeasurable.

SAFETY AND SECURITY: GANGS AND STREET VIOLENCE

Major cities across the country have long been the home of gangs, some of whom have been around consistently for 50 or more years. Gangs are usually composed of people of the same race or ethnicity.

Gangs: Gangs and gang violence have become a serious problem, particularly in large cities in the United States. However, gangs are not limited to cities. Some experts estimate that gangs account for as much as 40 percent of crime and violence in this country.

The economic, physical, and psychological costs of gangs and their activities to individuals and their families are extremely high. Gangs create an atmosphere of fear for individuals and families in many communities. Female gangs also exist, and can be very violent. Also, there is an increase in the global connection to gangs and gang activities in the United States.

Street Violence: The U.S. has an extremely high murder rate relative to other industrialized nations (twice as high as Northern Ireland, and eleven times higher than Japan).

Families living in big cities are especially affected by crime and random violence. Families with sons are especially at risk, particularly if they are African American, poor, and live in an inner city, and if sons are between the ages of 15 to 34. Half of all murder victims in the U.S. are black. Handgun violence is particularly extreme in the U.S.

America is characterized by a subculture of violence that is learned and embraced by many people in the society. This subculture is perpetuated and expressed throughout the mass media. Research that was once mixed now seems to suggest very strongly that there is a positive relationship between media violence and aggressive behavior, crime, and violence in the larger society.

While estimates of the economic damage done by violence in our society can be given, the physical pain and mental anguish suffered by families are incalculable.

TERRORISM AND WAR

Terrorism can be defined as *the employment or threat of violence, fear, or intimidation by individuals or groups as a political or revolutionary strategy to achieve political goals*. The goal seems increasingly to just intimidate.

Terrorism in the United States

In the past, American citizens were most vulnerable to terrorism and violence when traveling in foreign lands. In recent years, American citizens have become increasingly vulnerable to terrorism at home.

War

The intensity and frequency of wars have increased in the twentieth century. A major characteristic of contemporary war is that civilians are the primary victims. For example, one estimate holds that 40,000 Iraqi soldiers were killed in the 1991 Gulf War. However, 83,000 Iraqis, primarily women and children, were killed as a result of the war, 16 percent directly due to bombing and 84 percent resulting from the collapse of the health system.

Perhaps the most heinous war-related behavior, to date, is the mass rape of women and girls. For example, the Serbs have not only brutalized and murdered thousands of Muslim men but they have conducted mass rapes of Muslim women and girls. Entire villages became "rape camps," where women were raped and sodomized by as many as 20 men per night, every night. Many victims died. Historically, the sexual assault of women has been an integral part of war and conquest. *Table 11.4* (p. 295) presents a brief snapshot of some of the documented cases of war and mass rape in recent human history. Also, children around the world are bearing a disproportionate high cost of war.

FAMILIES COPING WITH LOSS: DYING AND DEATH

Death is a universal experience for families everywhere. All families must cope with the loss of a loved one and each culture must construct its own rules for mourning that loss.

The Process of Dying

Elizabeth Kubler-Ross has identified five stages through which she believed the dying patient moves: *denial, anger, bargaining, depression,* and *acceptance*. Critics reject the notion of a progression through stages. They see the dying person as experiencing a variety of feelings and emotions and engaging in psychological defenses and maneuvers.

The Needs and Tasks of the Dying

In the nineteenth century the overwhelming majority of Americans died at home, in the presence of family and friends. **Bereavement** refers to *the state of being deprived of a loved one*. While **grief** is *the emotional response to this loss*. Bereavement typically involves a period of confusion, difficulty in concentrating, and intense feelings of loss, depression, and loneliness. Helen Lopata pointed out the necessity of "grief work," confronting and acknowledging the emotions brought about by death. She suggests successful grief resolution involves four tasks: *accepting the reality of the loss, experiencing the pain of grief, adjusting to an environment in which the deceased is missing,* and *withdrawing emotional energy and reinvesting it in another relationship.*

How a person dies, the age of the person, and the relationship to the survivors all affect the nature of the grieving experience.

Death of a Child: The loss of a child is particularly devastating. Parents tell researchers that they never get over the death of one of their children. The two main causes of death of children are accidents and malignant disease.

Death of a Sibling: The well sibling of terminally ill children face many problems. When a child is dying the parents may be preoccupied with his or her care, and the well sibling may feel excluded or deprived of parental attention. When death occurs, the well child may feel guilt for the death, especially if there was any sibling rivalry in the past.

Death of a Parent: Reactions to the death of a parent vary depending on the age of the child. Illustrations are provided by the authors.

Death of a Spouse or Parent: The death of a spouse has been identified as the most stressful event that can occur in a person's life. The intensity of the grief reaction depends on a number of factors.

Suicide: Suicide is the ninth leading cause of death in the United States. The U.S. has a moderate rate of suicide among industrialized societies. Suicide has been documented throughout history. All grief work is difficult, but suicide is particularly stressful for survivors.

AIDS: Although there has been considerable medical progress in treating this disease, the death rate from AIDS remains high. Grief work is difficult in cases involving deaths resulting from complications related to AIDS, particularly because it is still considered by so many to be a "dirty disease."

Disenfranchised Grief: **Disenfranchised grief** involves *circumstances in which a person experiences a sense of loss but does not have a socially recognized right, role, or capacity to grieve.* Examples are discussed by the authors.

STRENGTHENING FAMILIES: A NEED FOR A GLOBAL RESPONSE

History teaches us that problems can be solved and that concerned people can find solutions to these problems. When national and international attention is focused on concrete targets--poverty, institutional racism and discrimination, and universal coverage of basic social services--much can be accomplished. The **Writing Your Own Script** box (p. 299) asks you to reflect further on how globalization has affected you and your family.

PART IV: KEY TERMS

drug use	drug abuse
alcoholism	drug
health	global interdependence
grief	disenfranchised grief
bereavement	grief work
closed adoption	open adoption
disability	terrorism
racism	individual racism
institutional racism	globalization

PART V: KEY RESEARCHERS

Carole McKelvey   Helen Lopata

Elizabeth Kubler-Ross   Joseph Shapiro

Lois Benjamin

PART VI. STUDY QUESTIONS

True-False

1. T   F   *Multinational corporations* are virtually always under the control of only one nation.
2. T   F   Females represent 70 percent of the *world's poor*.
3. T   F   The U.S. has the lowest *infant mortality rate* and the highest *life expectancy* of all industrialized societies.
4. T   F   The rate of poverty among the *disabled* is much higher than it is among the able-bodied.
5. T   F   Early research and treatment of *alcoholism* focused on the drinking alcoholic.
6. T   F   The idea behind *foster care* is that substitute families will provide short-term care until the children can be adopted or returned to their biological parents.

7.	T	F	Estimates are that about 80 percent of children currently in *foster care* are eligible to be adopted.
8.	T	F	Lesbians and gays are not legally allowed in the U.S. to become adoptive parents.
9.	T	F	Approximately 40 percent of the children eligible for adoption in the U.S. are African American.
10.	T	F	Half of all *murder victims* in the U.S. are black.
11.	T	F	According to the authors, the intensity and frequency of *wars* have increased in the twentieth century, and a major characteristic of contemporary war is that civilians are the primary victims.
12.	T	F	The U.S. has the highest *suicide rate* in the world.

Multiple-Choice

1. Today, the *wealthiest fifth* of the world's population controls about ____ percent of *total economic activity* as measured by gross national product, domestic savings, and investment, and world trade.

    (a) 50   (d) 85
    (b) 60   (e) 96
    (c) 70

2. The difference between the pay of the typical worker and chief executive today is more than _____ to one.

    (a) 100   (c) 20
    (b)   50   (d)   7

3. The *top .5 percent* of households in the U.S, own approximately _____ percent of the nation's *wealth*.

    (a) 10   (d) 40
    (b) 20   (e) 55
    (c) 30

4. Approximately one-half of the *world's poor* live in:

    (a) Africa   (c) South America
    (b) Asia   (d) North America and Europe

5. Approximately _____ percentage of our population do not have *health insurance*.

   (a) 4
   (b) 10
   (c) 15
   (d) 35
   (e) 23

6. The problems within the *child welfare system* are many and varied, including:

   (a) welfare workers continue to turn over at a high rate
   (b) the pool of foster families is shrinking
   (c) the needs of children in care are becoming increasingly complex
   (d) all of the above
   (e) none of the above

7. Which of the following is accurate concerning *adoptions*?

   (a) approximately 25 percent of the adoptions of children with special needs are by single women and men; five percent of other adoptions are by single people
   (b) private adoptions may be open or closed
   (c) couples who adopt are most commonly white and affluent, with at least some college education
   (d) it has only been recently that lesbians and gays have been allowed to become adoptive parents
   (e) all of the above are accurate

8. Some experts estimate that *gangs* account for as much as _____ percent of crime and violence in this country.

   (a) 40
   (b) 30
   (c) 60
   (d) 90
   (e) 10

9. Every _____ *hours* in this country a child or adolescent uses a handgun to end her or his own life.

   (a) 24
   (b) 18
   (c) 12
   (d) 6
   (e) 2

10. Which of the following is the *first stage* in Elizabeth Kubler-Ross' stage model of death?

   (a) denial   (d) depression
   (b) anger   (e) acceptance
   (c) bargaining

Fill-In

1. _____ _____ refers to a state in which the lives of people around the world are intertwined closely and in which any one nation's problems--unemployment, substance abuse, environmental pollution, etc.--increasingly cut across cultural and geographic boundaries.

2. The *poorest fifth* of the world's population control about _____ percent of the world's economic activity.

3. Approximately one in _____ people in the world today lives in *abject poverty*.

4. _____ is defined as a state of complete physical, mental, and social-being.

5. Three commonly used *indicators of well-being* include _____ _____, _____ _____ and access to primary _____ _____.

6. The most commonly *used* and *abused* drugs are: _____, _____, _____, _____, and _____.

7. Among *legal drugs*, _____ is the most commonly used, with 85 percent of respondents having used it at some time in their life; _____ are not far behind (73 percent).

8. The _____ code (circa 1758 B.C. in Babylon), contained laws regulating the operation and management of drinking establishments.

9. _____ is an *ideology* of domination and a set of social, economic, and political practices by which one or more groups define themselves as superior and other groups as inferior and then systematically deny the latter groups full access and participation in mainstream society.

10. In 1992, over _____ people lost their lives as a result of handgun violence in the U.S, compared to _____ in Britain.

11. The two leading *causes of death of children* in the U.S. are _____ and _____ _____.

12. *Suicide* is the _____ leading cause of death in the United States.

13. _____ _____ refers to circumstances in which a person experiences a sense of loss but does not have a socially recognized right, role, or capacity to grieve.

Short-Answer and Definition

1. What are the major indicators that a *global economy* exists today?
2. What is the evidence that there is inequality in *wealth* and *income* in the United states?
3. How is *health* defined by the World Health Organization? what is the evidence that there is global inequality in health?
4. What are the problems within the *child welfare system* operating in the U.S?
5. Differentiate between the concepts of *drug use* and *drug abuse*.
6. According to Helen Lopata, what are the four tasks for successful *grief resolution*?
7. Why is *grief work* so difficult in cases of death involving AIDS or suicide?
8. Differentiate between the concepts *grief, disenfranchised grief*, and *grief work*.
9. According to Elizabeth Kubler-Ross, what are the *stages of dying*? What are the criticism of this model?
10. What points are being made by the authors concerning *civilian casualties* in wars?
11. What is the nature of *racism* in the United States today?
12. Describe the major demographic patterns of *street violence* in the U.S. today? what factors seem to be helping to cause increases in violence in our society today?

PART VII. ANSWERS TO STUDY QUESTIONS

True-False

1.	F	(p. 278)		7.	F	(p. 286)
2.	T	(p. 279)		8.	F	(p. 287)
3.	F	(p. 280)		9.	T	(p. 288)
4.	T	(p. 282)		10.	T	(p. 293)
5.	T	(p. 285)		11.	T	(p. 294)
6.	T	(p. 286)		12.	F	(p. 296)

Multiple-Choice

1.	d	(p. 278)		6.	d	(p. 286)
2.	a	(p. 279)		7.	e	(p. 287)
3.	d	(p. 279)		8.	a	(p. 292)
4.	b	(p. 279)		9.	d	(p. 293)
5.	c	(p. 282)		10.	a	(p. 296)

<u>Fill-In</u>

1. Global interdependence (p. 277)
2. 1 (p. 278)
3. four (p. 279)
4. Health (p. 280)
5. life expectancy, infant mortality, health resources (p. 280)
6. narcotics, depressants, stimulants, hallucinogens, cannabis (p. 282)
7. alcohol, cigarettes (p. 283)
8. Hammurabi (p. 283)
9. Racism (p. 289)
10. 13,000, 33 (p. 293)
11. accidents, malignant diseases (p. 297)
12. ninth (p. 297)
13. disenfranchised grief (p. 298)

PART VIII. ANALYSIS AND COMMENT

<u>Critical Issues</u>

"Protecting Fetal Rights: The Case of Cocaine Babies"

Key Points:

Questions you have?

Writing Your Own Script

"Thinking Globally"

Violence and Abuse

12

PART II. LEARNING OBJECTIVES

1. To discuss the concept of family violence from historical and cross-cultural perspectives.
2. To discuss the prevalence of violence in U.S. culture.
3. To identify and refute common myths about violence and abuse.
4. To discuss in detail the social problem of woman battering.
5. To describe the myths and realities of rape in U.S. society.
6. To review evidence concerning the victimization of women within our criminal justice system.
7. To identify and describe the effects of and responses to violent abuse.
8. To discuss the prevalence and causes of child abuse, child sexual assault, sibling abuse, and elder abuse in U.S. society.
9. To consider the various explanations offered by researchers as to why these various types of violence occur so often in our society.

PART III. CHAPTER REVIEW--KEY POINTS

THE ROOTS OF FAMILY VIOLENCE: A HISTORICAL CONTEXT

Instead of havens into which we can retreat for comfort, safety, and nurturing, for many of us, families have increasingly become places of danger. Family violence has existed throughout history in cultures around the world. The extent of family violence in the U.S. is difficult to determine because official records were not always kept. Wife beating is the most common form of family violence. The opening vignette discusses common examples of family violence and abuse. You are asked to consider how you define these terms.

Violence Against Women

Violence against women has been part of the institutional structure of various societies throughout history. The folkways and mores of various cultures show the universality of violence in women's lives. Examples from India (suttee), China (binding of feet), and Africa (female circumcision) are used to illustrate this point.

As in the past, women continue to be the primary victims of violence. The United Nations has described the current global situation as an epidemic of violence against women.

The national cost of abuse in medical care for women alone is almost $900 million. The **Personal Reflection** box (p. 304) presents some historical facts about women and violence.

Violence Against Children

Throughout history, children have frequently been victims of violence and abuse, including sexual assault. Violence against children is linked to cultural values and attitudes that have defined children as the property of families. *Infanticide--the killing of infants and young children*--appears to have been widely practiced throughout much of history. Historically, much violence against children has been socially acceptable.

Violence Against the Elderly

Little is known about the historical incidence of elder abuse. Some historical examples of societal violence against the elderly include the practice of targeting older women as witches, and the high murder rate among older men. Elderly parents were often the target of violence from children who wanted their parents' wealth.

Violence Against Siblings

To date few systematic studies of nonfatal sibling violence in the United States have been conducted. Historically parents have considered sibling conflict to be "normal" behavior and therefore have not generally been reported.

FAMILY VIOLENCE AND U.S. CULTURE

We live in an increasingly violent culture and world. Crime statistics alone do not capture the full range of violent crime in this country. The Uniform Crime Reports indicate violent crime is very common in the U.S. For example, a violent crime is committed every 21 seconds, a forcible rape every 6 minutes, and a robbery every minute.

Despite our fears to the contrary, it is not a stranger but a so-called loved one or an acquaintance who is most likely to assault, rape, or murder us. We are only in recent times been aware of the seriousness and magnitude, and the multifaceted nature of domestic violence. This growing awareness is due, in part, to the efforts of the women's movement, but also to a number of events that have brought family violence into our living rooms on a daily basis. For instance, the high profile cases of O. J. Simpson, the Menendez brothers, and Mike Tyson. The nature and scope of the problem of domestic violence can be seen in the facts presented in *Table 12.1* (p. 306).

The Media

Today, violence pervades U.S. popular culture. Prime-time television transmits 13 acts of violence per hour, with even higher rates of violence in cartoons that are watched primarily by children. By the time they are 18 years old, most children will see 40,000 television murders.

Similar trends appear in contemporary music, particularly Rock and Rap videos. In addition to the visuals, the language itself is often violent and sexually explicit. Moreover, pornographic films are big business, outnumbering other films three to one.

The pervasiveness of sex and violence toward women in the media acts to desensitize both women and men to the seriousness and unacceptability of violence and assault against human beings. All these popular culture depictions of the violation of women contribute to what has been called a *rape syndrome*--or *men's proclivity to rape*.

MYTHS ABOUT VIOLENCE AND ABUSE

Myths concerning violence and abuse involve issues of race, class, gender, and the mental state of the abuser. As a result, much family violence and abuse goes unrecognized and unreported.

The major myths concerning family violence and abuse identified in the text include:

(1)   family violence is rare
(2)   only mentally ill or "sick" people abuse
        family members
(3)   family violence is essentially a problem
        of the lower classes
(4)   there is an absence of love in violent families

Referring to (1) above, each year, an estimated 6 million American women are battered by their husbands or partners; 40,000 of them are killed. The FBI reports that 30 percent of female homicide victims are killed by their husbands or boyfriends, and 6 percent of male homicide victims are killed by their wives or girlfriends.

Myth (2) above, is fueled by extreme cases of family violence that do not represent the nature of the vast majority of cases in our society. The vast majority of abusive family members are not mentally ill.

Data concerning myth (3) above indicate that family violence occurs throughout society, but is perhaps reported more often among lower classes. Research indicates that one out of four middle-class women reports physical abuse. But, many factors that are related to family violence are found to a greater degree among lower-class families (unemployment, lack of education, drug abuse, concern over economic security), so rates of violence are higher in the lower-class.

Finally, myth (4) above is closely related to the idea that abusive family members are mentally ill. The fact is that in spite of the horror of family violence, in most cases family members say that they love one another.

PHYSICAL ASSAULT: THE CASE OF BATTERED WOMEN

This section of the chapter focuses on the patterns of abuse and the strategies of resistance by victims of violence. Most experts agree that woman battering is probably the most common and one of the most underreported crimes in this country.

What Is Woman Battering?

In general, the pattern of the battering experienced by woman is referred to as the *battered woman syndrome*, and is defined in terms of frequency, severity, intent to harm, and the ability to demonstrate injury.

Battering is generally cyclical in nature. Family violence researcher Lenore Walker proposed a *cycle of violence theory*. According to Walker, the cycle of abuse includes three stages: (1) tension building, (2) acute battering, and (3) loving contrition.

Limiting battering or assault to discrete physical actions excludes a wide range of violence that women experience. Battering is often accompanied by verbal abuse, psychological abuse, and threats or actual violence toward children and other loved ones.

How Prevalent Is Woman Battering?

As of 1992, only three states had mandatory reporting laws for spousal violence. Researchers must rely primarily on crime statistics, police reports, and hospital records. Another major source of woman battering is the National Crime Survey sponsored by the Department of Justice. Statistics on woman battering are discussed in this section of the chapter, primarily focusing on data from self-reports.

Conservative estimates are that 25 percent to 35 percent of all U.S. women are battered at least once in the course of their intimate relationships. Unmarried cohabiting woman are twice as likely to be victims of battering than married women.

Theories of Spousal or Partner Abuse

Researchers have noted a number of variables conducive to violence in intimate relationships, including:

(1)   a high level of family or intimate conflict
(2)   a high level of societal violence
(3)   family socialization in violence
(4)   cultural norms that legitimate family or intimate violence
(5)   gender stereotypic socialization and sexual inequality
(6)   the privacy of the American family

The **For Your Information** box (p. 312) identifies four theories of spousal or partner abuse, including social stress, power, dependency, and alcohol.

Why Do Women Remain in Abusive Relationships?

Victim blaming--essentially, justifying the unequal treatment of an individual or group by finding defects in the victims rather than by examining the social and economic factors that contribute to their condition. Victim blaming is very common in cases of spousal abuse.

Women remain in battering relationships for a variety of reasons, including: fear, economic dependence and lack of community support, religious beliefs, their children, and love.

Confronting Intimate Violence

Table 12.2 (p. 314) lists some of the factors that might indicate that a woman is in an abusive relationship. Some of these are: she is withdrawn, seldom has money, has unexplained bruises, wear a lot of makeup, and seldom makes eye contact.

THE SEXUAL ASSAULT OF WOMEN

In the United States alone, it is estimated that between 1.2 and 1.5 million women are forcibly raped each year by their current or former male partners, some more than once. *Sexual assault* is a broad term that incorporates many behaviors, either physical or verbal, intended to coerce an individual into sexual activity against her or his will.

Rape is legally defined as *sexual assault in which a man uses his penis to vaginally penetrate a woman against her will by force or threat of force or when she is mentally or physically unable to give her consent.* This definition does overlook the fact that men and boys sometimes are victims of rape as well.

Rape is an act of violence, not sexual arousal. The overwhelming majority of rape victims are female. Most rapes are not committed by strangers but by people known to the victim. About 33 percent of all rapes in the U.S. take place in the victim's home, and 83 percent are perpetrated by husbands or acquaintances.

Of all types of abuse and violent crime, rape is the most frequently committed violent crime in the U.S. It is the least reported of all such crime: 9 out of 10 rapes go unreported. Females of all ages have been victims of rape. Men and boys are estimated to be victims in less than 10 percent of all rape cases.

Rape Myths

Two of the most persistent rape myths are that (1) male sexual violence is caused by the attitudes of female victims, and (2) African American males are the primary perpetrators of rape.

Rape and Race: The myth that African American males commit the majority of rapes diverts the attention of white women away from the most likely sources of their sexual assault: white men. At the same time, it serves as a justification for negative attitudes toward and treatment of African American males.

218

Blaming the Victim: Many believe that women act in a way to invite rape. The fact is women fear rape more than any other crime. *Table 12.3* (p. 316) provides a list of common rape myths.

Marital Rape

David Finkelhor and Kersti Yllo have classified marital rape in terms of the following categories: *force-only rape, battering rape,* and *obsessive rape.*

Researchers have identified several factors associated with marital rape. The four most important are:

(1)   the historical foundations of marriage
        in this country
(2)   the establishment of marital exemption
        in rape laws
(3)   the socially and economically disadvantaged
        position of women, and
(4)   the violent nature of U.S. society and its
        "rape culture"

In 1977, Oregon became the first state to repeal the marital exemption clause to its rape statute. Since that time, similar clauses have been eliminated or modified in half the states.

THE CRIMINAL JUSTICE RESPONSE TO WOMAN ASSAULT

The criminal justice response to woman assault is examined in terms of two categories: (1) the attitudes and behaviors of people involved in he criminal justice system, and (2) various court procedures and legal statutes that limit women's ability to receive redress.

Attitudes and Behaviors

Although some progress has been made toward sensitizing police to the issues and concerns of battered and sexually assaulted women, many police still do not understand the battering cycle. Most police calls for battering do not result in arrest. If an arrest is made, the likelihood of the case going to court is very low. If a woman's case gets to court, she often finds that she as much as her assailant is on trial. Fifty-four percent of all rape prosecutions end in either a dismissal or an acquittal. Almost 25 percent of convicted rapists are not sentenced to jail at all but rather are released on probation, and just about 50 percent of all convicted rapists are sentenced to less than 1 year in jail.

Court Procedures and Legal Statutes

In many states spouse abuse is considered simple assault. Currently, in some states, the police have the option of making an arrest if they believe there is "probable cause." Victims of battering and other violence can seek remedy in the criminal justice system through an *order of protection*, a court order that prohibits a person from threatening, striking, or harassing a victim.

The case of rape probably best illustrates women's continuing vulnerability in the criminal justice system. In recent years the treatment of rape and battered victims has improved somewhat. The **Critical Issues** box (p. 319) takes a look at a hypothetical robbery case in which a male victim is cross-examined during a trial in a manner similar to how rape victims are treated on the stand. On the national level, the country's first federal legislation dealing with domestic violence was introduced to Congress in 1991.

THE EFFECTS OF PHYSICAL AND SEXUAL ASSAULT ON WOMEN

Research indicates that violent abuse exacts a tremendous toll on women: physically, psychologically, emotionally, and financially. Illustrations are provided in this section of the chapter.

Coping and Survival Strategies

Although the ways individual women cope vary from situation to situation, their coping and survival strategies can be classified in the following ways: psychological and emotional, self-destructive, and fighting back.

Psychological and Emotional Strategies: Avoidance or prevention of violence is one strategy employed by women. Some women resort to dreams or fantasies in a relationship to help make it work. Some women block out or repress their experiences.

Self-Destructive Strategies: Various addictions such as alcohol and drug abuse, overeating, and suicide are all forms of coping, although most people consider them unhealthy, unwise, and ineffective.

Fighting Back: Self-defense is the strategy involved here. A small percentage of women who fight back actually kill their abuser. Most of these women are convicted and sent to jail.

Shelters for Battered Women

Although shelters vary in philosophy and approach, all share the conviction that no one deserves to be beaten and that battered women need special resources and support to end the violence in their lives. The ultimate goal of these shelters is to give women the power to make their own choices. Shelters appear to be successful in helping women break the chain of violence and abuse. There are three times more animal shelters in this country than women's shelters.

A COMPARATIVE LOOK AT BATTERED MEN

Suzanne Steinmetz was the first to call attention to the issue of male victims of spousal abuse. Some research suggests males are the victims or co-victims of spousal abuse in fifty percent of the cases. Critics of this idea caution that such data can be misinterpreted. Women usually suffer worse injuries than they inflict.

Many men each year turn to women's rape crisis centers as victims of sexual assault with no other place to go for help. According to national statistics, men (excluding prison inmates) accounted for 7 percent of all attempted rapes in 1993.

CHILD ASSAULT AND ABUSE

Child abuse has existed throughout history. In the U.S. it has only recently gained public interest and attention. During the 1960s, Dr. Henry Kempe published a national survey that described for the first time the series of behaviors known as the *battered-child syndrome*-- defined as *a clinical condition in children who have received severe physical abuse, primarily from a parent or foster parent.*

Research data indicate that cases of child abuse reported to social service agencies have risen at a rate of 10 percent each year since 1983. Estimates on the incidence of child abuse range from one to four million cases each year in the United States.

The Physical Assault of Children

Prevalence: Statistics we have on child assault and abuse are alarming. Most parents admitted using some kind of violence on their children during the preceding year. *Figure 12.2* (p. 324) gives information on the percentage of parents who said they had engaged in different disciplining strategies with their child(ren) during the past year. Parental violence is among the five leading causes of death for children between 1 and 18 years of age.

It is estimated that as many as one-third of all abuse and neglect cases go unreported or undetected, especially if they involve middle-class or wealthy families.

Who Are the Abused?: Current research seems to indicate that certain characteristics predispose a child to being abused. Such characteristics are identified in this section of the chapter.

Some researchers estimate that almost 2.5 million teenagers commit acts of violence against their parents each year in the United States.. Approximately 2000 parents die each year at the hands of a teenaged son or daughter, often in self-defense or in retaliation against abuse.

Who Are the Abusers?: In 90 percent of child abuse cases, the abuser is a member of the immediate family. Factors related to child abuse include spouse abuse, stress at work, young parents, and children of unemployed fathers. Rates of reported child abuse among lower-income families are two to three times those of upper-income families. Reported rates for black children is twice the rate for white children.

The Sexual Assault of Children

The term *child sexual abuse* refers to the use of a child for the sexual gratification of an adult. Such abuse can be divided into two basic categories depending on who the abuser is: familial abuse or extrafamilial abuse. Familial abuse is generally referred to as *incest--the sexual abuse by a blood relative who is assumed to be a part of the child's family.*

Prevalence: Many victims and perpetrators keep sexual abuse hidden. Official reports underestimate the rates of such abuse. National data suggests that incest occurs in 14 percent of U.S. families.

The sexually Abused Child and the Abuser: According to most research, the typical victim is female. Recent research suggests that boys are almost equally as vulnerable to incest as are girls.

A variety of factors have been identified that place some children at greater risk than others, including physical or emotional handicaps, uneducated parents, the presence of a stepfather in the home, having a parent who was abused as a child him or herself.

The Effects of Child Abuse: A large percentage of sexually abused children become prostitutes or drug users. Victims frequently suffer low self-esteem, severe depression, and alcoholism. Many attempt suicide.

ELDER ABUSE IN THE UNITED STATES

What is Elder Abuse

Elder abuse is a broad term that includes *the physical, psychological, and material maltreatment and neglect of older people.*

Who Are the Abused and the Abusers?

The most vulnerable to elder abuse are women, older people with physical or mental impairments, and those dependent on a caretaker to meet their basic needs. The abuser is most often a male spouse who abuses his elderly partner (58 percent of perpetrators) followed by children (28 percent of perpetrators).

SIBLING ABUSE

Surprisingly, the most common abusers are siblings. Boys of all ages are more likely than girls to initiate sibling violence, but the difference is relatively small. Some demographics of sibling violence are briefly discussed in this section of the chapter.

The **Writing Your Own Script** box (p. 328) asks you to consider some questions having to do with violence in intimate relationships. The test included in this box provides you with one way to identify if an intimate relationship you are involved in is violent or headed toward violence.

PART IV. KEY TERMS

infanticide

incest

elder abuse

battered-child syndrome

battered-woman syndrome

woman battering

rape syndrome

sexual assault

victim blaming

marital rape

PART V. KEY RESEARCHERS

Samual Radbill

David Levinson

Mary Daley

Lenore Walker

Erin Pizzey   Suzanne Steinmetz

David Finkelhor and Keersti Yllo   Henry Kempe

PART VI. STUDY QUESTIONS

True-False

1. T F Research shows that family violence is a *uniquely American* phenomenon that has come into being only in recent generations.
2. T F Half the *murdered women* in the United States are killed by a current or former partner.
3. T F According to the authors, the pervasiveness of sex and violence toward women in the media acts to desensitize *both* men and women to the seriousness and unacceptability of violence and assault against human beings.
4. T F *Cohabiting* women are more likely to be victims of battering than married women.
5. T F According to the text, a common reason why women *remain in violent relationships* is love.
6. T F Men and boys are estimated to be victims in less than 10 percent of all *rape cases*.
7. T F Most police calls for battering result in *arrest*.
8. T F Women who kill their husbands are *less severely* punished than men who kill their wives.
9. T F Most rape prosecutions end with either a dismissal or acquittal.
10. T F Most women who fight back against their abuser and kill them are convicted and sent to jail.

Multiple-Choice

1. According to anthropologist David Levinson, which of the following is the most common form of domestic violence around the world?

   (a) child abuse   (c) wives murdering husbands
   (b) wife beating   (d) husbands murdering wives

224

2. Not until the _____ was *wife beating* banned in the U.S.

   (a) 1880s   (c) 1950s
   (b) 1970s   (d) 1920s

3. By the time most U.S. children reach the age of 18 they have witnesses more than _____ *television murders*.

   (a) 10,000   (d) 40,000
   (b) 100,000   (e) 300,000
   (c) 20,000

4. Approximately _____ percent of all reported criminal assaults are *aggravated assaults between husbands and wives*.

   (a) 5   (d) 22
   (b) 11   (e) 30
   (c) 17

5. The *second stage* in Lenore Walker's cycle of violence theory is:

   (a) loving contrition   (c) tension building
   (b) unwanted attention   (d) acute battering

6. Conservative estimates are that as many as _____ of all U.S. women are battered at least once in the course of their intimate relationships.

   (a) 5 to 10 percent   (d) 80 to 90 percent
   (b) 10 to 20 percent   (e) 25 to 35 percent
   (c) 60 to 70 percent

7. Which of the following is *not* mentioned in the text as a major reason why women remain in *battering relationships*.

   (a) religious beliefs
   (b) economic dependence
   (c) fear of being alone
   (d) love
   (e) all of the above are reasons why women remain in battering relationships

8. It is estimated that _____ percent of *rapes* go unreported.

   (a) 30
   (b) 40
   (c) 90
   (d) 60
   (e) 70

9. On the national level, the country's first federal legislation dealing with *domestic violence* was introduced to Congress in _____.

   (a) 1991
   (b) 1820
   (c) 1935
   (d) 1790
   (e) 1865

10. According to national statistics, *men* (excluding prison inmates) accounted for _____ percent of all attempted rapes in 1993.

    (a) less than 1
    (b) 7
    (c) 15
    (d) 4

11. Research data indicate that cases of *child abuse* reported to social service agencies have _____ at a rate of ____ percent each year since 1983.

    (a) risen, 10
    (b) risen, 50
    (c) declined, 20
    (d) declined, 40

12. Estimates of the *incidence of child abuse* annually in the United States range from:

    (a) 100,000 to 250,000
    (b) 500,000 to 1 million
    (c) 1 million to 4 million
    (d) 5 million to 10 million

13. In _____ percent of the cases of *child abuse* the abuser is a member of the immediate family.

    (a) 50
    (b) 90
    (c) 99
    (d) 75

14. National data show that _____ percent of families in the U.S. are characterized by *incest*.

    (a) 1
    (b) 20
    (c) 8
    (d) 30
    (e) 14

1. Not until _____ was *wife beating* legally banned in the United States.
2. The pervasiveness of sex and violence toward women in popular culture contributes to what has been called a _____ _____ .
3. _____ percent of all spousal or partner assaults are committed by *men*.
4. In general, the pattern of the battering experienced by women is referred to as the _____-_____ _____ .
5. Battering is generally cyclical in nature. According to Lenore Walker, the three stages in the cycle of violence are _____ building, _____ battering, and _____ contrition.
6. In 1977, _____ became the first state to appeal the marital exemption clause to its rape statute. Since that time, similar clauses have been eliminated or modified by about _____ the states.
7. Three types of marital rape are identified in the test, including _____ rape, _____ rape, and _____ rape.
8. Victims of battering and other violence can seek remedy in the criminal justice system through an _____ _____ , a court order that prohibits a person from threatening, striking, or harassing a victim.
9. Just about 50 percent of all *convicted rapists* are sentenced to less than _____ in jail.
10. The coping and survival strategies used by women who are victims of sexual violence can be classified in the following ways: _____ and _____ , _____ , and _____ .
11. The ultimate goal of *women shelters* is to give women _____ .
12. Most elder abuse is perpetrated by _____ _____ (58 percent), followed by _____ (28 percent).

Short-Answer

1. What are some examples of folkways and mores in cultures around the world showing the universality of violence against *women*?
2. What are the historical indicators of how socially acceptable violence against *children* has been in our society?
3. What are some of the demographic facts that indicate the family is a *violent social institution* in our society?
4. What are the three *stages* of the cycle of violence theory?
5. Why do *battered women* remain in battering relationships?
6. What factors are related to *spousal abuse*?
7. What are some of the *signs* that a woman might be in an abusive relationship?
8. What are the different *coping and survival strategies* of women in abusive relationships? Describe each of these.
9. What are the *myths* about rape?

10. What is the *rape syndrome*? What are the cultural conditions that create and maintain this pattern in society?
11. What evidence is there that the criminal justice system discriminates against women in cases of *sexual assault*?
12. What is the *prevalence of child abuse* in our society? What factors help cause child abuse to occur?
13. What is the *prevalence of child sexual assault* in our society? What factors are related to this serious social problem?
14. What is *sibling abuse*? How common is this form of family violence?

PART VII. ANSWERS TO STUDY QUESTIONS

True-False

1.	F	(p. 303)	6.	T	(p. 316)
2.	T	(p. 306)	7.	F	(p. 317)
3.	T	(p. 307)	8.	F	(p. 318)
4.	T	(p. 311)	9.	T	(p. 318)
5.	T	(p. 313)	10.	T	(p. 321)

Multiple-Choice

1.	b	(p. 303)	8.	c	(p. 315)
2.	a	(p. 304)	9.	a	(p. 318)
3.	d	(p. 306)	10.	b	(p. 322)
4.	b	(p. 307)	11.	a	(p. 322)
5.	d	(p. 310)	12.	c	(p. 322)
6.	e	(p. 311)	13.	b	(p. 325)
7.	e	(p. 313)	14.	e	(p. 325

Fill-In

1. 1883 (p. 304)
2. rape syndrome (p. 307)
3. 95 (p. 309)
4. battered-woman syndrome (p. 310)
5. tension, acute, loving (p. 310)
6. Oregon, half (p. 317)
7. force-only, battering, obsessive (p. 317)
8. order of protection (. 318)
9. 1 year (p. 318)
10. psychological, emotional, self-destructive, fighting back (p. 320)
11. power to make their own choices (p. 321)
12. male spouse, children (p. 326)

PART VIII. COMMENT AND ANALYSIS

For Your Information

"Theories of Spousal or Partner Abuse"

    Key Points:

    Questions you have?

Critical Issues

"The Rape of Mr. Smith"

    Key Points:

    Questions you have?

Personal Reflection

"Some Historical Facts About Women and Violence"

    Key Points:

    Questions you have?

<u>Writing Your Own Script</u>

"Recognizing Abusive Behavior"

The Process of Uncoupling

PART I. CHAPTER OUTLINE

I. Historical Perspectives
    A. Divorce in Early America
    B. Divorce in Nineteenth-Century America
    C. Twentieth-Century America: Efforts at Reform
    D. Race, Ethnicity, and Divorce
II. Who Gets Divorced and Why?
    A. Factors Affecting Marital Stability
III. The Process of Divorce
    A. Stages in the Divorce Process
    B. The Six Stations of Divorce
IV. The Causes of Divorce
    A. Societal Factors
    B. From the Perspective of Divorced People
    C. From the Perspective of Family Therapists
V. The Impact of Divorce on Spouses
    A. Common Consequences of Divorce
    B. Gender Differences in Divorce
    C. Recovering from Divorce
VI. The Impact of Divorce on Children
    A. Short-Term Versus Long-Term Effects
    B. Changing Patterns in Child Custody
VII. Reaching Accord: Divorce Counseling and Mediation
VIII. The Divorce Debate Revisited
IX. Other Forms of Marital Disruption
X. Summary
XI. Key Terms
XII. Questions for Study and Reflection
XIII. Further Reading

PART II. LEARNING OBJECTIVES

1. To trace the demographic patterns of divorce in the U.S. from colonial times to today.
2. To describe the factors that affect marital stability.
3. To identify the stages of divorce.
4. To describe no-fault divorce and the effects it has on women.
5. To discuss the influences on divorce of race, ethnicity, and socioeconomic status.
6. To discuss the problems which family therapists believe are the most damaging to couple relationships, and also those problems that are believed to be the most difficult to treat.
7. To describe the consequences of divorce on both women and men.
8. To describe and differentiate between the short-term and long-term effects of divorce on children.
9. To describe the changing patterns of child custody.
10. To describe other ways, besides divorce, in which marriage may be disrupted.

PART III. CHAPTER REVIEW--KEY POINTS

HISTORICAL PERSPECTIVES

During the 1990s, approximately 1.2 million married couples in the U.S. divorce. In this chapter focus is given to historical controversies surrounding divorce, with an eye to understanding current divorce laws and social policies. The opening vignette presents a view of a seemingly ideal marriage that ends in divorce. Focus is given to the relationship between work and the family and the family life cycle.

Contrary to popular belief, divorce is not a modern phenomenon. It has been part of our history since 1639, when a Puritan court in Massachusetts granted the first divorce decree in colonial America.

Divorce in Early America

Divorce was allowed in New England colonies, but the grounds for divorce varied from one colony to another. Divorces were often adversarial. Divorce was granted more infrequently in the middle section of the colonies than in the north. For the most part the southern colonies did not enact divorce legislation until after independence was achieved.

Historian Glenda Riley sees a variety of social and economic factors interacting to put strains on marriages and families. For instance, the growing mobility of the colonists, the movement west, new technologies, and the emergence of a market economy.

Divorce in Nineteenth-Century America

The general trend in the nineteenth century was to liberalize divorce, except in New York (where adultery remained the only grounds for divorce) and South Carolina (where divorce was not permitted). These differing laws led to "migratory" divorce.

In 1887, Congress authorized a study of marriage and divorce. It was found that 68,547 divorces were granted between 1872 and 1876. Women obtained two-thirds of the divorces, desertion was the most common ground for divorce. Western states granted the most divorces, and southern states granted the fewest. More divorces occurred among the working class than among middle and upper classes.

Alimony was often granted by the states, but was difficult to enforce. Custody of young children, under the "tender years" principle, often went to mothers, but sometimes heated custody battles were fought. Split custody was sometimes awarded. Then as now, divorce often meant financial hardship (often poverty) for divorced women. While public attention focused on the issues of the frequency and availability of divorce, many other problems associated with divorce were being experienced.

The **Global Perspectives** box (p. 332) takes a look at divorce among the Hopi culture, the Yoruba culture, and certain Asian cultures. Among the matrilineal Hopi, the divorce rate was high--about one out of three marriages. The divorce rate was also high among the Yoruba, where women were economically independent from their husbands. Among Asian societies women had virtually no power to initiate a divorce, and men kept all property and custody of children after a marriage ended.

Twentieth-Century America: Efforts at Reform

During the 1960s public attention shifted from concern with the high rates to effects of divorce on spouses and children. The adversarial nature of divorce was of particular concern. The voices for divorce by consent culminated in California's *no-fault divorce* bill was signed into law in 1969 by Governor Ronald Reagan. Spouses no longer had to accuse each other of wrongdoing; instead, they could apply for a divorce on grounds of "irretrievable breakdown" or "irreconcilable differences."

Figure 13.1 (p. 334) summaries the changes in the *divorce rate--the number of divorces occurring annually for every one thousand people over the age of 15*--over the last century. The divorce rate reached an all-time high of 5.2 in 1980. Since then it has declined slightly.

Race, Ethnicity, and Divorce

Table 13.1 (p. 334) reveals several patterns in divorce. First, the divorce ratio has increased for blacks, whites, and Latinos, with the highest increase occurring between 1970 and 1980. Second, women in all groups had higher divorce ratios than men due to their lower incidence of remarriage. Finally, the ratios vary by race and ethnicity.

Divorce Among African Americans: Numerous studies support the argument that higher divorce rates among African Americans reflect greater economic hardships. For example, a significant amount of black-white differences in marital stability can be explained by differences in levels of education and income among the two groups.

Divorce Among Latinos: Because Latinos also experience higher rates of poverty and unemployment as a result of discrimination, we might assume that the Latino divorce ratio would be closer to that of blacks than to that of whites. Latinos have the lowest overall divorce rate of the three groups. Two factors are often cited to explain the relatively high level of marital stability among Latinos: a cultural tradition that emphasizes the importance of the family unit, and a religion (Catholicism) that prohibits divorce.

The Need for Further Research: More research is needed if we are to understand the interactive effects of economic status, race, and ethnicity on marital stability. In particular, more data are needed on groups such as Native Americans, who have high divorce rates, and Asian Americans, who have low rates.

WHO GETS DIVORCED AND WHY?

Factors Affecting Marital Stability

Age at First Marriage: Younger brides and grooms, especially those in their teens when they marry, are more likely to divorce. Similarly, marrying at a late age (35 plus) are at greater risk for divorce. *Figure 13.2* (p. 336) shows information in support of these conclusions. Rates of divorce for remarriage are higher than those for first marriages.

Education: A complex relationship exists between divorce and levels of education for women. Women who drop out of high school have the highest divorce rate,, whereas marriages of college graduates tend to be the most stable. Divorce rates are higher for women with 5 or more years of college education.

Income: Overall, the lower the income, the more likely a couple is to divorce. The significance of income is clearly shown in the fact that young couples with sufficient financial resources have more stable marriages than similar couples with inadequate resources.

Religion: Couples who attend religious services have lower rates of divorce than couples who do not attend religious service. Couples who share the same religion are more stable than mixed-religion marriages. Researchers have found differences among various religious groups. Protestant couples have the highest rates of divorce, Catholics are next, and Jewish couples have the lowest rates.

Parental Divorce: People whose parents divorced have higher divorce rates than do children who come from intact families. However, increased risk is not dramatic.

Presence of Children: A consistent research finding is that marital disruption is most likely when marriage is child-free and least likely when there is a child younger than three. This does not mean marriages with young children are happier than those without. Increasingly, however, married couples are less likely to stay together because children are present in the home. Approximately one-half of all couples recently divorced now have children under eighteen. Each year since 1972 more than one million children a year have been involved in divorce. The **Personal Reflection** box (p. 337) provides a question for you to complete to see if you are at risk for divorce during your lifetime.

THE PROCESS OF DIVORCE

Stages in the Divorce Process

Constance Ahrons and George Levinger identify three stages in the divorce process: (1) a period of marital conflict and unhappiness, (2) the actual marital dissolution itself, and (3) a postdivorce period. James Ponzetti and Rodney Cate see divorce as a four-step process: (1) recognition by one or both spouses of serious marital problems, (2) discussion of these problems with the spouse and possibly with family, friends, and counselors, (3) initiation of legal action to dissolve the marriage, and (4) the postdissolution period.

The Six Stations of Divorce

Anthropologist Paul Bohannan has identified six divorces that couples experience in dissolving their marital relationship, including: *emotional divorce, legal divorce, economic divorce, coparental divorce, community divorce, and psychic divorce.*

Emotional divorce involves *one or both spouses questioning the viability or quality of the relationship, and at some point shares this view with the other.* This condition can be present in a marriage for a long time before legal action is taken to end the relationship. **Legal divorce** refers to the *official ending of the marriage and gives the former partners the right to remarry.* **Economic divorce** involves the *settlement of property that often involves considerable conflict.* The **coparental divorce** involves *decisions concerning child custody, visitation rights, and the financial and legal responsibilities of each parent.* The **community divorce** involves *changing social relationships, including relatives and friends.* **Psychic divorce** involves a *redefinition of self away from the mutuality of couplehood and back to a sense of singlehood.*

THE CAUSES OF DIVORCE

Societal Factors

Several factors have contributed to the long-term trend of a rise in the divorce rate. These include: change in attitudes (as reflected in more liberal divorce laws), and changes in the economy (relationships between work and the family and the increase in the labor force participation of women).

From the Perspective of Divorced People

Paul Rasmussen and Kathleen Ferraro suggest that behaviors most commonly cited by divorced people as leading to divorce are *poor communication, extramarital sex, constant fighting, emotional abuse, drug and alcohol problems,* and *financial mismanagement.*

From the Perspective of Family Therapists

The ten areas rated as most managing by marriage and family therapists include:

(1)   communication,
(2)   unrealistic expectations of marriage or spouse
(3)   power struggles
(4)   serious individual problems
(5)   role conflicts
(6)   lack of loving feelings
(7)   lack of demonstration of affection
(8)   alcoholism
(9)   extramarital affairs
(10)   sex

The ten areas rated by marriage and family therapists as the most difficult to treat successfully include: alcoholism. lack of loving feelings, serious individual problems, power struggles, addictive behavior other than alcoholism, value conflicts, physical abuse, unrealistic expectations of marriage or spouse, extramarital affairs, and incest.

Implications for Strengthening Marriage: Therapists can intervene in distressed relationships to help people improve their relationships. Communication skills can be improved, unrealistic expectations can be identified and discussed, etc.

THE IMPACT OF DIVORCE ON SPOUSES

Common Consequences of Divorce

On the positive side divorce can free people from unhappy, conflict-ridden, or unsatisfactory relationships. On the negative side, divorce can produce considerable pain, guilt, and uncertainty. *Table 13.2* (341) lists the most frequently reported experiences of divorced persons. Researchers Cheryl Buehler and Mary Langenbrunner gave divorced people a list of 140 items and asked them to choose which ones they have experienced since they were separated from their spouses. The most commonly identified experience is "I have felt worthwhile as a person" (96 percent identified this experience).

Health Problems: The process of divorce involves a number of major lifestyle alterations: loss of a major source of intimacy, the ends of a set of daily routines, and a changed social status. Depression and despair are problems experienced by some divorced people.

Loneliness: Loneliness is especially true for childless couples and older couples whose children have left home.

Social and Sexual Readjustments: dating is not easy at any age, but it is particularly problematic for older divorced people. Newly divorced people must deal with two key issues: how to explain their unmarried status and whether to be sexually active.

Gender Differences in Divorce

"Her" *Divorce:* The most striking, even startling, difference between women and men following a divorce is a monetary one. According to some research, women suffer significant *downward social mobility.* The downward social mobility of women and their children is linked to two key factors: (1) the earnings gap between women and men, and (2) the failure of courts to award, and ex-husbands to pay, alimony and child support.

Researchers Frank Furstenberg and Andrew Cherlin suggest a shift in family resources take a characteristics form after a divorce. The focus of their research is on *the legal system and women's financial well-being.* Men typically become nonresidential parents and relinquish the principal responsibility for their support. The **Critical Issues** box (p. 344) presents data concerning child support. Among the fifty-four percent of custodial parents in 1991 who were awarded child support, only 51 percent received the full amount, and 25 percent received no payments. One explanation for why noncustodial fathers fail to pay child support is that they do not receive cooperation from their ex-wives in terms of visitation.

What are the *causes of inequality between divorced women and men?* Weitzman explains this economic discrepancy to no-fault divorce. Merely dividing material resources equally does not take into account such factors as earning power and educational background.

The consequences of divorce for women who experience downward mobility, especially those in traditional marriages, include suffering a loss in status, identity, and their domestic sphere--the home. Women with sole custody of children are often doubly burdened--they must be full-time parents as well as economic providers.

Despite their economic stress, evidence suggest that women fare better in terms of divorce adjustment than do men. According to Judith Wallerstein, women improve the emotional and psychological quality of their lives more than men do.

"His" *Divorce:* While the number of single-parent fathers has increased slightly, divorced men typically do not have custody of their children. Divorce men usually have more discretionary money than divorced women. Divorced men without custody may feel loneliness more intensely than their ex-wives. Divorce also has a negative effect on men's contact with their adult children and on their perception of their children as potential sources of support. Social policy must address divorced men's needs as well as those of divorced women.

Recovering From Divorce

Most people do recover from the trauma of divorce, although the process usually takes several years. Judy Wallerstein and Sandra Blakeslee studied families disrupted by divorce and found that women take an average of 3 to 3.5 years and men 2 to 2.5 years to reestablish a sense of external order after the separation.

Why do some people adjust more quickly than others? Younger people fare better than older people. This is particularly true for women. Other research suggests that women and men who are nontraditional in their gender role orientation adjust better and more quickly to marital breakdown.

THE IMPACT OF DIVORCE ON CHILDREN

Some research shows that none of ten black children and seven out of ten white children will spend part of their childhood in single-parent household, mainly because of divorce and births to unwed mothers.

Short-Term Versus Long-Term Effects

There is general agreement among researchers about the short-term effects of divorce on children---rejection, anger, denial, sadness, despair, and grief. Children frequently feel guilty, blaming themselves for the divorce. Research shows that the physical health ratings of children from divorced families are poorer than those of children from intact families.

Findings on long-term effects of divorce on children are not consistent. Some research finds children adjusting within one or two years, while other research show problems remaining for many years and interfering with normal social-emotional development. Most research to date has been cross-sectional and limited to comparisons between children from disrupted homes and those in intact families.

Does Divorce Affect Children's Behavior?: Findings are again inconsistent. However, unequal economic resources rather than difference in family structure may account for the observed differences in school performance.

Much of the research on children of divorce focuses on antisocial behavior. Misbehavior, especially among boys, increases following a divorce, but could be due to a lack of supervision. Not all effects of divorce are negative as single-parent families are better than conflict-ridden families.

Changing Patterns in Child Custody

Sole Custody: Today, approximately 90 percent of mothers get custody of their children following a divorce. Although most fathers do not request custody, those who do so are often successful. The odds of fathers gaining custody are enhanced when they pay child support, when the children are older, and when the oldest child is male. The father's better financial standing is often a factor in judges not awarding custody to mothers. The sexual orientation of a parent also has become an issue. Who will get custody may sometimes seem surprising. The **For Your Information** box (p. 348) tells the story of a convicted murderer who was awarded child custody.

Joint Custody: **Joint custody** means that *both parents are involved in child rearing and decision making.* Joint custody can take two forms: *joint legal custody*, in which both parents are to share decision making on such issues as education and health care, and *joint physical custody*, which covers how much time children will spend living with each parent.

Visitation Rights: Visitation for the noncustodial parent often becomes a source of stress and conflict.

REACHING ACCORD: DIVORCE COUNSELING AND MEDIATION

A growing number of marriage counselors and other professionals have shifted some of their practice into *divorce counseling*. Their efforts are aimed at helping people conclude the psychic divorce. Essentially, their goal is to replace the adversarial and often destructive aspects that can accompany the legal divorce with a more cooperative spirit.

Divorce mediation has a related but somewhat different emphasis. It is a procedure designed to help divorcing couples negotiate a fair and mutually agreed-upon resolution of such issues as mutual property distribution, child custody, visitation rights, and financial support.

THE DIVORCE DEBATE REVISITED

In recent years a movement to toughen state divorce laws has emerged. The principal target is the no-fault divorce statutes adopted by all states over the last 25 years. Another approach suggested is to have a two-tiered divorce law, keeping no-fault intact for couples without dependent children, but eliminating unilateral no-fault for couples with children.

OTHER FORMS OF MARITAL DISRUPTION

Separation refers to *the termination of marital cohabitation and can take a variety of forms.* *Desertion* refers to *the abandonment of a spouse or family.* *Civil annulment* *legally states that the marriage never existed and, thus, the parties are free to marry at will.* A civil annulment is distinct from the religious annulment granted by the Catholic church.

KEY TERMS

alimony	split custody
no-fault divorce	divorce rate
stations of divorce	emotional divorce
legal divorce	economic divorce

239

coparent divorce

community divorce

psychic divorce

sole custody

joint custody

conciliation counseling

divorce counseling

divorce mediation

desertion

annulment

separation

PART V. KEY RESEARCHERS

Glenda Riley

Frank Furstenberg and Andrew Cherlin

Judith Wallerstein

Paul Bohannan

Judith Wallerstein and Sandra Blakeslee

Paul Rasmussen and Kathleen Ferraro

Jesse Bernard   Cheryl Buehler and Mary Langenbrumer

James Ponzetti and Rodney Cate   Constance Ahrons and George Levinger

William Galston

PART VI. STUDY QUESTIONS

True-False

1.   T   F   *Divorce rates* among the Hopi has historically been extremely low relative to other cultures.

2.   T   F   *Desertion* was the most common reason women obtained divorces in nineteenth century America.

3.   T   F   Regionally, during the nineteenth century the *southern states* had a relatively high divorce rate compared to the rest of the United states.

4.   T   F   Relative to Native Americans and Latinos, Asian Americans have relatively high *divorce rates*.

5.   T   F   Divorce rates for *remarriages* are higher than for first marriages.

6.   T   F   Women with graduate degrees have a *higher* divorce rate than women with lower levels of education.

7.   T   F   Despite their economic stress, evidence suggests that women fare better in terms of *divorce adjustment* than do men.

8.   T   F   Judy Wallerstein and Sandra Blakeslee have research data that suggest men take longer than women to gain a sense of *external order* after a separation.

9.   T   F   Most research on the long-term effects of divorce on children has been *cross-sectional* and *limited* to comparisons between children from disrupted homes and those in intact families.

10.   T   F   *Joint custody* can take two forms, including *legal* and *physical*.

11.   T   F   *Divorce mediation* is defined as the process of helping people conclude the psychic divorce process.

1. Approximately _____ married couples *divorce* each year in the United States.

   (a) 200,000
   (b) 750,000
   (c) 1,200,000
   (d) 500,000
   (e) 1,900,000

2. According to historian Glena Riley, social and economic reasons for divorce during colonial times included:

   (a) growing mobility of colonists
   (b) emergence of a market economy
   (c) movement west
   (d) new technologies
   (e) all of the above

3. Which was the first state to recognize *no-fault divorce*?

   (a) New York
   (b) California
   (c) Nevada
   (d) Maine
   (e) Florida

4. Which of the following groups generally has the *lowest* divorce rate?

   (a) Latinos
   (b) African-Americans
   (c) whites
   (d) Native Americans

5. A number of factors identified as being associated with *divorce* have been found by family researchers, including:

   (a) education and religion
   (b) parental divorce
   (c) presence of children
   (d) income
   (e) all of these

6. Couples of which of the following *religious groups* have the lowest divorce rate?

   (a) Catholics
   (b) Jews
   (c) Protestants
   (d) all three groups have equivalent divorce rates

7. Paul Bohannan identified *six divorces experienced* by couples during the breakup of a marriage which he called the:

   (a) dissolution process
   (b) stations of divorce
   (c) push/pull factors of divorce
   (d) costs-benefits considerations
   (e) the uncoupling continuum

8. The American Association of Marriage and Family Therapists rated _____ as the most damaging aspect of couple relationships.

   (a) power struggles
   (b) lack of loving feelings
   (c) lack of demonstration of affection
   (d) communication problems

9. According to research in which divorced people are given a list of experiences to choose from, the most frequently selected one was:

   (a) I have felt insecure
   (b) I have felt angry toward my former spouse
   (c) I have felt worthwhile as a person
   (d) I have been depressed

10. The American Association of Family Therapists considered the problem of _____ in marriages to be the *most difficult* to treat.

    (a) lack of loving feelings
    (b) power struggles
    (c) value conflicts
    (d) alcoholism

11. Currently, the courts award *alimony* in approximately ____ percent of divorce cases.

    (a) 5   (d) 55
    (b) 15   (e) 25
    (c) 40

12. What is the procedure designed to *help divorcing couples* negotiate a fair and mutually agreed-upon resolution to their problems?

    (a) divorce mediation   (c) divorce counseling
    (b) conciliation counseling (d) articulation counseling

243

Fill-In

1.   Divorce has been part of U.S. history since _____ when a *Puritan court in Massachusetts* granted the first divorce decree in colonial America.

2.   The *divorce rate* reaches an all-time high in the U.S. in _____, and has declined slightly since.

3.   Two factors are often cited to explain the relatively high level of *marital stability* among Latinos include _____ _____ and _____.

4.   According to anthropologist Paul Bohannan, the *six stations of divorce* include: _____, _____, _____, _____, _____, _____.

5.   Two key societal factors affecting the divorce rate over the last generation includes changes in _____ and changes in the _____.

6.   The behaviors cited by divorced people as leading to divorce include: poor _____, _____ sex, constant _____, _____ abuse, _____ or _____ problems, and _____ mismanagement.

7.   According to researcher Jesse Bernard, the most striking difference between women and men following a divorce is a _____ one.

8.   Two key factors explain the *downward social mobility* of women and their children after a divorce: the _____ gap between women and men, and the failure of _____ to award, and the ex-husbands to pay, _____ and _____.

9.   *Joint custody* can take two forms: joint _____ custody, in which both parents share decision making on such issues as education and health care, and joint _____ custody, which covers how much time children will spend living with each parent.

10. _____ _____ legally states that the marriage never existed and, thus, the parties are free to marry at will.

Short-Answer

1.   Differentiate between *his* and *her* marriages as identified by Jesse Bernard.

2.   What are the general patterns concerning the *short-term* and *long-term* effects of divorce on children?

3.   What does the research show about the *negative consequences* of divorce on husbands and wives?

4.   What are the *stages* of divorce? What characterizes each stage? How does one move from one stage to another?

5.   What are the ten areas of marriage that are most damaging for couples experiencing marital difficulties?

6.   What are the major *societal factors* affecting divorce rate in our society?

244

7. What are the general demographic patterns of *divorce* in the U.S? That is, what characteristics of a person put them at high risk of divorce?
8. What factors do divorced people most commonly cite as leading them to *divorce*?
9. What factors do *family therapists* see as most likely to be related to divorce?
10. What doe the data show concerning how men and women *recover* from a divorce.

PART VII. ANSWERS TO STUDY QUESTIONS

True-False

1.	F	(p. 332)	7.	T	(p. 343)
2.	T	(p. 332)	8.	T	(p. 345)
3.	F	(p. 333)	9.	T	(p. 346)
4.	F	(p. 335)	10.	T	(p. 348)
5.	T	(p. 336)	11.	F	(p. 350)
6.	F	(p. 336)			

Multiple-Choice

1.	c	(p. 331)	7.	b	(p. 338)
2.	e	(p. 331)	8.	d	(p. 341)
3.	b	(p. 333)	9.	c	(p. 341)
4.	a	(p. 334)	10.	d	(p. 343)
5.	e	(pp. 335-37)	11.	b	(p. 343)
6.	b	(p. 336)	12.	a	(p. 350)

Fill-In

1. 1639 (p. 331)
2. 1980 (p. 334)
3. cultural traditions, religion (p. 334)
4. emotional, legal, economic, coparental, community, psychic (pp. 338-39)
5. attitudes, economy (p. 339)
6. communication, extramarital, fighting, drug, alcohol, financial (p. 340)
7. monetary (p. 342)
8. earnings, courts, alimony, child support (p. 343)
9. legal, physical (p. 348)
10. Civil annulment (p. 351)

PART VIII. COMMENT AND ANALYSIS

Global Perspectives

"Divorce in Other Times and Places"

    Key Points:

    Questions you have?

Personal Reflection

"Are You at Risk"

    Key Points:

    Questions you have?

Critical Issues

"Who Receives Child Support"

    Key Points:

    Questions you have?

For Your Information

"Convicted Murderer Awarded Child Custody"

    Key Points:

    Questions you have:

Writing Your Own Script

"Evaluating Relationships"

Remarriage and Remarried Families 14

PART I. CHAPTER OUTLINE

PART II. LEARNING OBJECTIVES

1. To discuss the concept of remarriage from an historical perspective.
2. To describe in detail the process of remarriage in the U.S.
3. To identify and describe the five stations of remarriage.
4. To provide an overview of the typical reactions to and consequences of parental remarriage for children.
5. To discuss the problems associated with stepsibling relationships.
6. To analyze the roles performed by both stepmothers and stepfamilies.
7. To identify and discuss the positive aspects of remarried families.
8. To discuss the overall quality and stability of remarried families.

PART III. CHAPTER REVIEW--KEY POINTS

Over 40 percent of recent marriages in the U.S. involved a second marriage for at least one of the partners. A *remarried family* has been defined by Esther Wald as *a two-parent, two-generation unit that comes into being on the legal remarriage of a widowed or divorced person who has biological or adopted children from a prior union with whom he or she is regularly involved.* The opening vignette asks you to consider what problems are faced by couples who are thinking about marrying, and who have been married before and have children from the previous marriage. *Figure 14.1* (p. 355) illustrates an example of overlapping households created in remarriages.

Despite the large number of remarriages, however, social and legal changes have not kept pace with this new family form. William Beer has identified ten fundamental ways in which the remarried family is different from the nuclear family, including: *complexity, a changing cast of characters, unclear boundaries, undefined rules, undefined laws, a lack of kinship terms, instant families, guilt, grieving,* and *myth of recreated nuclear family.* Each of these characteristics is defined in this section of the chapter.

HISTORICAL PERSPECTIVE

During the seventeenth and eighteenth centuries the proportion of remarriages among all marriages was approximately 20 to 30 percent. The circumstances leading to remarriage were quite different then, however. In early America the vast majority of remarriages followed the death of a spouse, whereas today remarriages typically involve divorced individuals. In early America marriages were likely to last an average of only 7 years and had only a 33 percent chance of lasting 10 years before one spouse died.

CULTURAL IMAGES OF STEPFAMILIES

The terms *stepchild, stepparent,* and *stepmother* have conveyed negative connotations from earlier times. Most of these images derive from folklore and fairy tales. Maternal loss and cruel replacement dominant many traditional children's stories.

In an attempt to correct negative stereotypes more neutral terms are being used to describe stepfamilies: reconstituted, blended, merged, binuclear, and remarried. The authors of the text prefer the term *remarried families*, agreeing with Esther Wald that the use of this term is "accurately descriptive, nontechnical, and value-free, and does not imply goals achieved."

THE PROCESS OF REMARRIAGE

Dating and Courtship Patterns

Older adults report many of the same anxieties about dating that adolescents do. Adults with children may find dating even more complicated. Divorced and widowed individuals who remarry tend to spend only half the time in dating and courtship that they did preceding their first marriage.

Frank Furstenberg and Graham Spanier found that dating among divorced people was guided more by pragmatic than by romantic considerations. The style of dating among the divorced is more informal, and courtship often involves living together before marriage.

The Decision to Remarry

Among divorced people, marriage is still perceived as a major cultural value and as the normal way to form an intimate connection with another person. Reasons for remarriage, especially for women, include very practical reasoning--improving their economic standing and gaining help with raising their children.

Patterns of Remarriage

Figure 14.2 (p. 358) show marriage rates fell and then remained relatively stable in the 1980s. Divorced people marry at a much higher rate than widowed people. This is in part due to the fact that divorce generally occurs at a younger age than widowhood, and strong emotional attachments to deceased partners often keep widowed people from being interested in establishing another relationship. Age is a key factor in remarriage, especially for women. Three out of four divorced women under thirty remarry, but only one of four divorced women over forty remarry.

Social Class and Education: Social class may be more important than age in the decision to remarry. Men with higher incomes are more likely to remarry than are men with lower incomes. Women with lower incomes are more likely to remarry. Women with higher levels of education tend to remarry later or not at all. Women without college education tend to remarry quickly.

Social Class: Race and Ethnicity: Rates of remarriage vary across social class, race, and ethnicity. Sociologist Andrew Cherlin suggests that the overall disadvantaged economic position of blacks has led many of them to see the marital relationship as less effective than the larger kin network in providing support. *Table 14.1* (p. 359) shows the percentage of divorced people of color under age 45 who are currently married with spouse present, by sex. Considerable variation exists among Latino groups. Variation is also found among Asian Americans.

The presence of children: Divorced men with custody of children tend to remarry sooner than their female counterparts. Among women, those with young children or no children are more likely to remarry than those with older children or large families. The **Critical Thinking** box (p. 360) presents information about the complexity of weddings involving couples with children from previous marriages. Involving children in decision making regarding the wedding is important. Adult children celebrating their own weddings have many issues to confront as well. For example, who to invite from the potentially larger pool of relatives created by the remarriages of their parents.

The Stations of Remarriage

Ann Goetting found that there is similarity between the developmental tasks that must be mastered in the divorce process and the many personal changes and adjustments that accompany the process of remarriage. She has identified six remarriages derived from Bohannan's stations of divorce.

Emotional Remarriage: Reestablishing a bond of attraction, love, commitment, and trust with another person is involved in this station of remarriage.

Psychic Remarriage: Psychic remarriage requires moving back from the recently acquired identity as a single person to a couple identity.

Community Remarriage: Reentering the couple world may result in reverting back to less intimate and more couple-oriented relationships. The frequency and nature of contact with relatives and friends changes after a divorce. A new network must be established for the remarried couple.

Parental Remarriage: Remarriage in which one or both spouses have children from a previous relationship is known as a remarriage. Establishing good working relationships with stepchildren is perhaps the most challenging and emotionally trying aspect of remarriage. This station of marriage usually receives the most attention in social science literature.

Economic Remarriage: This station of remarriage involves the establishment of a unit of economic productivity and consumption while at the same time working out mutually agreeable earning and spending habits. Barbara Fishman found that the "common-pot" approach is more likely to unify the stepfamily than the "two-pot" approach.

Legal Remarriage: Taking on new responsibilities as a spouse does not absolve one from responsibilities that accompanied the first marriage. Court-awarded payments of alimony and child support remain in effect. Ambiguity surrounds many other issues. For example, insurance benefits for children of noncustodial parents, inheritance from noncustodial parents or former partners, stepchild-stepparent relationships, and guidelines for sexual relationships for different members in remarried families.

REMARRIED FAMILIES: ROLES, INTERACTIONS, AND REACTIONS

Children in Remarried Families

Divorce and remarriage create two separate but overlapping households, with children having membership in both. Adjusting to two different sets of rules is difficult for most children. Whether overlapping households are beneficial to children depends, in large measure, on the attitude and behavior of the adults involved. Children play a key role as well. They can cooperate or be a source of friction in overlapping families.

Children's Perceptions of Family Membership: A study by Penny Gross used structured interviews with children to learn about parent-child relationships. Four patterns emerged in terms of who children considered family members: *retention, substitution, reduction,* and *augmentation.*

Consequences of Parental Remarriage for Children: A review of an extensive number of studies found that the majority of children in stepfamilies did not have any more psychological or behavioral problems than did children from nuclear families.

Studies suggest that if parental remarriage occurs early in the child's life (before age 5) it has few adverse effects. Older children experience more stress. Research consistently finds that boys have more problems adjusting to divorce than do girls. In contrast, in stepfamilies girls experience more adjustment problems and report poorer relationships with parents than do boys. The most common structure in remarried families is a biological mother, her children, and a stepfather.

Stepsiblings Relationships: Rivalry or Solidarity: A significant part of the tension in remarried families is centered on stepsibling relationships. *Stepsibling rivalry* can be a serious problem in remarried families. One main difference between siblings and stepsiblings is the origin of their relationships. Sharing living space can be a problem, especially if one part of the remarried family moves into the residence of the other. There is also a "them" and "us" feeling in many remarried families. Household rules and differential treatment can also be problems in such families.

Changes in Age-Order often occurs in remarried families and this can seriously disrupt the ranking system among siblings (stepsiblings).

Stepsibling Sexuality is also a critical issue in remarried families. When a teenaged boy and girl who have not grown up together come to live in the same residence, they may become sexually attracted to each other. Often these feelings are converted into hostility.

The Role of Half Siblings cannot be overlooked in the remarried family. One way in which remarried parents try to overcome difficulties in establishing a cohesive family is by having a mutual child that will provide a blood tie among all members of the remarried family. Half of all women who remarry will bear a child with their spouse. Research shows that remarried parents who had a mutual child reported much more often than parents who did not have a mutual child that relationships among the siblings were excellent.

Stepsibling Relationships Over Time is another important area of concern for remarried families. Most adults still keep in contact with step-/half siblings. Contact seems to be affected by three key factors: race, gender, and proximity.

Stepmothers: A Bad Rap?

Margaret Draughon suggests three possibilities for a new stepmother role: *primary mother, other mother*, and *friend*.

Stepmothers and Mothering: The nurturing expectations for women are so strong that stepmothers often assume that they should love the children instantly. Regardless of how fast a stepmother may get involved, there are likely to be problems. There are even more challenges if the children live with their biological mother and just visit their father. It most be remembered though that not all stepparenting situations are alike. The **Family Profile** box (p. 367) takes a look at one example of a remarried family and issues its members are confronted by over time.

Stepfathers: Polite Strangers?

Stepfather families are the most common remarried family structure. Overall, stepfathers tend to be more positive and responsive and less negative and directive toward children than are biological fathers. Stepfathers generally enjoy better relations with their stepchildren than do stepmothers.

Elizabeth Einstein has identified three areas of difficulty for stepfathers: *sex, money,* and *discipline*. Each of these areas of difficulty is discussed in this section of the chapter.

Ex-spouses: Do They Fade Away?

Research findings differ with respect to ongoing conflicts between divorced parents. Many labels have been attached to ex-spouse relationships, including *fiery foes, angry associates, cooperative colleagues,* and *perfect pals*.

THE STRENGTHS AND BENEFITS OF REMARRIED FAMILIES

Some recent empirical studies have identified several strengths of remarried families, particularly the remarried couples. Remarried couples have identified three important ways in which their marriages are stronger than their first marriages. These include, being more realistic about the existence of conflict in marriage, better communication skills, and the balance of power in decision making is more equal in the remarriage.

Benefits: Benefits include a sharing of responsibility, companionship, continuity of sexual relationship, and a sense of partnership.

THE QUALITY OF THE REMARITAL RELATIONSHIP

Despite all the problems we have just discussed, most remarried couples seem to find happiness in their new relationship. When gender is examined, however, differences in levels of happiness and satisfaction emerge. In both first marriages and remarriages men report higher levels of satisfaction than women. Patricia Kelley found general agreement among the respondents that it works best not to define gender roles as distinctly as they are in many families. The presence of children can affect the quality of family life.

Stability in Remarriage

Historically, research has suggested that divorced people who remarry have a higher divorce rate than first marriages. However, recent research has shown that remarriages dissolve at approximately the same rate as first marriages do. About 40 percent of all remarriages end in divorce.

Factors Affecting Stability: Remarriage is a complex process, requiring a number of adjustments not necessary in first marriages. For example, how to address stepparents and how to integrate grandparents into the family.

Outside support and pressures are also important factors to take into account. Positive and supportive reactions from friends and relatives contribute to success. Conversely, disapproval puts added stress on the relationship.

Attitudes toward divorce are also important to consider. Remarried white men are more likely to redivorce than remarried white women. More black women than men divorce a second time.

The presence of children also affect stability in remarriage. The divorce rate is higher in remarriages with stepchildren. The presence of children makes adjustment harder for remarried couples. They limit privacy, engage in disruptive behavior, and cause conflict over discipline. Children can be manipulative and can create a tense and hostile environment.

RECOMMENDATIONS FOR SOCIAL POLICY

Clarification of Legal Norms

Researchers have identified three ways in which state laws affecting parent-child relationships could be modified to meet the needs of stepfamilies. There could be a form of legal guardianship that would allow stepparents to function more effectively in families. Lawmakers and judges need to be aware of the probability of a second divorce and take steps to ensure that the desires of stepparents and stepchildren regarding visitation rights be incorporated into divorce decrees. To reduce ambiguities and sexual tensions incest laws could be broadened to include stepparents and their children and quite possibly stepsiblings as well.

Modification of the Tax Code

Currently, dependent children can be claimed as a deduction for only one household when, in fact, two households frequently share financial responsibility. This tax structure of which such policy is a part needs to be revised.

Education

Forms could be changed to eliminate confusion about surnames, and when students are asked to make cards or gifts for parents or grandparents, steprelationships could be included on a routine basis.

The **Applying the Sociological Imagination** box (p. 372) asks you to consider greeting cards, and to visit card shops to see if card companies recognize stepfamilies in their cards. The **Writing Your Own Script** box (p. 373) asks you to think about remarriage.

PART IV. KEY TERMS

remarried family

emotional remarriage

psychic remarriage

community remarriage

parental remarriage

economic remarriage

legal remarriage

overlapping households

PART V. KEY RESEARCHERS

Esther Wald

Barbara Fishman

Margaret Draughon

Elizabeth Einstein

Frank Furstenberg and Graham Spanier

William Beer

Lynn White and Agnes Riedman

PART VI. STUDY QUESTIONS

True-False

1. T   F   The U.S. has the highest *remarriage rate* in the world.
2. T   F   In *colonial America* remarriage following the death of a spouse was not socially acceptable, especially for women.
3. T   F   Older adults report many of the same anxieties about *dating* that adolescents report.
4. T   F   Divorced and widowed individuals tend to spend more time in *dating and courtship* than they did preceding their first marriage.
5. T   F   Divorced people remarry at a much *higher rate* than do widowed people.
6. T   F   *Rate of remarriage*, while varying by age, do not vary very much across social class, race, or ethnicity.
7. T   F   Studies suggest that if parent remarriage occurs *early* in a child's life, the child experiences few adverse effects.
8. T   F   Research has consistently shown that *girls* have more problems adjusting to divorce than do boys.
9. T   F   The most common structure in *remarried families* is a biological mother, her children, and a stepfather.
10. T   F   In *both* first and remarriages men report higher levels of satisfaction than women.
11. T   F   Remarriage ends in *divorce* at a significantly higher rate than first marriages.

1. Approximately what percentage of marriages in the U.S. today involved a *second marriage* for at least one of the partners.

   (a) 3
   (b) 15
   (c) 30
   (d) 40
   (e) 65

2. In which of the following ways, according to William Beer, does the *remarried family* differ from the nuclear family.

   (a) lack of kinship terms
   (b) complexity
   (c) guilt
   (d) grieving
   (e) all of these

3. In the early colonies, *marriages* were likely to last ____ years.

   (a) 3
   (b) 7
   (c) 16
   (d) 23
   (e) 42

4. Which of the following *terms* is preferred by our authors?

   (a) remarried family
   (b) blended family
   (c) binuclear family
   (d) merged family
   (e) aggregate family

5. In the U.S., approximately _____ percent of *women 40 years of age or older* remarry.

   (a) 25
   (b) 35
   (c) 45
   (d) 55
   (e) 65

6. The ____ *remarriage* generally receives the most attention in social science literature and in the media.

   (a) emotional
   (b) economic
   (c) parental
   (d) psychic

7. Barbara Fishman found that a(n) _____ *approach* to family finances is the most likely to unify a stepfamily.

    (a) "two-pot"   (c) "common pot"
    (b) economic   (d) legal

8. Which of the following patterns emerged *least frequently* in Penny Gross's study on children and parent-child relationships in remarried families?

    (a) retention   (c) reduction
    (b) augmentation   (d) substitution

9. Which of the following was *not* one of the themes in the research on *stepsiblings* conducted by William Beers?

    (a) the role of half siblings
    (b) stepsibling rivalry
    (c) changes in age order
    (d) stepsibling sexuality
    (e) all are themes in this research

10. Approximately _____ *percent* of women are likely to have a child after remarrying.

    (a) 40   (c) 70
    (b) 20   (d) 50

11. Margaret Draughon suggested all of the following *except* _____ as possible relationships between *stepmothers* and *stepchildren*.

    (a) primary mother   (c) counselor
    (b) friend   (d) other mother

12. Which of the following was *not* one of the areas of difficulty between stepfathers and stepchildren as outlined by Elizabeth Einstein?

    (a) rivalry for the mother's attention
    (b) money
    (c) discipline
    (d) sex

13. Ways in which couples in remarried families may be stronger than nuclear families include:

   (a) they are more realistic about the existence of conflict in marriage
   (b) they report better communication skills
   (c) the balance of power in decision making is more equal in remarriages
   (d) all of the above
   (e) none of the above

Fill-In

1. During the seventeenth and eighteenth centuries the proportion of remarriages among all marriages was approximately _____ to _____ percent. Whereas in early America the overwhelming majority of remarriages followed the _____ of a spouse, today remarriages typically involve _____ individuals.

2. In the early colonies the average *marriage* lasted _____ years, and had a 33 percent change of lasting _____ years.

3. *Divorced* and *widowed* individuals who *remarry* tend to spend _____ _____ the time in dating a courtship that they did preceding their first marriage.

4. For both women and men _____ _____ may be more important than *age* in the decision to remarry.

5. Ann Goetting found that there is a similarity between the developmental tasks that must be mastered in the _____ *process* and the many personal changes and adjustments that accompany the *process* of _____.

6. Remarriage in which *both spouses have children from previous relationships* is known as a _____ *remarriage*.

7. Utilizing a structured interview technique that focused on parent-child relationships, researcher Penny Gross asked children who they considered to be family members. Four patterns emerged, including _____, _____, _____, and _____.

8. _____ of all women who *remarry* will bear a child with their spouses.

9. Margaret Draughon suggests three possibilities for *stepmother roles*: _____ mother, _____ mother, and _____.

10. Elizabeth Einstein identified three *areas of difficulty* for *stepfathers*, including _____, _____, and _____.

11. The *recommendations for social policy* change concerning remarriages presented in the text include: _____ _____, _____ _____, and _____.

Short-Answer

1. William Beer suggests that *remarried families* differ from nuclear families in what ways?

2. Briefly recount the *history* of remarriage from early colonial times to today.

3. What generalizations are being made about the *characteristics* of divorced people in dating and courtship relationships?
4. How do *remarriage rates* vary by such variables as *age, race, ethnicity, social class,* and *education*.
5. What are the ways in which *remarriage* may be *stronger* than first marriages?
6. What are the *social policy recommendations* regarding remarriages?
7. What does research show about *stability* in remarriages as compared to first marriages?
8. What are the effects of a remarried couple having a mutual child on the relationships among stepsiblings?
9. What are the *consequences* of parental remarriage for children?
10. What are the issues raised in the text concerning the status of *stepmother*?
11. What are the issues raised in the text concerning the status of *stepfather*?
12. What factors seem to be related to half-/stepchildren relationships over time?

PART VII. ANSWERS TO STUDY QUESTIONS

True-False

1.	T	(p. 355)	7.	T	(p. 363)
2.	F	(p. 356)	8.	F	(p. 363)
3.	T	(p. 357)	9.	T	(p. 364)
4.	F	(p. 358)	10.	T	(p. 369)
5.	T	(p. 358)	11.	F	(p. 370)
6.	F	(p. 359)			

Multiple-Choice

1.	d	(p. 355)	8.	d	(p. 363)
2.	e	(p. 355)	9.	e	(p. 364)
3.	b	(p. 356)	10.	d	(p. 365)
4.	a	(p. 357)	11.	c	(p. 366)
5.	a	(p. 359)	12.	a	(p. 368)
6.	c	(p. 361)	13.	d	(p. 369)
7.	b	(p. 361)			

Fill-In

1. 20, 30, death, divorced (p. 356)
2. 7, 10 (p. 356)
3. Only half (p. 358)
4. social class (359)
5. divorce, remarriage (p. 360)
6. parental, psychic (p. 361)

7. retention, substitution, reduction, augmentation (p. 363)
8. Half (p. 365)
9. other, primary, friend (p. 366)
10. sex, money, discipline (p. 368)
11. legal norms, tax code, education (p. 372)

PART VIII. COMMENT AND ANALYSIS

Critical Issues

"Children and the Remarriage Service"

    Key Points:

    Questions you have?

Family Profile

"The Maring family"

    Key Points:

    Questions you have?

Applying the Sociological Imagination

"What's in a Card?"

    Key Points:

    Questions you have?

<u>Writing Your Own Script</u>

"Thinking About Remarriage"

Marriages and Families In Later Life

15

PART I. CHAPTER OUTLINE

XII. Summary
XIII. Questions for Study and Reflection
XIV. Further Reading

PART II. LEARNING OBJECTIVES

1. To describe the demographic and social characteristics of families in the later stages of the family life cycle.
2. To identify and describe the most widely recognized age categories of the elderly.
3. To discuss the myths and realities of housing patterns among the elderly.
4. To discuss the nature of marriage in later life with respect to the quality, satisfaction, and adjustment to retirement.
5. To describe the essential characteristics of grandparenting in U.S. society.
6. To describe the realities of health, illness, and caregiving with regard to the elderly in the U.S.
7. To discuss the experience of widowhood in U.S. society.

PART III. CHAPTER REVIEW--KEY POINTS

In 1900 only 4 percent of the U.S. population was over the age of 65. Today, thirty-three million people, 13 percent of our population is in this age group. By the year 2050 the number of *elderly* is expected to climb to more than 80 million, over 20 percent of the population. The **Personal Reflections** box (p. 376) provides a five question quiz for you to test your knowledge of the elderly.

CHARACTERISTICS OF LATER-LIFE FAMILIES

According to Timothy Brubaker, *later-life* families exhibit three characteristics: (1) They are mutligeneration, (2) they have a lengthy family history, and (3) they experience a number of new life events for which they may have little preparation.

The Sandwich Generation

The middle-aged generation, sometimes called the *sandwich generation* because of the pressures its members experience from both sides of the age spectrum, finds itself playing many roles. Many young adults are finding difficulties today in gaining financial success. They have been labeled the *boomerang generation*. In 1994, 12 percent of young adults aged 25-34 lived with their parents. While there are difficulties, many parents report spending enjoyable time with their co-resident adult children. Three factors affected the level of parental satisfaction: *younger siblings, employment status,* and *grandchildren.*

Diversity in the Family Life Cycle

The U.S. culture has always emphasized youth, and there have been negative stereotypes of the elderly. Robert Butler coined the term **ageism** to describe these *stereotypes and discriminatory treatment applied to the elderly.*

Social gerontology, *the study of the impact of sociocultural conditions of the process and consequences of aging*, show us that the impact of aging on marriages and families is multifaceted. The approach taken in this chapter is to present a balance concerning the strengths and satisfactions of the elderly with the real problems many of the elderly confront on a daily basis.

Changing Age Norms

Age norms refer to *expectations of how one is to behave at any stage in life.* These age norms currently show signs of being less restrictive than in the past. Timing of marriages, births, and remarriages are identified as examples of such changes.

THE DEMOGRAPHICS OF AGING: DEFINING "OLD"

In 1935 the government arbitrarily selected 65 as the age at which a worker could receive full social security retirement benefits. Defining old age is more difficult than this. **Functional age**, or an *individual's physical, intellectual, and social capacities and accomplishments*, seems more important today than chronological age.

Age Categories of the Elderly

Significant differences in the social realities of older people exist. Gerontologists now speak of three distinct categories: the *young-old* (ages 65-74), the *middle-old* (ages 75-84), and the *old-old* (ages 85 and over). The older population itself is aging at a rapid rate. *Figure 15.1* (p. 379) shows the changes expected in these age categories by the year 2050. By that time 22 percent of the elderly are expected to be 85 years of age or older. Today that figure is just over 10 percent. The health-care requirements of this age group, along with other social services must be prepared for by society. The **Applying the Sociological Imagination** box (p. 379) takes a look at the issue of *ageism*. A 26 year old female researcher presented herself to people in different social situations as either 26 years old or as an old woman of 85 years of age. She was treated quite differently depending on how old she appeared.

Gender and Marital Status

Six out of every ten older Americans are female. This pattern is a relatively recent historical phenomenon. Only since the 1930s did women's life expectancy increase more rapidly than men's as female deaths connected with pregnancy, childbirth, and infectious diseases declined dramatically. *Table 15.1* (p. 380) shows the changing sex ratios in the older population in 1960 and 1990, that women clearly have a longevity advantage over men. Researcher Erdman Palmore attributes half of the difference to genetics and the other half to social roles and environmental factors.

In 1994 there were almost five times as many widows as widowers. *Figure 15.2* (p. 380) shows the marital status for all elderly people in the U.S. for 1994. Gender differences in survivorship rates are significant because women of all racial and ethnic groups have fewer financial resources and are more likely than men to experience poverty in old age. In 1994, the median income for female householders living alone was $9,980, compared to $13,896 for male householders living alone.

Race, Ethnicity, and Class

In 1995, the overall racial composition of the U.S. population 65 and older was 85 percent white, 8 percent black, 2 percent Asian Pacific Islander, and less than 1 percent Native American. Latinos, who are classified as either black or white, constituted 5 percent of the elderly population. By 2050 people of color will constitute almost 34 percent of the aged population in the United States. People of color in 2050 will constitute almost 48 percent of the total U.S. population. *Figure 15.3* (p. 381) show population patterns and projections for 1995 and 2050.

Although the gap in life expectancy rates for the white population and people of color is narrowing, these rates remain lower for people of color. For example, in 1993 life expectancy at birth was 79.5 for white females and 73 for white males. In contrast, it was only 73.7 for black females and 64.7 for black males. One major factor accounting for these differences is social class. For example, in 1993 the median income for black householders 65 and over was $11,926, for Latinos $13,284, and for whites it was $18,471.

Poverty Among the Elderly

Almost 42 percent of households headed by an elderly person had incomes less than $42,000. Although a smaller proportion of the elderly are poor today than in the past, poverty remains a problem for millions of elderly people. Today 12 percent of the elderly are classified as being poor. *Table 15.2* (p. 382)show the poverty status of the elderly by race and Latino origin, 1959-1993. Rates are two to three times higher for people of color.

LIVING ARRANGEMENTS

Only 5 percent of the elderly live in nursing homes, but because people are living much longer there will be a greater need in the future for good nursing home care. Most older people live with a spouse or alone. *Figure 15.4* (p. 382) shows data concerning the living arrangements of the elderly by sex and race for 1994. Difference exists between women and men and between different age categories among the elderly.

Housing Patterns

Seventy-seven percent of the elderly own their homes. The income level of the household is a key factor for homeownership. Although the elderly are less likely to be living in physically deficient housing than past generations, a significant portion of the housing occupied by the elderly (perhaps 20 percent) is of poor quality.

The situation for renters can be worse. Some renters are boarders, and others live in residential hotels, including single-room residences (SROs). Increasingly, SROs, especially those that cater to low-income elderly men, have been demolished to make room for urban renewal projects.

As the family life cycle changes so too do housing needs. Houses can become too big, too isolated, too expensive, or too difficult to maintain for a retired couple or the widowed after children have left home. The vast majority of the elderly do not want to live with their children. Race and ethnicity also effect housing decisions.

MARRIAGES IN LATER LIFE

Marital Quality and Satisfaction

Studies which gauge marital satisfaction show inconclusive results (some show improvement over time, some show a decrease over time, and some show no difference). Karol Ade-Ridder found that sexual activity was related to marital satisfaction, but it is not essential. The **Family Profile** box (p. 384) focuses the challenges and relationship philosophy of a couple who have been married for 54 years.

Adjustment to Retirement

In 1994, 3.8 million (12 percent) of persons aged 65 and older were either working or looking for work. Younger elderly men are the most likely to work. Like so much of social life in the United States, the experience of retirement is affected by an individual's race, class, and gender.

Type of Retirement: Timothy Brubaker has identified four patterns of retirement among older couples:

> *Single or traditional*: In this pattern, one spouse, usually
> the husband, has been employed and thus only one spouse
> retires from paid employment.
> *Dissynchronized--husband initiated*: Here, the husband retires
> before the wife. She is usually younger and started her
> career later.
> *Dissynchronized--wife initiated*: In this pattern, the wife
> retires first. This case is rare.
> *Synchronized retirement*: In this situation both the husband
> and wife were employed, and they retire at the same time.

Most studies on retirement do not take these variations into account. Marital satisfaction may be affected by the circumstances of retirement, not just retirement itself. Gary Lee and Constance Shehan found that wives who continue to work after their husbands retired have lower levels of marital satisfaction than wives in couples with any other employment status combination.

Other factors affecting marital satisfaction after retirement include a couple's financial status and health. According to Judith Treas, most older people see their incomes decline by one-third to one-half after retirement. Different patterns exist for blacks and whites. In general, when people have control over the timing of their retirement they are more likely to feel satisfied with this stage in their lives.

INTERGENERATIONAL RELATIONSHIPS

Studies have consistently found that 50 percent to 60 percent of older people with children have at least one child within 10 minutes of their home. Although considerable diversity exists, norms of complimentarity and reciprocity dominate family relationships.

Quality of Relationships

Gender seems to play an important role in the quality of relationships between elderly people and their adult children. Most adult children and their elderly parents like one another and express satisfaction with their relationships.

Patterns of Support

Study after study indicate that families, not the formal system, provide the bulk of care for the elderly across all cultural groups.

Racial and Ethnic Variations: Families of color, especially among the poor, have developed a wider range of informal support systems than have whites. For example, blacks have a higher incidence of extended family households than whites. Blacks also rely more heavily on family, friends, and neighbors than whites, though when social class is controlled the differences are not pronounced.

EVOLVING PATTERNS OF KINSHIP: GRANDPARENTHOOD

Changing mortality and fertility rates can have enormous consequences for kin networks. There are far more grandparents today than at the turn of the century. In fact, approximately 50 percent of all older adults with children are great-grandparents. These social roles are fairly recent ones and therefore are not well defined.

Styles of Grandparenting

People become grandparents at ages ranging from the early 30s to 60s and 70s. This diversity in ages contributes to the ambiguity surrounding this role. Bernice Neugarten and

Karol Weinstein classified the interactions of grandparent couples with their grandchildren into one of the following five categories: *formal, fun seeker, distant figure, surrogate parent,* and *reservoir of family wisdom.* These researchers found that age is a factor in the development of grandparenting styles.

Andrew Cherlin and Frank Furstenberg found three styles of grandparenting: *remote, companionate,* and *involved.* These three styles correspond roughly to Neugarten and Weinstein's grandparenting styles of distant figure, fun seeker, and surrogate parent.

Benefits and Conflicts

The presence of grandchildren can make a number of contributions in a person's life. Grandchildren can contribute to a sense of immortality and self-esteem, and can keep the grandparents up to date on cultural and social changes. Grandparents can provide love and guidance minus the intensity, responsibility, and tension that frequently exist in parent-child relationships.

Such benefits, however, can also produce tension and conflict. Parents and grandparents may disagree about child-rearing strategies. Parents may resent what they perceive as interference by their parents. Jealousy for parents due to the child's affection for grandparents may also be a problem.

Research indicates that there is more contact with maternal grandparents and that the maternal grandmother was consistently listed as the grandparent whom grandchildren felt closest.

Race and ethnicity play a role in the degree of involvement in the grandparent role. Vira Kivitt found that the grandfather role was more central in the lives of black men than it was for white men.

Unplanned Parenting: In a growing number of cases, grandparents assume sole responsibility for their grandchildren. Both positives and negative outcomes for the caregivers. Such caregiving can provide more purpose to life and keep grandparents active. However, caregiving can be exhausting and economically costly.

Great-Grandparenthood

Studies show that a majority of great-grandparents express positive feelings about the experience. However, most great-grandparents have only limited and mostly ritualistic contact with their great-grandchildren.

THE CHILD-FREE ELDERLY

In 1990, 25 percent of white women and 33 percent of black women either never had children or had children who had already died. Childlessness is a predictor of social isolation in later life. The unmarried elderly have actively created support network of friends and neighbors. The child-free elderly have a greater chance of being institutionalized.

SIBLING RELATIONSHIPS

Sibling relationships are valuable because siblings share a history and because these are potentially the longest-lasting relationships an individual will ever have. Seventy to eighty percent of all elderly adults have at least one living sibling.

HEALTH AND ILLNESS

Although health problems increase with age, the health status of today's elderly is varied and not as negative as is popularly portrayed. Surveys have found that 70 percent of the noninstitutionalized elderly describe their health as good or excellent. A common measure of health among the elderly is the activities of daily living.

Despite he publicity about the health-care system, the majority of care is still being provided at home by informal. *Figure 15.5* (p. 392) shows the percent of informal caregivers by type--daughter, wives husbands, sons, and other females and males.

The Spouse as Caregiver

Wives make up the majority of spousal caregivers. The degree of satisfaction found in such relationships is affected by the severity of the illness or disability. Caregivers can become overwhelmed by the demands of caregiving and become "hidden patients."

Adult Children as Caregivers

It is estimated that five million adult children care for parents at any one point in time. A wide range of studies has consistently shown that across all racial and ethnic groups the role of caretaker is most frequently filled by daughters.

The Stresses of Caregiving: Although most children willingly help their parents when the need arises and express satisfaction in doing do, parental care can be stressful. The time demands of caring for an adult patient compete with other responsibilities and may result in conflict, particularly with regard to employment.

In extreme situations elder abuse may result from the stress and strains of the caretaker role. Another phenomenon, referred to as "granny dumping," involves caretakers abandoning an elderly relative at a hospital emergency room.

THE EXPERIENCE OF WIDOWHOOD

In the United States today there are few norms to guide the newly widowed person. After the death of a spouse and the loss of their main support, widowed persons become more isolated past social networks. Helen Lopata found that only 25 percent of widows saw their husbands' families on a regular basis.

270

Stages of Widowhood

Robert DiGiulio described four stages that widowed people experience. These stages include:

(1) *Encounter:* In this stage people may experience depression, shock, rage, loss of appetite, insomnia, and frequent crying.

(2) *Repondence:* During this stage there is a recognition of the reality of the spouse's death.

(3) *Emergence:* Over time the widowed come to realize that death is a natural outcome of life, and that although they have lost someone they loved, they can move on with their lives.

(4) *Transformation:* At this point, the grief work is over. Many widowed see themselves as changed people, as having grown from their experience.

Gender Differences in Widowhood

Figure 15.6 (p. 395) shows that widowhood is largely a female experience. Among women aged 65 and over, 47 percent of whites, 56 percent of blacks, and 44 percent of Latinos are widowed. In contrast, the rates for men in the same age categories are 13 percent for whites, 23 percent for blacks, and 17 percent of Latinos.

Special Problems of Widows: Besides the adjustments associated with bereavement and grief, widows are likely to face two major problems: changes in their self-identity and changes in their financial situation.

Special Problems of Widowers: Many widowers are ill-prepared for domestic matters and have fewer contacts with their families and receive less social support from them following the death of their spouse.

Beyond Widowhood

As already mentioned, there are many traumatic aspects of widowhood. However, many widowed people return to school, take up a hobby, do volunteer work, travel, and in some cases, remarry. While the changes in women tend to be more internal (more self-confidence), men focus more externally (becoming more aware and appreciative of friendships).

IMPLICATIONS FOR SOCIAL POLICY

Tomorrow's elderly, particularly women and people of color, should be provided with better education, job-training, and more extensive pension plans. The health-care system must be changed to better accommodate the increasing numbers of elderly who will use it in the future. More preventative medicine is needed. Today 15 percent of the population is without health insurance coverage. Besides increasing and developing support systems for the elderly, society needs to find ways to use the reservoir of skills that they possess.

PART IV. KEY TERMS

sandwich generation

ageism

boomerang generation

social gerontology

age norms

bereavement

grief

euthanasia

functional age

PART V. KEY RESEARCHERS

Timothy Brubaker

Elizabeth Kubler-Ross

Erdman Palmore

Linda Ade-Ridder and Timothy Brubaker

Robert Rubinstein

Judith Treas

Gary Lee and Constance Shehan

Vira Kivitt

Linda Ade-Ridder

Bernice Neugarten and Karol Weinstein

Robert Rubinstein

Robert DiGuilo

Elizabeth Murran

Helen Lopata

Felix Berado

PART VI. STUDY QUESTIONS

True-False

1. T   F   By the year 2050 it is expected that most elderly people in the U.S. will be over the *age of 85*.
2. T   F   In 1994 there were almost five times as many *widows* than *widowers* in the U.S.
3. T   F   Most men over the age of 65 in the U.S. are *married*.
4. T   F   *Poverty rates* among the elderly are higher today than in the past.
5. T   F   The vast majority of older people maintain their independence in the community, living *alone* or in a household *with a spouse*.
6. T   F   The elderly today are *less likely* to live in deficient housing than in generations past.
7. T   F   Most older people live at least 100 miles from their adult children.
8. T   F   The weight of evidence in study after study indicates that *families*, not the formal system, provide the bulk of care for the elderly across all cultural groups.
9. T   F   Research indicates that there is more contact with *maternal grandparents* and that the *maternal grandmother* was consistently listed as the grandparent to whom grandchildren felt closest.
10. T   F   Upward of 70 to 80 percent of all elderly adults have at least one living sibling.

Multiple-Choice

1. Approximately _____ percent of the U.S. population today is *over the age of sixty-five*.

   (a)   5
   (b)   8
   (c)   13
   (d)   18
   (e)   23

2. According to Timothy Brubaker, *later-life families*:

   (a)   have a lengthy family history
   (b)   are multigenerational
   (c)   experience a number of new life events for which they have little preparation
   (d)   all of the above
   (e)   none of the above

3.   By the year 2050 the number of elderly Americans is expected to be approximately
      ____ *million*.

      (a)   58   (d)   98
      (b)   80   (e)   90
      (c)   45

4.   The *boomerang generation* refers to:

      (a)   the large percentage of young adults today moving back into the residence of
            their parents
      (b)   older people remarrying after the death of a spouse and repeating earlier
            stages in the family life cycle
      (c)   the tendency of relationships with kin, especially ones children to be "patched
            up" before the death of an aged relative
      (d)   the pattern whereby each generation, as they age, begins to develop attitudes
            and behaviors similar to generations past

5.   In 1994, approximately _____ percent of unmarried adults aged 25-34 *lived with
      their parents*.

      (a)   12   (c)   32
      (b)   22   (d)   42

6.   Which of the following is *not* one of the categories of older people currently
      recognized by gerontologists?

      (a)   old-old   (c)   newly-old
      (b)   young-old   (d)   middle-old

7.   Approximately _____*percent* of older Americans are *female*.

      (a)   45   (c)   55
      (b)   50   (d)   60

8.   The vast majority of older people live:

      (a)   in nursing homes
      (b)   with members of their extended families
      (c)   alone with their spouse
      (d)   none of the above

9. At any given time, what percentage of the elderly in the U.S. live in *nursing homes*?

(a) 5
(b) 10
(c) 15
(d) 20
(e) 25

10. According to research by Linda Ade-Ridder and Timothy Brubaker, *marital quality* _____ with age.

(a) improves
(b) remains the same
(c) declines
(d) there was no consensus on this question

11. Which of the following patterns of *retirement* among older couples was *not* identified by Robert Brubaker?

(a) dissynchronized-husband initially
(b) dissynchronized-wife initiated
(c) dissynchronized-jointly
(d) single or traditional retirement

12. Which of the following situations has been found to produce the *least amount* of marital satisfaction among American wives?

(a) husband working-wife retired
(b) wife working-husband retired
(c) husband and wife both working
(d) husband and wife both retired

13. According to Bernice Neugarten and Karol Weinstein, older grandparents are most likely to adopt the approach _____ approach to *grandparenting*.

(a) formal
(b) surrogate parent
(c) distant figure
(d) fun seeker
(e) reservoir of family wisdom

14. Which of the following is *not* a style of grandparenting according to research by Andrew Cherlin and Frank Furstenberg?

(a) remote
(b) involved
(c) companionate
(d) removed

276

15. Robert DiDiulo described four stages that *widowed* people experience the final stage is called:

(a) emergence
(b) catharsis
(c) encounter
(d) reponderence
(e) transformation

Fill-In

1. Three key factors affecting the level of *parental satisfaction* for parents with adult children living at home are: _____ _____, _____ _____ and _____.

2. _____ _____ is the study of the impact of sociocultural conditions on the process and consequences of *aging*.

3. _____ _____ are expectations of how one is to behave at any *stage of life*.

4. _____ _____ refers to an individual's physical, intellectual, and social capacities and accomplishments.

5. Women have a *longevity* advantage over men. Researcher Erdman Palmore attributes half of this difference in longevity to _____ and the other half to _____ _____ and _____ factors.

6. In 1993, *life expectancy* at birth was _____ for white females, and _____ for white males. For black females it was _____ and for black males _____.

7. Today in the U.S. approximately _____ percent of the elderly *own their own homes*.

8. In 1994, approximately _____ percent of persons aged 65 and older were either working or looking for work.

9. Andrew Cherlin and Frank Furstenberg found three *styles of grandparenting*, including _____, _____, and _____.

10. Vira Kivitt's research found that the _____ role was more central in the lives of black men than it was for white men.

11. Approximately _____ percent of *white women* and _____ percent of *black women* aged 85 and older either never had children or had children who have already died.

12. Approximately _____ to _____ percent of all elderly adults have a least one *living sibling*.

13. It is estimated that _____ million adult children are currently *caring for parents*.

14. According to Robert DiGuilio, a person in the _____ *stage of widowhood* has come to realize that death is a natural outcome of life and, although they have lost someone they loved, they can get on with their lives.

15. Besides the adjustments associated with bereavement and grief, *widows* face two additional major problems, including changes in their _____ and changes in their _____ situation.

16. Approximately _____ percent of Americans have *no health insurance coverage*.

<u>Short-Answer</u>

1. What are the current *demographics* concerning the aged in the U.S? What are the projections for the next fifty or so years?
2. What is meant by the term *sandwich generation*? What is the *boomerang generation*?
3. What are *age norms*? Provide two illustrations.
4. Discuss the issue of *gender and marital status* in the U.S. today for people over the age of sixty-five. What are the demographic patterns found?
5. What are the three *categories of the aged* identified today by gerontologists? What are the changing demographic patterns for these categories among the aged?
6. What are the significant demographic characteristics of the aged by *race, ethnicity,* and *social class*? What is the current demographic portrait for *poverty* among the elderly in our society?
7. Briefly describe the patterns in *living arrangements* among the aged, differentiating between those for women and those for men.
8. What are the *types of retirement* identified by Timothy Brubaker? Describe and illustrate each of these.
9. What does research tell us about the *quality of marriage* after retirement? What are the factors associated with higher level of marital satisfaction in old age?
10. What are the different *styles of grandparenting* identified by sociological research? Define and illustrate these different styles.
11. What are the *benefits* and *conflicts* involved in grandparenting?
12. Discuss the nature of *sibling relationships* among the elderly.
13. Describe the general patterns of *health* and *illness* among the elderly in the U.S.
14. What are the patterns in *caregiving* among the elderly in our society? What are the stresses involved for adult children as caregivers?
15. Identify and describe the experience of *widowhood*. What are the *stages* of widowhood?
16. What are the *gender difference* in the experience of widowhood.

PART VII. ANSWERS TO STUDY QUESTIONS

<u>True-False</u>

1.	F	(p. 379)
2.	T	(p. 380)
3.	T	(p. 380)
4.	F	(p. 381)
5.	T	(p. 382)

6.	T	(p. 383)
7.	F	(p. 386)
8.	T	(p. 387)
9.	T	(p. 389)
10.	T	(p. 391)

Multiple-Choice

1.	c	(p. 376)
2.	d	(p. 376)
3.	b	(p. 376)
4.	a	(p. 377)
5.	a	(p. 377)
6.	c	(p. 379)
7.	d	(p. 380)
8.	c	(p. 382)
9.	a	(p. 383)
10.	d	(p. 384)
11.	c	(p. 384)
12.	b	(p. 385)
13.	a	(p. 388)
14.	d	(p. 389)
15.	e	(p. 394)

Fill-In

1. Younger siblings, employment status, grandchildren (p. 377)
2. Social gerontology (p. 377)
3. Age norms (p. 378)
4. Functional age (p. 378)
5. genetics, social roles, environmental (p. 380)
6. 79.5, 73, 73.7, 64.7 (p. 381)
7. 77 (p. 383)
8. 12 (p. 385)
9. remote, companionate, involved (p. 390)
10. grandfather (p. 390)
11. 25, 33 (p. 391)
12. 70, 80 (p. 391)
13. 5 (p. 393)
14. emergence (p. 394)
15. self-identity, financial (p. 395)
16. 15 (p. 396)

PART VIII. COMMENT AND ANALYSIS

Personal Reflection

"What Do You Know About the Elderly?"

  Key Points:

  Questions you have?

Applying the Sociological Imagination

"Is Ageism Dead?"

  Key Points:

  Questions you have?

Family Profile

"The Gottlieb Family"

  Key Points:

  Questions you have?

Writing Your Own Script

"Thinking About Later Life"

Marriages and Families In the Twenty-First Century

16

PART I. CHAPTER OUTLINE

PART II. LEARNING OBJECTIVES

1. To review major changes in marriages and families in the U.S. over the last several decades.
2. To review and analyze predictions concerning future trends in marriages and families.
3. To discuss the issues of race, class, and gender as they relate to the experience of family life in our society.
4. To review data concerning satisfaction with family life in contemporary U.S. society.
5. To consider five major family-related problems--the declining economic well-being of families, the politics of welfare, the right to privacy versus the right to know, the growing numbers of elderly, and the ongoing challenges of living in a global economy.

PART III. CHAPTER REVIEW--KEY POINTS

In the opening vignette to this chapter we are introduced to two young college graduates who are in love, but hesitant to marry. Linda and Joe have had different family life experiences and each has somewhat different expectations for family life in the future.

This chapter begins with a brief review of the major changes that have occurred in marriages and families since the 1950s. Following this review, major trends that likely will carry us into the twenty-first century will be considered, highlighting the major family-related problems that currently confront the nation.

The most significant changes in marriages and families over the last several decades in our society include:

-The proportion of people living in family households, especially in traditional nuclear families, has declined.
-The number of families in which both parents work has rose sharply.
-The average size of families has decreased as couples are choosing to have fewer children or remain childless.
-New reproductive technologies are allowing more women to have children.
-People are marrying at later ages.
-The percentage of people who have never married has increased.
-The number of marriages ending in divorce has increased dramatically. One in two marriages now end in divorce.
-The rate of remarriages climbed during the 1960s and 1970s and leveled off somewhat in the 1980s. Forty percent of remarriages end in divorce.
-The number of single-person households has increased dramatically.
-Single-parent households more than doubled between 1970 and 1990. A significant number of single-parents are created by births to unmarried mothers.
-Both heterosexual and homosexual cohabitation has increased.
-Although growing in number, interracial marriages continue to represent only a small fraction of all marriages.
-Over the last two decades, economic inequalities have intensified both in the United States and throughout the world.
-Due to the shortage of healthy babies, adoption has become a competitive and controversial process.

MARRIAGES AND FAMILIES IN THE TWENTY-FIRST CENTURY

The scope and magnitude of change in marriages and families over the past several decades has been dramatic. These trends will likely continue, though at a slower pace. For example, the increase in the number of working mothers has slowed, and the divorce rate has declined slightly.

The decline in the divorce rate may or may not be a long-term trend. However, several factors may explain the current decline: people are marrying later, cohabiting more, and public awareness that divorce often involves significant adverse consequences, especially for children, has increased.

RACE, CLASS, AND GENDER

How family life is experienced is affected by race, class, and gender. Over the decades some of these diverse experiences have converged, while others have diverged.

American racial categories are extremely rigid, and they impose identities on individuals that do not fit them. There is a growing population of biracial and multiracial individuals in this country. In a world of racial and ethnic antagonisms, conflict, and prejudice, biracial and multiracial families have an added and unique set of challenges and concerns revolving around their "racial difference."

SATISFACTION WITH FAMILY LIFE

National survey data consistently shows that the vast majority of people report a great deal of satisfaction with their family lives. A supportive environment to provide a sense of identity, emotional closeness, and security for family members is critical.

FAMILY-RELATED PROBLEMS

The Declining Economic Well-Being of Families

Donald Barlett and James Steele have documented a major transfer of wealth to the rich, resulting in a decline in the standard of living for the middle and working classes. Families with children, families of color, families headed by women, and the unmarried elderly are especially vulnerable.

Managing Finances: Social researchers consistently have found that finances are a major source of tension and conflict within families. The **For Your Information** box (p. 404) provides a standard budget form to get you started on the road to sound financial planning.

The Politics of Welfare

The current debate over welfare seldom acknowledges the basic social and political structures in society that produce and sustain poverty in the first place and welfare dependency secondarily.

Welfare Dependency: Welfare dependency has become a fact of life in many poor neighborhoods in the U.S. According to Loic Wacquant and William Julius Wilson, during the past decade, the nations 10 largest metropolitan areas contained over half of the poor living in the 50 largest cities in this country and over one-third of all urban poor. These pockets of poverty and welfare dependency are located in areas where the employment infrastructure has collapsed.

Recent surveys show that the public generally believes that the welfare system is ineffective and that people receiving such assistance should be forced to work like the rest of us. Most people feel that welfare recipients are taking advantage of the system. Contrary to myths, the welfare family is getting smaller, and now averages fewer than two children per family. Further, the real monetary value of welfare benefits has declined 40 percent over the past 2 decades.

Retrenchment: Retrenchment is a pattern that is beginning to emerge across the United States and in other countries that discourages services for the homeless and indigent. Many communities are rezoning areas to exclude services for the homeless.

The Declining Welfare of Children: The economic shifts and family changes over the last two decades have had a negative impact on the lives of children. Economist Sylvia Ann Hewlett cites a number of statistics that describe the plight of many children today:

-Twenty percent of all children are growing up in poverty.
-Some 330,000 children are homeless.
-The rate of suicide among adolescents has tripled since 1960.
-Forty-two percent of fathers fail to see their children in
 the wake of divorce.
-Twenty-seven percent of teenagers drop out of high school.

According to Hewlett, the United States ranks second worldwide in per capita income but is not among the top teen in any significant indicator of child welfare. She claims hat American society over the past 25 years has been tilting in an ominous new direction-- toward the devaluation of children.

One of the obstacles we face in trying to improve the welfare of children is the deeply embedded notion that child rearing is a private endeavor that should result in a public benefit. Hewlett argues that child rearing must be seen as a collective responsibility and that public policies must be redrawn in the direction of supporting children through a variety of means. Several of these are outlined in this chapter (p. 406).

The Right to Privacy Versus the Right to Know

Adoptive parents face some unique problems. Today, child experts advice parents to tell the child right from the beginning about the adoption, at a level she or he can understand. This often leads though to the child questioning the circumstances of their birth.

Policies concerning adoption records and privacy versus the right to know vary from state to state. Twenty-one states, for example, have mutual consent registries.

Contested Adoptions: Although the majority of adoptions proceed relatively smoothly, sometimes problems do arise. Recently publicized cases are discussed in this section of the text.

The Growing Numbers of Elderly

More and more families, especially female family members, will find themselves facing the demands of caring for elderly relatives. The new generation of elderly will be at greater risk of being without needed support than is the current generation because there will be fewer children to care for them. Furthermore, in the future, more of the elderly will have experienced divorce and remarriage.

The Right-To-Die Movement: With the advent of modern medical technologies, it is possible to sustain life under conditions that would have led to death in the past. Increasingly people are questioning the wisdom of such action when any meaningful gain in the quality of life is unlikely. The 1976 landmark case of Karen Ann Quinlan is discussed in this section of the chapter.

Euthanasia, or "mercy killing," is briefly discussed. Euthanasia can take two forms: passive and active. In passive euthanasia, medical treatment is terminated, and nothing is done to prolong the patient's life artificially. Active euthanasia refers to action deliberately taken to end a person's life. Doctor Jack Kevorkian has fueled the debate over this latter form of euthanasia. Public opinion appears to be moving toward acceptance of euthanasia, though the active type is seen as controversial.

The Ongoing Challenges of Living in a Global Economy

Families everywhere are experiencing the challenges of living in a global economy. A major challenge to the well-being of families is the unequal valuation of women's and men's labor and contributions to families and societies. For example, the United Nations Development Program in its 1995 report suggested:

(1) Women work longer hours than men in nearly every country of the world.

(2) In industrialized countries, roughly two-thirds of women's total work burden is spent on unpaid activities and one-third on paid activities; for men the shares are reversed.

(3) In developing countries, two-thirds of women's total work is also spent on unpaid labor but less than one-fourth of men's work is unpaid.

The chief author of this report, Mahbub ul Haq, makes it clear that this inequity is harmful to the interests of everyone. A clear example of the denial of full participation of women in society is the fact that of the nine hundred million people who are illiterate in the world, women outnumber men two to one.

The trends identified in this chapter are complex and multifaceted. Social policies that are truly "profamily" will recognize the diversity of the world's families and our connections to one another.

286

PART IV. KEY TERMS

retrenchment   euthanasia

PART V. KEY RESEARCHERS

Donald Barlett and James Steele   Sylvia Ann Hewlett

Loic Wacquant and William Julius Wilson   Mahbub ul Haq

PART VI. STUDY QUESTIONS

True-False

1.	T	F	The average size of families in the U.S. has *decreased* since the 1950s.
2.	T	F	In comparison with previous decades, Americans are marrying at *later ages*.
3.	T	F	Approximately eighty percent of *remarriages* end in divorce.
4.	T	F	*Single parent households* more than doubled between 1970 and 1990.
5.	T	F	Approximately 75 percent of adults in the U.S. say that they would *marry the same spouse* if they had it to do over again.
6.	T	F	according to the authors, *welfare dependency* has become a fact of life in many poor neighborhoods in the United States.
7.	T	F	Recent surveys show that the public generally believes that the welfare system is ineffective and that people receiving such assistance should be forced to work like the rest of us.
8.	T	F	The average size of *welfare families* has been increasing over the last decade with more and more families having three or more children.
9.	T	F	Today, child experts advice parents to tell *adopted children* right from the beginning at a level they can understand.
10.	T	F	Research shows that in industrialized societies, roughly two-thirds of women's total work burden is spent on *unpaid* activities and one-third on paid activities; for men, the shares are reversed.

Multiple-Choice

1. The ___*family* currently represents the most common married family unit in the U.S.

    (a)   dual-earner   (c)   single breadwinner
    (b)   single parent   (d)   remarried

2. The *average size of families* in the U.S. has _____ since the 1950s.

    (a)   increased
    (b)   decreased
    (c)   remained constant
    (d)   decreased but has begun to increase

3. Current estimates are that one out of every ____ marriages will end in *divorce*.

    (a)   two   (d)   five
    (b)   three   (e)   six
    (c)   four

4. What percentage of American couples rate their marriage as *very happy*?

    (a)   35   (c)   43
    (b)   50   (d)   67

5. What percentage of adults surveyed said that they would *choose the same* spouse if they had to do it over again.

    (a)   59   (c)   75
    (b)   98   (d)   45

6. According to Donald Bartlett and James Steele, early next century the top 4 percent of individuals and families drawing a paycheck will earn as much on the job as _____ *percent* of the rest of American workers.

    (a)   35   (c)   100
    (b)   43   (d)   60

7. According to the authors of the text, _____ are a major source of *tension* and *conflict* within families.

    (a)   finances   (c)   in-laws
    (b)   careers   (d)   extramarital affairs

288

8. What percentage of all children in the U.S. are growing up in *poverty*?

(a) 5　　　　　　　　　　　　　(c) 21
(b) 45　　　　　　　　　　　　(d) 14

9. What percentage of teenagers today *drop out of high school*?

(a) 6　　　　　　　　　　　　　(c) 18
(b) 13　　　　　　　　　　　　(d) 27

10. According to Sylvia Ann Hewlett, over the past 25 years, America has been moving toward:

(a) increased individual and national debt
(b) the devaluation of children
(c) a greater inequity between the rich and the poor
(d) a disintegrating society

11. Sylvia Ann Hewlett argues that *public policy* must be redrawn using which of the following means?

(a) free access to parental and maternity care and state mandated parenting leave
(b) investment of a higher percentage of public money on child care and education
(c) encouragement of employers to design family-friendly workplaces
(d) provision of substandard housing subsidies for families with children
(e) all of the above

12. The 1976 landmark case of Karen Ann Quinlan gave public recognition to:

(a) the debate over the right to die
(b) the issue of privacy in adoptions
(c) the devaluation of children
(d) the problem of welfare dependency

Fill-In

1. Two key *themes* have characterized U.S. marriages and families over the centuries: _____ and _____.
2. The _____-_____*family* currently represents the most common married-family unit in the U.S.
3. Although growing in number, _____ *marriages* continue to represent only a small fraction of all marriages.

289

4. If current trends continue, early in the next century the top _____ *percent* of individuals and families drawing paychecks will earn as much on the job as _____ *percent* of the rest of American workers.

5. _____ refers to a pattern that is beginning to emerge across the United States and in other countries that discourages services for the *homeless* and *indigent*.

6. The real monetary value of *welfare benefits* has declined _____ *percent* over the past two decades.

7. The *rate of suicide* among adolescents has _____ since 1960.

8. One of the obstacles we face in trying to improve the *welfare of children* is the deeply embedded notion that child rearing is a _____ endeavor that should result in a _____ benefit.

9. The term _____ derives from Greek words meaning "good death," or dying without pain or suffering.

10. *Euthanasia* takes two forms: _____, in which medical treatment is terminated, and nothing is done to prolong the patient's life artificially, and _____ which refers to actions deliberately taken to end a person's life.

Short-Answer

1. What are the general *demographic changes* that have characterized the U.S. family since the 1950s? Which ones do you think are most significant, and why?

2. What is happening to *satisfaction* with family life in our society? What factors seem to most affect a person's satisfaction with family life?

3. In what ways do *gender*, *class*, and *race* affect the experience of family life in our society?

4. What factors today are related to the recent decline in *divorce rates*?

5. What is the meaning of the term *retrenchment* as used in the context of the politics of welfare.

6. What evidence is provided by economist Sylvia Ann Hewlett that there is a *devaluation* of children in our society?

7. What are the main issues being raised by the authors concerning *adoption* and the right to know versus privacy with adoptions?

8. What are the issues being raised in our society given the *growing numbers* of elderly?

9. What are the *challenges of the global economy* as identified by the authors?

PART VII. ANSWERS TO STUDY QUESTIONS

True-False

1.	T	(p. 400)	6.	T	(p. 403)
2.	T	(p. 400)	7.	T	(p. 405)
3.	F	(p. 400)	8.	F	(p. 405)
4.	T	(p. 400)	9.	T	(p. 406)
5.	T	(p. 402)	10.	T	(p. 408)

Multi-Choice

1.	a	(p. 400)	7.	a	(p. 403)
2.	b	(p. 400)	8.	c	(p. 405)
3.	a	(p. 400)	9.	d	(p. 405)
4.	d	(p. 400)	10.	b	(p. 406)
5.	c	(p. 402)	11.	e	(p. 406)
6.	d	(p. 402)	12.	a	(p. 407)

Fill-In

1. diversity, change (p. 400)
2. dual-earner (p. 400)
3. interracial (p. 400)
4. 4, 60 (p. 402)
5. Retrenchment (p. 405)
6. 40 (p. 405)
7. tripled (p. 405)
8. private, public (p. 406)
9. euthanasia (p. 407)
10. passive, active (p. 408)

PART VIII. COMMENT AND ANALYSIS

For Your Information

"Calculating a Monthly Budget"

Key Points:

Questions you have?

Notes

Notes

Notes